St. Louis Community College

Forest Park
Florissant Valle
Meramec

Instructional Re
St. Louis, Misso

The Fiction of Ellen Gilchrist

photo by Andrew Kilgore

THE FICTION OF
ELLEN GILCHRIST

Margaret Donovan Bauer

University Press of Florida

Gainesville · Tallahassee · Tampa · Boca Raton

Pensacola · Orlando · Miami · Jacksonville

04 03 02 01 00 99 6 5 4 3 2 1

Library of Congress Cataloging-in-Publication Data

Bauer, Margaret Donovan, 1963–

The fiction of Ellen Gilchrist / Margaret Donovan Bauer.

p. cm.

Includes bibliographical references and index.

ISBN 0-8130-1699-1 (alk. paper)

1. Gilchrist, Ellen, 1935– —Criticism and interpretation.

2. Women and literature—Southern States—History—20th century.

3. American fiction—themes, motives. I. Title.

PS3557.I34258Z74   1999

813'.54—dc21   98-50943

The University Press of Florida is the scholarly publishing agency for the State
University System of Florida, comprising Florida A&M University, Florida
Atlantic University, Florida International University, Florida State University,
University of Central Florida, University of Florida, University of North Florida,
University of South Florida, and University of West Florida.

University Press of Florida
15 Northwest 15th Street
Gainesville, FL 32611–2079
http://www.upf.com

I dedicate this manuscript to the influential women in my life,
particularly my mother, Jane Colvin Desonier,
my grandmothers, Rebecca Donovan Colvin
and Margaret Wooster Bauer,
my mentor, Dorothy Scura, and my friends Susan McFatter,
Tanya Long Bennett, Lynne Vallone, and Cynthia Ryan.

CONTENTS

ACKNOWLEDGMENTS

I would like to express my deepest gratitude to Dorothy Scura for her generosity in guiding my course of study while I was in graduate school and my career since. She has been an invaluable mentor. I appreciate, too, the valuable revision suggestions I received from Luke Whisnant, B. J. Leggett, Mary Papke, and James Cobb. I also thank Darrell Bourque for introducing me to the work of Ellen Gilchrist and providing me the opportunity to interview her. Finally, I wish to express my gratitude to the people who read my manuscript for the University Press of Florida, particularly Carolyn Perry, copyeditor Sally Antrobus, and the anonymous reviewer who suggested I consult Nancy A. Walker's *The Disobedient Writer*.

Most important, I am overwhelmingly grateful to my parents, Jane Colvin Desonier and Carl W. Bauer, for their bountiful love and never-ending encouragement throughout my life.

The following material has been published as indicated. The discussion of "The Blue-Eyed Buddhist" in chapter 1 is taken almost verbatim from my article in *Louisiana Literature*. Discussions of some of Gilchrist's "New Orleans stories" in chapter 2 have been largely excerpted from my article in the *Xavier Review*. Much of the discussion of "Traveler" in chapter 2 was used in my analysis of the story for *Masterplots*. An early version of chapter 4 appeared in the *Southern Literary Journal*. (See appendix of available criticism on Gilchrist for full citations.)

ABBREVIATIONS

The following abbreviations are used with page numbers when quoting from primary sources by the major authors covered in this study. Complete citations are in the bibliography.

Books by Ellen Gilchrist

LDD	*In the Land of Dreamy Dreams*
A	*The Annunciation*
VJ	*Victory over Japan*
DL	*Drunk with Love*
FS	*Falling through Space*
AP	*The Anna Papers*
LWP	*Light Can Be Both Wave and Particle*
IC	*I Cannot Get You Close Enough*
NJ	*Net of Jewels*
AM	*Age of Miracles*
SC	*Sarah Conley*

Books by Ernest Hemingway

IOT	*In Our Time*
DA	*Death in the Afternoon*
MF	*A Moveable Feast*
MWW	*Men without Women*
NAS	*The Nick Adams Stories*
WTN	*Winner Take Nothing*

Works by Katherine Anne Porter

CE   *The Collected Essays and Occasional Writings of Katherine Anne Porter*

CS   *The Collected Stories of Katherine Anne Porter* (All quotations from Porter's stories and novellas are copied from this collection.)

Books by William Faulkner

SF   *The Sound and the Fury*

PF   *The Portable Faulkner*

Works by Kate Chopin

CW   *The Complete Works of Kate Chopin* (All quotations from Chopin's stories and her novel *The Awakening* are copied from this volume.)

1

Tradition and an Individual Talent

No poet, no artist of any art has his complete meaning alone. His significance, his appreciation is the appreciation of his relation to the dead poets and artists. You cannot value him alone; you must set him, for contrast and comparison, among the dead.

T. S. Eliot, "Tradition and the Individual Talent"

For books continue each other, in spite of our habit of judging them separately. And I must also consider her—this unknown woman [writer]—as the descendant of all those other women whose circumstances I have been glancing at and see what she inherits of their characteristics and restrictions.

Virginia Woolf, *A Room of One's Own*

I first encountered the fiction of Ellen Gilchrist by way of a short story entitled "Revenge," in her collection *In the Land of Dreamy Dreams,* about a little girl who successfully pole-vaults, despite her brother's insistence that such is not an activity for girls. After reading the story's last line, "Sometimes I think whatever has happened since has been of no real interest to me" (*LDD* 124), I was overwhelmed by a sense of triumph, of empowerment. If it had been in vogue at the time, I would have shouted aloud, "You go, girl," to the child protagonist. But it was only 1986 or so, and I, significantly, had no such phrase of approval and affirmation at the tip of my tongue for the actions of women. Even had I one, I would later realize, it would have been misdirected, for after a subsequent reading of "Revenge" some years later, I would recognize that the story is not, after all, triumphant—at least not for the protagonist, the little girl named Rhoda, who would reappear, in various stages of her life, throughout Gilchrist's canon. Rhoda is suggesting in this line that an accomplishment that occurred when she was ten years old seems to remain the high-light of her life. "Revenge" is, however, an example of the writer's ac-complishments: her depiction of the limitations upon girls and women who grew up during and following World War II and the consequences, particularly to strong girls and women, of those limitations.

In the almost twenty years since the University of Arkansas Press pub-lished Ellen Gilchrist's first book of fiction, a collection of short stories entitled *In the Land of Dreamy Dreams* (1981), which includes the short story "Revenge," Gilchrist has produced seven additional volumes of short fiction and six novels. Her canon also includes two collections of poetry, both of which appeared before *In the Land of Dreamy Dreams* won her instant attention; a collection of her journal entries and National Pub-lic Radio broadcasts; and poems and essays published in a number of different popular and literary magazines. Although no one can foresee the future of an author's critical reputation, my study of Ellen Gilchrist's fiction leads me to believe that she will emerge as a major figure in con-temporary southern literature.

Introducing Gilchrist's Organic Story Cycle

In addition to widespread praise, *In the Land of Dreamy Dreams* won its creator a contract with Little, Brown and Company to publish a novel and a second collection of stories. In his review of *In the Land of Dreamy Dreams,* novelist Mark Childress remarks that Gilchrist's stories "breathe new life into the idea of a short-story collection" (60). I agree and would credit the intratextual nature of her work for much of its appeal. I use the term *intratextual* here as it is used by Thaïs Morgan to refer to the relationships "among earlier and later texts by the same author" (241). The interrelatedness of the individual works within Gilchrist's canon makes it particularly interesting, unique, and worthy of critical analysis. Her narrative technique is not, of course, innovative only because her stories and novels are interrelated; writers have been writing interrelated stories for some time. Indeed, all four of the writers whose works are read intertextually with Gilchrist's in the following four chapters—Ernest Hemingway, Katherine Anne Porter, William Faulkner, and Kate Chopin—have written interrelated stories or novels. Gilchrist's point of uniqueness is that *all* of her work is interrelated to the extent that her whole body of work—that which she has already published and prob-ably that which she will publish—is part of an *organic story cycle,* a story cycle that continues to evolve as each new book appears, comparable to the *roman-fleuve*. It is a story *cycle* in the full sense of the word: there are no definite endings to the individual books and, distinguishing her work from the *roman-fleuve*, there is no clear beginning to the cycle. For the most part, there is no order in which Gilchrist's books should be read, a characteristic of her canon that reflects the chaotic contemporary world in which the author sets her fiction (with the single exception of her historical novel *Anabasis*, set in ancient Greece).[1]

Childress's praise for Gilchrist's first book of fiction was to be echoed by reviewers of her later collections of short stories who argue that Gilchrist is at her best with the short story. A more specific point of praise for this first volume of stories is directed toward Gilchrist's criticism of southern aristocracy and the caste system still operating within the contemporary South. Reviewers of *The Annunciation* (Little, Brown, 1983) also appreciate the focus on these subjects in Gilchrist's first novel. Fiction writer Rosellen Brown, for example, remarks that "Gilchrist describes again, effectively, the codes of the class system, and of the religious system as it is distorted by privilege" (53).

The overall critical reception of *The Annunciation* was mixed, however. A few reviewers speculate that the novel might not suit Gilchrist's talents as well as the short story does, an opinion which would seem to be reinforced by the resounding success of *Victory over Japan*, Gilchrist's second collection of short stories (Little, Brown, 1984), and which would then be repeated after the publication of her second novel.[2] As is discussed in chapter 5 in relation to this second novel, *The Anna Papers* (Little, Brown, 1988), the negative reviews reveal more about reader response to strong women characters who are satisfied, even happy with themselves—or who ultimately achieve self-satisfaction: readers seem disturbed by such positive self-images, reflecting the still prevalent attitudes of this country's Puritan roots.

Gilchrist apparently did not lose heart upon reading the negative comments within the reviews of her first novel, as is indicated in particular by a short story in *Victory over Japan*, in which she humorously parodies herself, *The Annunciation*, and the reviewers who criticized her novel (this story, "Looking over Jordan," is analyzed in chapter 3). Reviewers began to comment upon Gilchrist's interrelated stories and books with the appearance of this volume. Perhaps one might even argue that the 1984 American Book Award for Fiction granted to *Victory over Japan* is testimony for the theory that it is what I term the organic nature of

Gilchrist's story cycle that makes her fiction innovative. This characteristic of her fiction may also be largely responsible for its appeal to the reading public, which usually prefers the novel to the short story, and to the literary community, which often seems to value the novel as the superior form of fiction.

Surprisingly, although Gilchrist's first novel was criticized as inferior to her short stories, at least one reader of *Victory over Japan* praised the interrelated stories because they give one the sense of reading a novel: at the end of his glowing review of the collection for the *Washington Post*, Jonathan Yardley comments that "because many of the stories are connected in ways both obvious and subtle, you feel as though you are reading a novel; at the end you have that satisfied, contented feeling only a good novel can give" (B10). It is interesting to note that Yardley had ended his earlier critical review of *The Annunciation* saying that "perhaps, like a number of other gifted writers, Gilchrist is simply more suited to the short story than the novel" (3). Also somewhat ironic in light of the reviews of Gilchrist's novel the year before, the reviewer for *Publishers Weekly* notes how the stories of *Victory over Japan* "feel like sketches for a novel" and wonders if "perhaps Gilchrist needs the space of a novel to develop her characters and our sympathy for them" (rev. of *Victory* 136). I disagree with the implication that a consequence of the serial nature of Gilchrist's work is that a reader of a single story will not care about the characters within it. At the same time, I would answer this reviewer by pointing out that Gilchrist is taking even more space than that of a novel to develop her plot lines. In spite of the point of contrast noted earlier (the absence of any definite beginning to the story cycle), her organic story cycle is something like a *roman-fleuve*, the appeal of which Lynette Felber relates to its resemblance to the soap opera: "Much of its popularity is based upon its creation of an extended relationship between readers and characters; our familiarity with these seemingly real friends compels us to 'tune in' week after week or year after year to see what becomes of them" (4). Also comparable to the *roman-fleuve*, many different plot lines and characters are found in each book Gilchrist writes, some of which are returned to in later books, while others are dropped.

While the reviews of Gilchrist's first two story collections are overwhelmingly positive, the reviews of her third collection, *Drunk with Love* (Little, Brown, 1986), are mixed. Whereas reviewers enjoyed the stories about recurring characters in Gilchrist's body of work thus far, they are discomforted by some of the other stories—in particular, those that deal with race issues. I respond to the misgivings about these stories in chapter 3. For my purposes in this introduction to Gilchrist's fiction, it is interesting to note that the stories in *Drunk with Love* that most clearly continue her evolving story cycle are the reviewers' favorites, again supporting my theory about the appeal of this element of her fiction. Similarly, the few reviewers who liked Gilchrist's journal entries and National Public Radio broadcasts, collected under the title *Falling through Space: The Journals of Ellen Gilchrist* and published by Little, Brown in 1987, were those who enjoyed finding the geneses of Gilchrist's stories in the recollections of the author's own past included in this volume. Most reviewers, however, criticized this autobiographical collection as simplistic and self-aggrandizing; they were apparently discomforted by the author's positive self-image.

Although at least one reviewer, short story writer David Walton, considers *The Anna Papers* the "most balanced, emotionally accomplished sequence in all Gilchrist's fiction" (an opinion with which I wholeheartedly agree) and wishes it had "been another 50 or even 100 pages longer" (6–7), others criticize Gilchrist's self-aggrandizement in the characterization of the obviously autobiographical Anna and express distaste for Anna's egotism. Whereas reviewers of the earlier works did not seem to mind the fact that several of Gilchrist's characters seem to be autobiographical, reviewers of this novel were troubled by the autobiographical element. They argue that Gilchrist does not achieve the objective distance from Anna that she demonstrates in her stories about such other autobiographical characters as Rhoda and Crystal Manning. As is proposed in chapter 5, it seems that they are troubled by the character—and perhaps the writer—liking herself. I, in contrast, find it refreshing for its implicit rejection of self-deprecating humility as a feminine virtue.

After *The Anna Papers*, Little, Brown next published a fourth collection of Gilchrist's short fiction entitled *Light Can Be Both Wave and Particle* (1989). The reviews of this book are overwhelmingly favorable. Reviewers again expressed their approval of Gilchrist's return to the short story form. Indeed, the stories liked least in this volume, according to the reviews, were the two that provide a new ending to *The Annunciation* and the long story or novella "Mexico." Reviewers clearly favored the new stories about Rhoda Manning's childhood, some commenting that Gilchrist is at her best not only with the short story but also with child and adolescent protagonists. In "Mexico," Rhoda is a fifty-three-year-old woman whom reviewers did not find as appealing. It is true that Gilchrist is not able to achieve the distance from adult characters living in the present or recent past that she is able to achieve with her child characters growing up in the post–World War II South. I suggest later in this chapter, however, that the source of the readers' preference is their disappointment at finding in such stories as "Mexico" that, in spite of her vivacity and strong will, Rhoda has not overcome the limitations to women's opportunities in the patriarchal South.

Following *Light Can Be Both Wave and Particle* is *I Cannot Get You Close Enough* (Little, Brown, 1990), a collection of three novellas, in two of which Gilchrist focuses mainly upon a new generation of protagonists. This volume also received praise from reviewers for the depiction of youth and was criticized for the development of the older characters. Here, I would suggest that what may actually trouble readers is the absence of Gilchrist's usual humor in these novellas, as is suggested in the concluding chapter of this study. The author does not present a very uplifting picture of growing up in the 1990s.

In 1992, Little, Brown published Gilchrist's "first Rhoda novel," as her readers tend to call her third novel, *Net of Jewels*. Readers who have followed Gilchrist's work faithfully, anxious to receive a new installment of the life of perhaps her most intriguing, definitely her most popular recurring character, appreciate the author's full development of quite formative years in this character's life (as is adddressed more fully in the forthcoming section on Gilchrist's evolving prototype). Again, however, some reviewers commented that the author should confine herself to the short story form, and others lamented the character's lack of development in the course of the novel. As I discuss later, this complaint also seems related to readers' apparent desire for a more optimistic view of Rhoda's adult life.

After *Net of Jewels*, Gilchrist returned to the Hand family's story in her fourth novel, *Starcarbon, a Meditation on Love* (Little, Brown, 1994). At least two reviewers believe that the novel is still autonomous: Victoria Jenkins states early in her review that "previous acquaintance with the Hand family is not a prerequisite for understanding *Starcarbon*" (5), and the *Publishers Weekly* reviewer believes that "Gilchrist skillfully makes [the] complicated relationships [between various characters whose histories are found in earlier books] clear even to those who haven't read her earlier books" (rev. of *Starcarbon* 74). However, the mixed reception of this novel reflects an issue I address in the next section of this introduction to Gilchrist's canon: the decreasing autonomy of her individual volumes as her organic story cycle evolves. One can infer from the reviews of *Starcarbon* that some believe the novel will be particularly enjoyable only to the readers already familiar with Gilchrist's characters, while other readers may become bogged down by the number of different characters. Both Sarah Ferguson, in the *New York Times Book Review*, and the reviewer for the *Kirkus Review*, for example, remark upon the Gilchrist fan's pleasure in receiving a new installment on the Hand family (rev. of *Starcarbon*), while Trev Broughton complains in his *Times Literary Supplement* review about "excess personnel"(21). Returning to the *Publishers Weekly* review quoted previously, one will find, however, an understanding of Gilchrist's achievement with her "multi-volume narrative"—that is, what I consider the story cycle made up of her many volumes of fiction (74). This reviewer argues that Gilchrist's work "offers a tart antidote to the rootlessness of so much American fiction" (74), another way of suggesting that the appeal of her work lies largely in her fiction's kinship to the *roman-fleuve* and the soap opera.

I agree with this reason for Gilchrist's appeal; however, in my assessment of her fiction, *Starcarbon* marks a negative turning point, for I find that the weaknesses of this novel continue to infect her later books. Victoria Jenkins sums up the first weakness most succinctly when she characterizes Gilchrist as a "fairy godmother" to her characters, "an overly fond *deus ex machina* who lets her charges teeter on the brink of disaster but can't bear to see anyone topple. She snatches them back in the nick of time to avert catastrophe. The gun discharges harmlessly, the tornado is selective in its path, children and parents forgive and embrace" (5).[3] Whereas I noted earlier previously that the author's fondness for her protagonists has a refreshing appeal for me, it has unfortunately gotten out of hand in her recent fiction, beginning with *Starcarbon*: Gilchrist seems to have become *too* fond of her characters. She won't let anything "bad" happen to them; consequently, since bad things happen to likable people in real life, her work has become less credible (as well as less interesting). Indeed, while reading the novel, Trev Broughton, who complained about too many characters, admits to longing for "a bout of bloody feuding to dispose of [the] excess personnel" (21).

Another weakness of this novel, which can also be found in the works to follow, is Gilchrist's development of the central character, Olivia de Havilland Hand, whose voice simply does not ring true. It becomes evident when reading this book not only that Gilchrist's strongest medium is the short story but also that her strongest characters are the women she creates of her own generation, whether they be middle-aged women of the 1980s and '90s or young girls growing up in the 1940s and '50s. At the same time, however, the women of Gilchrist's own generation created for this novel (for example, Olivia's therapist and professor) and the volumes to follow are not so appealing to this reader. Like Gilchrist's fondness for her characters, her characters' fondness for themselves has gotten out of hand. Their sense of self-worth has become increasingly narcissistic, the third weakness of Gilchrist's recent fiction (i.e., her post–*Net of Jewels* books). Due to these weaknesses, the consequence of which is that these volumes do not measure up to the quality of Gilchrist's early fiction, I do not treat them in this study as specifically or fully as I treat the early work.

Also in 1994, the University Press of Mississippi published Gilchrist's *Anabasis, a Journey to the Interior*, a historical novel set in ancient Greece. The author explains in a note preceding the beginning of the tale that she had begun making up this story during her childhood. The reviewer of *Anabasis* for *Kirkus* considers its departure from the usual setting and characters something of a relief (rev. of *Anabasis*, 867). Another admires the author's "enthusiasm for her heroine" (S. Smith 128), and a third praises the "uplifting tale of a valiant young woman" (Joyce 23). It is disturbing to me that appreciation of a woman character's strong self-image is so late in coming and directed to a character in a fantasy—indeed one who, as the reviewer for *Publishers Weekly* points out, is not "wholly credible" (rev. of *Anabasis* 382)—when it was denied to the more realistic Anna Hand.

With the publication of *The Age of Miracles* (Little, Brown, 1995), Gilchrist returns to the medium of the short story; to her first recurring characters, Rhoda, Crystal, and Nora Jane; and, in most of the stories, to New Orleans and Fayetteville, Arkansas. Seemingly as a result, it is the strongest of her recent works, and the reviewers concur with this opinion.[4] At the same time, one can still find in this volume the weaknesses already examined: unbelievable characterizations of young women and narcissistic characterizations of older women—the problem with the latter being that the author does not seem aware of these women's narcissism. She and her characters have lost the self-knowledge praised by such early reviewers as Thulani Davis, who once remarked of Gilchrist's characters, "terrible as they are, these people see themselves so clearly they are both interesting and sympathetic" (12).

In the same year, Little, Brown published a volume entitled *Rhoda, a Life in Stories*, in which Gilchrist has collected and organized in chronological order most of the Rhoda stories from her previous books, an excerpt from *Net of Jewels*, and two additional Rhoda stories. Upon examination of this collection, it is interesting to note that Rhoda's life adventures during her forties are missing, leaving the reader to wonder about how she developed from a philandering wife who is burdened by motherhood (except when she hands her children over to her father, mother, or husband's care), who drinks too much, and who is obsessed with her weight, to the Rhoda approaching her sixties, who is no longer obsessed with finding the perfect lover or escaping her father's influence and who is devoted to her grandchildren.[5] This transition (or rather, lack thereof) is analyzed in the final chapter of this study. The collection itself demonstrates microcosmically the point made repeatedly here regarding how Gilchrist's canon is an organic story cycle. Even after the publication of this collection, because of the missing decade the reader does not feel that Rhoda's story is complete and thus waits for further installments in later books.

Gilchrist's next collection of short stories, *The Courts of Love* (Little, Brown, 1996), provides one such installment, although half of this volume continues the adventures of another set of recurring characters—Nora Jane, her husband Freddy, her twins, her former lover Sandy—and includes some spin-off tales involving the people they meet during their new adventures. There are dark moments in these stories, but again, everything works out well for those characters in whom Gilchrist has the most invested—that is, Nora Jane, Freddy, and the twins.

Gilchrist's most recent book, the novel *Sarah Conley* (Little, Brown, 1997), is reminiscent of her first two novels, *The Annunciation* and *The Anna Papers*, in that at its center is a strong female writer. Like the characters in her more recent fiction, however, the title character of this novel never really suffers. Her father's death occurs "off-stage" before the novel's opening, and just after it opens she finds a surrogate father in her best friend's home. The only crisis in her life is that she and her apparent soulmate realize they are in love with each other just before she is to marry his brother and he is to marry her best friend. They consummate this love once, she gets pregnant (although since she has sex with his brother later that same evening, she never knows which brother is the father), and then they marry their original intendeds. The novel then jumps ahead twenty years to just before the death of this same best friend, after which Sarah and her one-time lover rekindle their relationship (she is divorced from his brother by this time). Although most of the novel develops the conflict involved when two career-oriented people try to make a life together, still there is little tension, little of the angst involved in deciding whether to compromise one's career goals for love, and all eventually winds up happily: Sarah gets to keep both her lover and her career.

If one recalls how, early in her career, Gilchrist responded to negative reviews of her novel with a short story that simultaneously parodied the novel and mocked the reviewers, it is troubling to realize that she seems, in most recent years, to be allowing her readers to dictate the tone of her writing. One can find evidence of this as early as *Light Can Be Both Wave and Particle,* in which she published two more chapters to *The Annunciation.* In an essay for *Southern Magazine,* Gilchrist refers to having "confuse[d] and sadden[ed her] readers" when she killed off a main character in *The Annunciation* ("White" 66). This reference to her readers' disappointment with the novel's original ending supports the view that she wrote the "new ending" to please them. Then one notices that it is after the negative response to the dark tone of *I Cannot Get You Close Enough* and *Net of Jewels* that Gilchrist began—to borrow Victoria Jenkins's analogy—playing fairy godmother to her characters. But rather than focus on the weaknesses of Gilchrist's recent fiction, I turn now to one of her achievements in her early work: the evolution of the composite personality at the center of her organic story cycle.

Gilchrist's Evolving Prototype

Although Gilchrist's stories and novels can be read and appreciated individually, recognizing their *intratextual* nature reveals the increasing interdependence of each story and novel upon her other works published both earlier and later, which, in turn, contributes to one's sense that the organic story cycle is evolving. So, too, is the composite personality at its center, the initial prototype for which is Rhoda Manning. Rhoda is the protagonist of four stories in Gilchrist's first book of fiction. She appears in most of Gilchrist's subsequent volumes of short fiction and is the central character of one of Gilchrist's novels, but the details of her life are not always consistent, reminding the reader that the individual works are to some extent autonomous. It is undeniable, however, that they are also interrelated; thus, the inconsistencies give the reader pause to consider their significance.

Like Faulkner, Gilchrist sometimes changes the circumstances of Rhoda's life from one work to another. In *The Faulkner-Cowley File*, Cowley lists several discrepancies between details in the novel *The Sound and the Fury* and the appendix Faulkner wrote to the novel for the Viking *Portable Faulkner*, which Cowley edited (41–42). An example of a more significant inconsistency might also be noted between the same novel and the short story "That Evening Sun": although Quentin Compson commits suicide at nineteen years old in the novel, a twenty-four-year-old Quentin Compson narrates the short story. If Faulkner can raise a character from the dead, then Gilchrist can give a character back her lost virginity, which is perhaps the most significant instance of an inconsistency from one work to another in her fiction: she presents nineteen-year-old Rhoda as a virgin in the beginning of *Net of Jewels*, in spite of the story "Music" in *Victory over Japan*, in which fourteen-year-old Rhoda loses her virginity.

It is not my intention to repeat (within my analysis of Gilchrist's work) Malcolm Cowley's quest to pin Faulkner down on his inconsistencies from one work to another. I will instead borrow from Faulkner's response to Cowley's endeavors to explain Gilchrist's inconsistencies here and elsewhere in her canon. Referring to the appendix he wrote to *The Sound and the Fury* for Cowley's *Portable Faulkner*, Faulkner explained,

> The inconsistencies in the appendix prove to me the book is still alive after 15 years, and being still alive is growing, changing; the appendix was done at the same heat as the book, even though 15 years later, and so it is the book itself which is inconsistent: not the appendix. That is, at the age of 30 I did not know these people as at 45 I now do; that I was even wrong now and then in the very conclusions I drew from watching them, and the information in which I once believed. (Cowley 90)

Similarly, explaining Rhoda's reinstated virginity, Gilchrist herself has said, "The more I've written about Rhoda, the more I know about her" (W. Smith 46), a statement that prepares for my perception of an evolving prototype at the center of the larger story cycle made up of Gilchrist's whole body of fiction.

Although the Gilchrist enthusiast looks forward to reading new installments of Rhoda's life, knowledge of the events already narrated is not necessary to the understanding and enjoyment of any of the Rhoda stories, until, perhaps, the novella "Mexico" (which closes *Light Can Be Both Wave and Particle*) and the novel *Net of Jewels*. To appreciate fully these two later works, both of which have received negative reviews, the reader's understanding of the character of Rhoda Manning, as it has been established in the earlier Rhoda stories, is helpful. Without having read these stories of an intelligent, strong-willed, for the most part likable young girl's battles against the sexism of her community and family, one might have difficulty sympathizing with the spoiled young woman and frustrated older woman she becomes.

Net of Jewels covers Rhoda's life from her college years through the early years of her first marriage. In the beginning of the novel, Rhoda's character is shown to be quite like that of the Rhoda in many short stories that recount this protagonist's childhood and adolescence. As a young adult, she is precocious and spoiled and yet, for a while, still endearing because of her vivacity and strong will. Her major weakness is that she allows her concern about winning her father's approval to dictate her life. The reader familiar with Rhoda's childhood and adolescence knows that for many years she has fought the propensity within herself to worship a father who constantly manipulates and criticizes her and rarely recognizes her talents and achievements. Gilchrist shows in the course of this novel, however, that even as strong a person as Rhoda cannot continue to withstand the constant rejection of her achievements by one so loved and revered as a parent, particularly since that rejection seems based solely on the fact that Rhoda is a daughter, rather than a son, and is, for that reason primarily, viewed to be naturally lacking. Rhoda becomes less and less sympathetic to the reader as the novel progresses and she continues to call on her father for help, regardless of the price she knows she will be made to pay: her independence. The reader wants her to learn to be smarter than that but should realize that her reliance upon her father is a learned behavior after many years of oppression under his empowered will.

In "Mexico," too, Gilchrist shows the consequences to Rhoda's development of her not receiving the love she longs for from her father. In her fifties in this novella, Rhoda feels that she has spent her whole life looking for a man who would love her—and the reader familiar with her past knows this to be true. Thus, even at fifty-three she has not matured very far beyond the little girl of the early stories. At the end of the novella, however, Rhoda considers finally growing up, and the result, if one considers the works intratextually, is the novel *Net of Jewels*, which Rhoda has ostensibly written at the age of fifty-five or sometime thereafter, perhaps as a step in that direction. Then, in three of the stories in *The Age of Miracles* ("A Wedding in Jackson," "Paris," and particularly "The Uninsured"), the reader sees the completion of Rhoda's journey. Rhoda seems in these works, in which she is approaching sixty, as vital as ever but more content with herself than she has ever been. This way in which the novella, the novel, and these stories work together again illustrates the cyclical nature of Gilchrist's fiction.

When Rhoda Manning is introduced in *In the Land of Dreamy Dreams*, she is immediately revealed to be an important figure in Gilchrist's fiction: in that collection, she is the only character to appear in more than one story. Another character in that volume later becomes a recurring figure in Gilchrist's body of work: Nora Jane Whittington of the story "The Famous Poll at Jody's Bar." The development of Nora Jane's character from this story to her appearances in *Victory over Japan, Light Can Be Both Wave and Particle,* and *The Courts of Love* is further evidence of the growing interdependence of Gilchrist's work. Nora Jane's reappearance in two of the stories in *Victory over Japan,* Gilchrist's second collection, is preceded by a note from the author in which she reviews for the newcomer to her fiction Nora Jane's adventures in the earlier collection. This is the only time Gilchrist includes such a note in one of her books. In later works, when knowledge of events from earlier stories is necessary or relevant to what is happening to the protagonist in the present work, she merely sums up those events within the story she is currently telling, often changing or elaborating upon details to suit the goals of the moment.

As a recurring character Nora Jane is different from Gilchrist's other recurring protagonists in another way as well. She is the only one whose story is told chronologically from story to story, book to book, with two exceptions: "The Blue House" of *The Age of Miracles* and "New Orleans" of *The Courts of Love,* which are both prequels to the rest of her stories.[6] Still, she is the only one of these characters whose stories could be easily put together into a chronologically consistent novel. Consequently, however, one might not appreciate as fully later Nora Jane stories without knowledge of details in the preceding ones. Also, the prequels might not be so poignant to readers not familiar with her later life adventures.

Thus, her stories do not contribute to the cyclical nature of Gilchrist's organic story cycle as well as do the stories of the other recurring characters.

Nora Jane herself differs from other major recurring characters in that she belongs to a generation younger than theirs. In that way, she anticipates, as early as Gilchrist's first book of fiction, a new generation of female protagonists who have stepped to the front of the stage in Gilchrist's more recent works.

But long before she turned her attention to this younger generation, Gilchrist introduced another recurring character, Crystal Manning Mallison Weiss, a cousin and contemporary of Rhoda Manning. Crystal is introduced in *Victory over Japan* by her black maid and closest companion, Traceleen, who narrates several of the five stories in which she appears in this volume and many of the other segments of Crystal's life to follow in later books. The relationship between these two women is perhaps the most positive relationship between any two people in all of Gilchrist's work. Traceleen loves and accepts Crystal as she is, and rather than playing upon Crystal's weaknesses to manipulate her, as Crystal's husband, ex-husband, son, and brother do, Traceleen helps Crystal to overcome these weaknesses.[7]

More Crystal/Traceleen stories can be found in *Drunk with Love* and *Light Can Be Both Wave and Particle*. In between these two volumes, in *The Anna Papers*, Crystal and her family appear as minor characters who attend the funeral of Anna Hand, another Manning cousin. The Weisses and some of the Hands come together again, this time sharing the spotlight more evenly, in "Summer in Maine," the last novella of *I Cannot Get You Close Enough*. And finally, Crystal's family appears sporadically in the latest Hand-focused novel, *Starcarbon*; they are the central focus of one of the stories in *The Age of Miracles* ("Too Much Rain, or The Assault of the Mold Spores"); and they play a minor role in another story in that collection ("The Raintree Street Bar and Washerteria").

Anna Hand is the fourth of Gilchrist's major recurring characters and the apex of Gilchrist's development of her prototype. Anna is introduced in "Looking over Jordan" in *Victory over Japan* (the story mentioned previously in which Gilchrist makes fun of her first novel and its reviewers: Anna is an author whose novel *The Ascension* is harshly reviewed by the protagonist of this story). Anna is also the main character of the story "Anna, Part I," which closes *Drunk with Love* and, by its title, anticipates

The Anna Papers. With the characterization of Anna in the novel, Gilchrist reveals the full potential of her prototype: she can overcome social obstacles and limitations when she recognizes her strengths and does not focus on her weaknesses, and when she uses those strengths toward the creation of her art (Rhoda and Anna are writers, and Nora Jane sings, to name only the creative pursuits of recurring characters),[8] rather than to attract the attention of a man (indeed, men come to Anna; she does not go after them). As is explored in chapters 5 and 6, Anna is not only a development of the prototype as it is manifested in such characters as Rhoda and Crystal; she can also be viewed as a new prototype upon whom the women she leaves behind when she dies—including women from both her own generation and the next generation—will model their lives. Her role as such for her sister, cousins, friends, and nieces begins within *The Anna Papers* and continues to be evident within the novellas of *I Cannot Get You Close Enough*.

Before pursuing further Anna's role as Gilchrist's second, revised or evolved prototype, one needs to understand Gilchrist's development of an initial prototype. In the tradition of Hemingway's Nick Adams stories, as is examined in chapter 2, Gilchrist created a composite personality for her first collection of stories, which is in itself a story cycle. As Nick Adams is the prototype upon which the other characters in *In Our Time*, the collection in which he first appears, are based, as well as the prototype for the Hemingway hero in general, so is Gilchrist's Rhoda Manning the prototype for the other protagonists in *In the Land of Dreamy Dreams* and her later works of fiction. In preparation for his analysis of Faulkner's various manifestations of a particular character type, John T. Irwin explains, "Sometimes a writer gets an idea for the structure of a character, and one fictional incarnation isn't enough to exhaust the possibilities inherent in it, possibilities for its development that may often be mutually exclusive" ("Horace" 543). Crystal Manning, for example, is another manifestation of the Rhoda character type; so, too, are many one-time-only protagonists, such as the women and girls at the center of the other stories in *In the Land of Dreamy Dreams*; Lady Margaret Sarpie of "Looking over Jordan" (discussed in chapter 3), Diane of "The Gauzy Edge of Paradise," and Lilly Kase of "Crazy, Crazy, Now Showing Everywhere" in *Victory over Japan*; and Annalisa Livingston of "First Manhattans" (discussed in chapter 3), JeanAnne Lori Mayfield of "The Last Diet," and Helen Altmont of "Belize" in *Drunk with Love*. However, one might turn to Faulkner's *development* of a character type for an analogy of how Gilchrist's prototype also *evolves* in a way that the Hemingway hero does not (as argued more fully in chapter 2).

Critics agree that Faulkner's Horace Benbow and Gavin Stevens share quite similar personality traits with his Quentin Compson. Unlike Quentin, however, these two men live past the age of nineteen, though Horace is emotionally destroyed by the end of the novel *Sanctuary*, in which work he is forty-three.[9] In contrast to both Quentin and Horace, then, Gavin is somehow able to survive physically and emotionally through several works, in spite of the romantic nature and strong attachment to his sister that make him so like his two precursors.[10] The reason that Horace is able, for a while at least, to maintain his idealism and to defy the sister with whom he is unconsciously obsessed is that he is an *evolution* of the Quentin prototype. Gavin, a further evolution of the same prototype, suffers only in that he appears and feels foolish after his romantic escapades chasing after Eula Varner Snopes; also, he is merely close to rather than obsessed with his own sister. With each manifestation of the prototype subsequent to Quentin, Faulkner's characterization reveals growth in the original spirit, as though each character were able to learn from the mistakes of the earlier version(s) of himself.

Similarly, a few of Gilchrist's protagonists evolve from rather than merely being more manifestations of the Rhoda Manning prototype, as I show in the following chapters. The evolution begins with Amanda McCamey of *The Annunciation* and the two additional chapters to the novel included in *Light Can Be Both Wave and Particle*.[11] As John Irwin sees "Horace Benbow as a transitional figure between Quentin Compson and Gavin Stevens" ("Horace" 544), so, too, can Amanda McCamey be seen as a transitional figure between Rhoda Manning and Anna Hand. In the beginning of her novel, Amanda's character has much in common with Rhoda's: she, too, is spoiled and headstrong and longs for love to replace the parental love she missed out on as a child (due to her father's death and her mother's perpetual mourning). Halfway through *The Annunciation*, however, Amanda focuses her energy upon her power to create art, leaving behind a rich but incompatible husband, as well as the memory of the male cousin with whom she was obsessed for most of her life up to that point, to pursue a career as a translator, with a plan to proceed from translating to writing her own poems and novels. She regresses somewhat when she meets a young man and becomes so caught up in her affair with him that she is unable to work for a while. At the end of her novel, however, Amanda is able to regroup her strengths and is preparing to try again to live her own life as she determines it should be lived. This resolve includes having the baby she conceives even though she is unmarried and in her forties and also finding the daughter she gave up for adoption, under family duress, when she was a teenager. Indeed, she is further empowered by her ability to have children, whereas Rhoda finds pregnancy and motherhood to be debilitating.

Another protagonist whose character is a development of Rhoda's and an anticipation of Anna's is Sally Lanier Sykes of "The Blue-Eyed Buddhist" in *Drunk with Love*. As I have argued elsewhere, this story anticipates in a number of ways *The Anna Papers* ("Water" 88–89). "The Blue-Eyed Buddhist" opens with the fact stated simply that thirty-four-year-old "Sally Lanier Sykes was going to die" (*DL* 161). Sally is another of Gilchrist's headstrong women who love life, but her kidneys are failing; so she plans one last adventure before settling herself into the room her husband is equipping with her new dialysis machine. Before allowing herself to be imprisoned to await death, she attempts to set free the sea animals fenced in by a research facility, a feat she "can brag about . . . till the day [she] die[s]" (*DL* 183). Ironically, she drowns while trying to accomplish the task. Though not a suicide, her death foreshadows the death that Anna Hand will choose when she learns that she has cancer. That Sally's death is accidental reflects the fact that her character is merely a step toward Anna's. She has not consciously chosen to end her life rather than live it less fully, as Anna does.

Following Anna's development in *The Anna Papers* (analyzed in chapter 5), the women characters in Gilchrist's fiction can be divided into two groups: the women of Anna's own generation, like her sister Helen, Rhoda, Crystal, and Crystal's friend Lydia, who on the one hand are angered by her death but who, on the other, compare themselves to her and strive to be more like her;[12] and the women of the next generation, including, for example, Anna's nieces Olivia and Jessie, Traceleen's niece Andria, and Crystal's daughter Crystal Anne, all of whom take center stage in *I Cannot Get You Close Enough* and appear in *Starcarbon*, though the latter focuses primarily on Olivia alone. One can further classify Gilchrist's new generation of young women characters in these and her other post–*Anna Papers* works into those whose characters are based upon the evolution of the prototype—Anna Hand—and those whose characters are more similar to the original prototype—Rhoda Manning—again reflecting the recursive nature of this organic story cycle.

Recognizing the Intertexts, Hearing the Dialogues

The interconnectedness of Gilchrist's cast of characters reveals that, like her four precursors who are discussed in subsequent chapters, she has created a community of characters, like Faulkner's Yoknapatawpha County, only extending beyond Mississippi into Louisiana, Arkansas, North Carolina, Indiana, Oklahoma, and even California and New York, to name only those states in which several or major works are set. The large area of her fictional "county" is indicative of the postmodern world she and her characters inhabit. The presence of many of these characters in regions of the country outside the South (occasionally even outside the country, though only temporarily so) reflects both the expansion and the assimilation of the South, just as Gilchrist's connection to Hemingway as well as to Faulkner, Porter, and Chopin reflects her position in the American as well as southern literary traditions.

Within her canon, Gilchrist's works engage provocatively in various dialogues with several literary traditions as they are represented by these writers whose work is analyzed intertextually with hers in the next four chapters. Before proceeding further, given the various ways in which critics have employed the term *intertext* and the various definitions of *intertextuality*, I will define my own use of the term and my method of intertextual criticism as it is practiced in the following four chapters. Put simply, as Michael Riffaterre has done, "the intertext proper is the corpus of texts the reader may legitimately connect with the one before his[/her] eyes, that is, the texts brought to mind by what he[/she] is reading" (627).[13] As my explanation of method to follow will reveal, I have combined various critics' theories regarding intertextuality into a practice that allows me to illustrate the way that Gilchrist's works are similar to and/or deviate from other writings within two different traditions of American literature: the short story tradition, specifically the development of a composite personality within a story cycle; and southern literature, specifically the development of female characters and feminist issues within southern literature.

In her explanation of "Textual Feminism," Nelly Furman argues that the work of a woman writer should "be construed as the product of a prior reading" (50). She supports making this assumption of a literary historical sense (as T. S. Eliot would call it): "Writing is an inscription within an existing literary code, either in the form of an appropriation or a rejection. To study women writers as readers is to analyze their interaction with the cultural system, and to determine how their texts propose a critique of the dominant patriarchal tenor of literary expression" (Furman 50). Such is my intention with Gilchrist's work. To accomplish this goal, my approach to Gilchrist follows the example of Nancy A. Walker, who shows in *The Disobedient Writer* "some of the ways in which women writers have worked against, revised, and reinterpreted some of the literary traditions they have known" (18).

Like Walker, I do not spend time in my study proving authorial intention. I have not, for example, found quotations from interviews in which Gilchrist admits that she modeled her first collection of short stories upon Hemingway's *In Our Time* or her prototype upon either Nick Adams or Porter's Miranda Gay; nor have I interviewed the author myself to ask her if she consciously drew her conflicts for her first novel from Faulkner's *The Sound and the Fury* and began her second novel where Chopin ended *The Awakening*. My contentions may therefore seem presumptuous. In the passage quoted previously, Furman condones the presumption that women writers are also readers, but for those uncomfortable with assumptions not based on concrete evidence, I support my methods with reader-centered intertextual theories. John Frow explains that "the identification of an intertext is an act of interpretation" rather than an argument for influence: "The intertext is not a real and causative source but a theoretical construct formed by and serving the purposes of a reading" (46).

Such perceptions of the intertexts in a work of literature focus on what Jonathan Culler refers to in *The Pursuit of Signs* as the "prior body of discourse" (101) that exists before the text in question. Culler explains that "literary works are to be considered not as autonomous entities, 'organic wholes,' but as intertextual constructs: sequences which have meaning in relation to other texts which they *take up, cite, parody, refute*, or generally *transform*. A text can be read only in relation to other texts" (38, emphasis added). As Susan Stanford Friedman has noted, this perception of the literary tradition transforms Harold Bloom's theories of influence into theories of intertextuality (156). Roland Barthes, in fact, goes so far in his emphasis upon the *reader's* part in the making of the meaning of the text (as opposed to the *writer's*) as to contend that the "site where this multiplicity [of the text, which he notes "consists of multiple writings, proceeding from several cultures and entering into dialogue, into parody, into contestation"] . . . is not the author, as has hitherto been claimed, but the reader" (54). As a reader of the "texts" of Ellen Gilchrist,

I hear the echoes of other writers and explore their significance. To a greater extent, then, than Walker, whose primary focus is on the writer's subversive nature, my focus includes the reader's role in recognizing intertextual relationships between texts. I treat these earlier texts by Hemingway, Porter, Faulkner, and Chopin as existing together with the new texts by Ellen Gilchrist within the reader's literary history, and I show how the reader's knowledge of these earlier texts affects one's reading of Gilchrist's work and, conversely, how reading this relatively new writer's work leads one to re-view the work of her more established forebears.

Already one can see how my *practice* of intertextual criticism is derived from several sources, perhaps beginning with *Desire in Language: A Semiotic Approach to Literature and Art,* in which Julia Kristeva employs Bakhtin's theory of the dialogic nature of words to set up her own theories of intertextuality (as I employ both of their theories and others to set up mine). Kristeva notes that "Bakhtin situates the text within history and society, which are seen as texts read by the writer, and into which he[/she] inserts him[/her]self by rewriting them" (65). Kristeva concludes from Bakhtin's "conception of the 'literary word' as an *intersection of textual surfaces*" that each text is "a dialogue among several writings: that of the writer, the addressee . . . and the contemporary or earlier cultural context" (65), which would include the past reading of writer and readers (addressees, as Kristeva calls them). Kristeva, then, supports my combination of textual feminist assumptions about writers' intentions with intertextual critics' focus on the reader.

My employment of Bakhtin's theories by way of Kristeva's is perhaps most akin to Jay Clayton and Eric Rothstein's theories of intertextuality. In the first chapter of their collection of essays entitled *Influence and Intertextuality in Literary History,* Clayton and Rothstein show how Kristeva's theories of intertextuality, which are usually focused on the historical, social, and cultural intertexts within a literary work, can be employed to examine *literary* intertexts: the history of which the writer and her work is a part includes the literature of and available to that writer's culture. Hence, these literary works are also inevitably being rewritten by the writer (18–20). Clayton and Rothstein turn to Bakhtin, too, then, to allude to the impossibility of critics divorcing themselves from literary history when preparing to assess a particular text:

> Bakhtin authorizes this attention to history by shifting linguistic analysis from the grammatical, atemporal plane to that of the indi-

vidual utterance, which is always caught up in a context of other utterances. A sign can never be analyzed in isolation, for its meaning is always informed by the many other conflicting ways it has been used by other speakers. Thus one focuses not on the usual linguistic unit, the sign, but on the relation of one sign to other signs. (18)

In other words, an analysis of a new writer's work *should* include, as this study of Gilchrist's work does, the relation of the work to what has preceded it, indeed has apparently played some role in its existence being what it is. The literary text, as Kristeva notes, "does not simply *exist* but is generated in relation to *another* structure" (64–65). But Bakhtin has noted the reciprocal benefits of reading works of literature together. According to Bakhtin, "every word is directed toward an *answer* and cannot escape the profound influence of the answering word that it anticipates" (Bakhtin 280).

As already indicated, another influence upon my practice of intertextual criticism is Barthes's explanation of the function of the reader in determining the meaning of a text: "the reader is the very space in which are inscribed, without any of them being lost, all the citations out of which a writing is made; the unity of a text is not in its origin but in its destination" (54). My employment of Barthes's theory in relation to intertextuality has been anticipated by Tilottama Rajan, who explains the role of the reader in recognizing literary intertexts and thereby justifies intertextual readings by critics. Rajan casts the literary text onto two planes: the horizontal, on which it "operates exclusively as an interchange between the text and contemporaneous writings," and the vertical, on which it "functions . . . in relation to previous and future history" (67). Due to this vertical plane, Rajan says, "it becomes necessary to posit a reader who will effect the transposition of the horizontal into the vertical" (67). This explanation of intertextuality calls to mind T. S. Eliot's notion of the presence of the past and the present's ability to affect the past. Rajan points to that "aspect of the vertical dimension [which] is the reinsertion of the writer's own scripts in that text which calls them into being and also marks their limits and complicities" (67).

In sum, examining Gilchrist's work intertextually with the work of various other writers—that is, examining dialogic relationships between her works and the works of others as well as echoes of other writers' works in her stories—both enhances her themes and conflicts and provides a fresh reading of the themes and conflicts of her predecessors. In

"Weavings: Intertextuality and the (Re)Birth of the Author," Susan Fried-man defines the purpose of an intertextual reading most succinctly: "The interesting question for the critic [is] how the successor(s) adapted, as-similated, revised, transformed, altered, reshaped, or revised the precursor(s)" (155). Clayton and Rothstein have provided a method for such intertextual readings of literary works akin to the deconstruc-tionist's approach: they suggest that the critic follow Derrida's "active intertextual practice, in which intertextuality becomes the critic's method of probing, fissuring, disorienting, and dangerously supple-menting the text at hand so as to exhibit its implications and impli-catedness" (19). For example, reading Gilchrist together with these other writers reveals, first of all, how she has transformed the traditions out of which she is writing: the American patriarchal short story tradition as it is epitomized in the work of Ernest Hemingway, whose female charac-ters are usually among those who would thwart his male characters' ide-als, and the southern patriarchal literary tradition as it is epitomized in the work of William Faulkner, who, even as he depicts the oppression of women, objectifies his female characters. Second, one can see how, as she develops her craft within these traditions, her writings deviate from the examples set by these male models. One is therefore not surprised to find similarities between her work and the work of two southern women writers, Katherine Anne Porter and Kate Chopin. However, Gilchrist also transforms these women's techniques, characters, and themes, at times allowing for more positive development of her characters, reflecting a lessening of female oppression in the more recent South, and at other times showing the continuing, if not increasing, oppression of women in a patriarchal society.

2

Gilchrist's Composite Personality and Story Cycle

Transforming Ernest Hemingway

Re-vision—the act of looking back, of seeing with fresh eyes, of entering an old text from a new critical direction—is for us more than a chapter in cultural history: it is an act of survival.

Adrienne Rich, "When We Dead Awaken: Writing as Re-Vision"

It was Ernest Hemingway's new book, and it had come from the book club the day she left North Carolina. She had been waiting for it to come for weeks. Now she opened it to the first page, holding it up to her nose and giving it a smell. . . . "This is going to be a good one. I can tell."

Ellen Gilchrist, *In the Land of Dreamy Dreams*

In Gilchrist's "1957, a Romance," as Rhoda Manning begins to read *Across the River and into the Trees*, she tells her father that Ernest Hemingway is her "favorite writer" (*LDD* 85). In light of this detail about Gilchrist's admittedly most autobiographical character, it is not as surprising as it might otherwise be to find that a contemporary southern woman writer's story cycles have been created in the tradition of the story cycles of Ernest Hemingway and that her prototypical character Rhoda Manning has much in common with Hemingway's Nick Adams. However, the allusions to and parallels with works by Hemingway throughout Gilchrist's work reveal, in addition to Gilchrist's development of story cycles and composite personalities in the tradition of Hemingway, the deconstruction of the Hemingway hero.

Writing of Hemingway's first story cycle, Clinton S. Burhans, Jr., argues that "*In Our Time* is indeed a consciously unified work . . . containing the careful artistry and the central vision of the world and the human condition which characterize Hemingway's writing from beginning to end. As such, *In Our Time* is not only the first of Hemingway's major works but also the best introduction to his thought and art in the rest" (88). Similarly, Gilchrist's first collection of short stories, *In the Land of Dreamy Dreams*, provides several avenues of introduction into her canon. First of all, the collection is a well-crafted short story cycle, a medium with which Gilchrist continues to experiment. Second, in *In the Land of Dreamy Dreams*, Gilchrist begins to develop a composite female personality, which she will continue to draw on in creating other female protagonists for her later stories. Third, this collection introduces two of the major recurring characters of her fiction: Rhoda Manning and Nora Jane Whittington. Fourth, within many of the stories of this volume, one can find the genesis for still other works and characters. And finally, the themes developed in these stories—particularly those concerning issues of class, race, gender, and people's unwillingness to face truths about themselves or others—are all themes Gilchrist will return to again and again in her fiction.

Like *In Our Time*, *In the Land of Dreamy Dreams* is a rendition of a particular kind of short story collection, what Carl Wood calls "a fragmentary novel" and what other critics have termed a short story cycle. Whichever term one prefers, Wood's definition, which he applied to *In Our Time*, can be used to describe *In the Land of Dreamy Dreams*: "a collection of short stories which are unified, not merely by a common theme or subject matter, but also by a discernible plot development dealing with a single character or a single personality type represented in several characters" (725).[1] It seems, therefore, that Gilchrist has written her first collection in the same form with which Hemingway began.

As Hemingway did with Nick Adams, then, Gilchrist placed at the center of several of her stories in this collection a single character who ultimately emerges as the prototype for the other characters in the collection, as well as for most of the protagonists of Gilchrist's entire body of fiction. Susan Garland Mann feels that Nick's "presence is almost continuously felt" throughout *In Our Time*. The unnamed protagonists, for example, "so closely resemble [Nick] Adams that many readers assume he is the character involved. Also, some of the other [named] protagonists . . . remind us of Nick because even if they differ from him in some important ways, they still resemble him since they share similar experiences, personality traits, and family or social backgrounds" (Mann 75). Therefore, Mann concludes from Hemingway's use of a "composite personality," "the reader is almost always in the presence of Nick or someone who invites a comparison with Nick" (75). The same can be said of Rhoda Manning. Her presence in four of the fourteen stories in this collection catches the reader's attention. Her character is reinforced each time she appears. The comparisons between Rhoda and many of the other stories' main characters thereby become more significant, and the reader recognizes the unity of the collection. The stories repeatedly show a type of person who resists maturity and reality. In the stories featuring a child protagonist, the reader can either see or infer the consequences of such resistance in whatever circumstances the protagonist finds herself. In the stories featuring an adult protagonist, Gilchrist depicts the inevitable fate of this type of character.

Illustrating how the adult protagonists of several of the stories of *In Our Time* share a single personality, Carl Wood describes them all as "drifting and disillusioned member[s] of the lost generation who [are] unhappily married and whiling away [their] time in Europe" (722). He then notes that "when Nick appears in an identical situation in . . . 'Cross Country Snow,' the cycle of alternative versions of the same personality is complete" (722). Not only are Gilchrist's characters similar in nature, but also, in the stories with adult protagonists in her first collection, one can see that she, too, has created almost "interchangeable characters in a narrative of the development of a single central personality" (C. Wood 722). Lelia of "The President of the Louisiana Live Oak Society," Alisha of "There's a Garden of Eden," Nora Jane of "The Famous Poll at Jody's Bar," LaGrande of "In the Land of Dreamy Dreams," and Melissa's mother (unnamed) of "Indignities" anticipate the prototype Rhoda Manning, who will be introduced to the reader as an adult in the story "1957, a Romance." Even closer in character to Rhoda, particularly the child Rhoda who is the central character of the three other Rhoda stories from this collection—"Revenge," "1944," and "Perils of the Nile"—are the young girls Helen of "Rich," Margaret of "Generous Pieces," LeLe of "Traveler," and Matille of "Summer, an Elegy." As Wood says of the resemblance of Hemingway's Harold Krebs to Nick Adams in "background and predicament," these girls and women "may [each] be regarded in some sense as an alternate version of the personality Nick [or, in this case, Rhoda] represents" (721).

Although the development of a composite personality in the course of these two story cycles is similar, the two authors' arrangement of the stories in these volumes is exactly opposite. Susan Mann points out that the stories of *In Our Time* "are arranged so that the composite protagonist gradually grows older" (10). In *In the Land of Dreamy Dreams*, on the other hand, the protagonists of the first half of the stories are adults, while the protagonists of the second half are children. Reading the two works intertextually, then, illuminates via contrast what Gilchrist achieves by ordering her stories as she does. Hemingway's order shows the gradual development of a personality type out of the character's experiences from childhood, adolescence, and young adulthood. Gilchrist chooses, rather, to present the shocking adult personalities first and then to illustrate how these women are products of their common upbringing. In this way, Gilchrist emphasizes the sinister role that society (the same social system that tortures her adult protagonists) plays in the development of her child protagonists.

In comparison, both authors interrupt the chronological progression forward (in Hemingway's case) or backward (in Gilchrist's). Hemingway places "My Old Man," with its adolescent protagonist, toward the end of his collection, surrounded by adult Nick Adams stories. Positioning this story of the boy Joe Butler in between these Nick Adams stories, Hemingway recalls to the reader's mind the boy Nick of the early stories, thereby reminding the reader of the early experiences that contributed to the development of the adult personality. In the first two stories of Gilchrist's collection, "Rich" and "The President of the Louisiana Live Oak Society," the narration diverges briefly from the adult protagonists' points of view to their children's perspectives. Similar to what Hemingway has done, Gilchrist is thereby reminding the reader that the adults of these stories were once children growing up within the same social setting, a fact which seems to contribute significantly to their present state of mind. Even more in keeping with Hemingway's interruption of his adult stories with "My Old Man," after the first story with a protagonist based on the child Rhoda prototype, Gilchrist interrupts the (again, backward) progression (or regression, one might say) with a final story with an adult protagonist who looks back on her childhood, during which she suffered "Indignities" (the story's title) similar to those the children in the surrounding stories are suffering. The placement of "Indignities" again reminds the reader that the little girl in the preceding story and those who will appear in the next stories, Rhoda included, will grow up and continue to be affected by the events of their childhoods.

Clinton Burhans notes of *In Our Time* that, as well as through the use of either the recurring character Nick Adams or "a central character like him in all but name" and the almost consistent chronological order of the stories, unity is achieved by "themes introduced and developed" throughout the collection, by Hemingway's "pattern of alternating locales" (90), and by the vignettes that focus "even more specifically on various ways in which men immediately threatened by [the] human condition respond to it. . . . Together, these vignettes show men responding to harsh experience with fear, drunkenness, disillusion, hypocritical prayer, and dissociation" (92). Gilchrist's collection is also unified by its composite personality, as pointed out by Jeanie Thompson and Anita Miller Garner: "In gathering for the reader a whole cast of female characters in various stages of life, with the character Rhoda appearing by name in four of the stories, Gilchrist achieves a kind of coherence of style and voice that is absent from many first collections of short fiction" (104–5). I would add that this unity is enhanced through the employment of all three of the additional methods that Hemingway uses to achieve unity. Gilchrist develops several recurring themes, including class consciousness and familial discord. The stories in the opening section are all set in New Orleans, and after that, most of them are either set in the South or center around southerners living outside the South. Finally, one can find in these stories all of the responses to the human condition that Burhans lists, though most of the characters whose "respon[ses] to harsh experience" are the focus of Gilchrist stories are women. Gilchrist thereby shows that male and female reactions to the "human condition" are not necessarily distinctive.

As already mentioned, Susan Mann explains Hemingway's accomplishment with *In Our Time*'s recurring character and character type: a "composite personality" at the center of a collection that includes several different protagonists. Mann explains that "with Nick Adams, Hemingway provides a substantial, psychologically complex protagonist; and since most of the other major characters closely resemble Nick, the author also successfully creates a composite personality: the Middle American who is wounded in battle and has difficulty readjusting after the war is over" (71). Hemingway's development of a composite personality illuminates the common experiences and attitudes of the male members of the generation of World War I. Upon recognizing that Gilchrist develops a Hemingway-like composite personality in her own collection, the reader should then note how she even draws upon and then transforms his characterization of his composite personality to suit her own purposes. To start, one might note that many of Gilchrist's stories with child protagonists, including several of the Rhoda stories in this first and the later collections, are set during World War II. Although Gilchrist alludes to the war going on in Europe and Asia, she is more concerned with those who stayed at home: the children and wives of soldiers. In her short story "Revenge," for example, Rhoda is staying at her grandmother's house while her father is overseas; her consequential sense of displacement is aggravated by being the only girl among several male cousins. Furthermore, she is confused by the discrepancy between women being in charge now that most of the men are away and yet nothing changing in her favor; she is still marginalized and limited because of her sex. In this story, as well as in "1944" from this same collection, "Victory over Japan" from the next, and the novel *The Annunciation*, Gilchrist alludes to war widows (those who are temporary widows while their husbands are overseas and those who are made widows permanently by the war), though they are not the works' central characters. Still, the child protagonists see the effect of the war on these women; therefore, these women's reactions to their losses are also part of the children's own war experiences.[2]

Also as in Hemingway, then, many of the adult protagonists in Gilchrist's stories who are members of Rhoda's generation have the experience of a world war, though in their case World War II and not combat experience, as part of their implied pasts—which Hemingway would refer to as the part of the iceberg underwater. Of "Big Two-Hearted River," for example, Hemingway explains in *A Moveable Feast*, "The story was about coming back from the war but there was no mention of the war in it" (*MF* 76), though in this case it is a part of the iceberg that would not have concerned him. His view of women during war is confined to the women his soldier characters meet during their adventures or who are not able to understand their veteran sons', husbands', or lovers' angst following the war.

Hemingway elaborates upon his method of omission in *Death in the Afternoon:* "If a writer of prose knows enough about what he is writing about he may omit things that he knows and the reader, if the writer is writing truly enough, will have a feeling of those things as strongly as though the writer had stated them. The dignity of movement of an ice-berg is due to only one-eighth of it being above water" (*DA* 192). Gilchrist also employs the iceberg theory. Consequently, the reader must recognize from the tip of the iceberg provided in a single story that there is much more beneath the surface of that story, which will aid in understanding her characters and their actions. As Sally Helgesen explains in her review of *Victory over Japan*, Gilchrist's stories seek to answer the question asked by her character Traceleen, "How come they went and did that way?" (*VJ* 223). Helgesen writes, "Gilchrist has found a perfect vehicle for answering this question. Characters from one story meet characters from another, destinies cross, and random events are later seen to make sense" (55). Thus, much of the iceberg beneath the surface of a single Gilchrist story is the material found in other Gilchrist stories. However, just as in "Big Two-Hearted River" one does not have to know that Nick has recently returned from fighting in World War I to appreciate much of what the story does, neither does one have to have read Gilchrist's earlier fiction to understand a later work. On the other hand, just as realizing the historical intertext of Hemingway's story does enhance one's appreciation of it, so too does knowledge of the events that have occurred to a Gilchrist protagonist in an earlier work enhance one's reading of a later one.

Recognition of Gilchrist's entire canon as an organic story cycle provides further evidence that she is writing in the tradition of Hemingway, for Hemingway's prototype also continues to develop with each of his books. Joseph DeFalco explains, "The complete journey of Nick Adams is not contained in a full cycle of stories; rather his ultimate destiny is involved with that of the other characters. All are to some extent victims of the same plight, and Nick's fate can be judged according to the reactions of characters with a similar background" (3). The similar development of Gilchrist's Rhoda Manning prototype should be assessed, therefore, not only by her experiences within the stories in which she appears but also by the author's development of her prototype as it is manifested in each new character she creates. As Jeanie Thompson and Anita Garner point out in their discussion of *In the Land of Dreamy Dreams*, Gilchrist "invites us to compare these women with each other and determine whether or not the sum of their experiences adds up to more than just their individual lives" (105).

In subsequent works Gilchrist transforms this Hemingway technique as the character of her later manifestations of the prototype evolves. In contrast, Hemingway's prototype does not *evolve*. Perhaps Hemingway was happy with his initial development of the prototype's personality; he did, after all, focus most of his criticism outward on the *causes* of the character's conflicts (the demands of his parents, the war, women upon him). His protagonists turn inward for the strength to deal with their troubles. Hemingway offers, via their actions, a mode of behavior—always to exercise grace under pressure—for men. Gilchrist's development of her characters' conflicts also reveals society's role as antagonist; however, she makes clear her protagonists' responsibility for what befalls them as well. As her later characters recognize their own culpability, they are able to learn from their mistakes and grow from their experiences. Gilchrist seems, therefore, more interested than Hemingway in having an individual recognize what she can do to improve rather than merely "gracefully" endure her life.

As she allows her prototype to evolve—from Rhoda to Anna Hand—Gilchrist undermines the Hemingway hero's philosophizing about life and death. In her first two novels, *The Annunciation* and *The Anna Papers*, the central characters echo the older waiter of Hemingway's "A Clean, Well-Lighted Place" in *Winner Take Nothing*. Alluding to Hemingway in these works, Gilchrist mocks his character's fear of death in the face of no danger, reducing it to being afraid of the dark. Kenneth G. Johnston explains that at the end of the Hemingway story, the old waiter's "reluctan[ce] to leave the well-lighted café" is due to his lack of a "comforting belief in God, the protecting Father and Shepherd," a lack Johnston sees reflected in the old waiter's parody of the Lord's Prayer and the Hail Mary effected by his "substitut[ing] *nada* for every important word in the prayers" (163). At the end of *The Annunciation*, Amanda, too, transforms the Lord's Prayer to reflect her own state of mind—not at the end of an ordinary day's labor but after the labor of childbirth. Feeling empowered and awed by the experience of giving birth, she changes the words of this patriarchal prayer to "My will be done. . . . My life on my terms, my daughter, my son. My life leading to my lands forever and ever and ever, hallowed be my name, goddammit, my kingdom come, my will be done, amen, so be it, Amanda" (*A* 353). This is, however, neither parody nor blasphemy. Like the old waiter, Amanda does not believe in God, but unlike him, she does have another source of strength: her faith in herself.[3] She, an evolved manifestation of the Rhoda prototype, achieves this feeling of self-worth by the end of her novel. She has decided to have this baby by herself and for herself and is thus empowered rather than entrapped and endangered by pregnancy and childbirth. Thus, her development reflects an evolutionary step in the development of the prototype.

In a less uplifting echo of the old waiter, Anna Hand leaves a doctor/ friend's office at the beginning of *The Anna Papers* after refusing an examination to find out what is wrong with her. She thinks, "No doctors. . . . No checkups. No hospitals, no operating rooms, no chemicals, no nothing. *Nada, de nada, de nada.* . . . You are not sick. There is nothing wrong with you" (*AP* 20).[4] However, there *is* something very much wrong with her—not the fact that she is going to die "someday," which is at the root of what troubles Hemingway's protagonist, but that she is going to die soon. In Hemingway's story, the older waiter tells the younger waiter, "I have never had confidence and I am not young" (*WTN* 22). If one substitutes the word "faith" for "confidence," which is an appropriate substitution given his later ruminations that "it was all a nothing and a man was nothing too" (*WTN* 23), and then notes his reference to his age, one understands that his insomnia reflects his fear of dying and the "*nada*" which follows. In contrast to the old waiter, who may have many years still ahead of him, Anna has cancer, and no amount of positive thinking is going to stop it from growing within her. But like Amanda, Anna has "confidence"—not in a religious faith but in herself and in the order of things in the universe. She will accept her death as part of that order. In fact, she will walk right into it—committing suicide by stepping off a pier with a cyanide tablet in her mouth—rather than try to hide from it in lighted rooms (in her case operating rooms) as the old waiter does in "A Clean, Well-Lighted Place." She is both much like Rhoda—a redhead, a writer, a reader of Hemingway, an overbearing personality, in conflict with her father and brother—and yet an evolution of Rhoda and, even, of Amanda. At the start of her novel, she has achieved the self-acceptance that Amanda reaches only at the end of hers.

Parallels between Prototypes

In spite of this significant contrast in the authors' development—and lack thereof—of their prototypes, something else beneath the surface of Gilchrist's stories is the similarities between the personalities of the original prototypes Nick Adams and Rhoda Manning. Recognizing the parallels prepares the reader for the conflicts that burden the Gilchrist protagonists, though as already suggested, Gilchrist ultimately transforms the Hemingway hero into a more positive heroine. Susan Mann provides three characteristics of the protagonists of *In Our Time:* "they are generally expatriates, committed to some sport, and unhappily married or unhappy in some other relationship" (75). The Gilchrist protagonists in *In the Land of Dreamy Dreams* share at least two of these characteristics, the first and third: they are often outsiders, in attitude if not in actuality, and they suffer in unhappy relationships. Ironically, their communal conflicts and failed relationships are a result of the very kind of male-centered society that Hemingway lauded in his fiction. Perhaps to emphasize this connection, Gilchrist draws upon the second characteristic of Hemingway's protagonists that Mann mentions. In several of the stories of *In the Land of Dreamy Dreams*, some sport plays a significant role: tennis in "The President of the Louisiana Live Oak Society" and "In the Land of Dreamy Dreams," both of which take place among the New Orleans upper class; swimming in "1957, a Romance" and "Traveler," both of which are set in the Deep South in the summer, the latter in the Mississippi Delta; and pole-vaulting in "Revenge," a story in which the end of World War II is prematurely anticipated so that the characters look forward to the 1944 Olympic Games.

Since three of the Rhoda stories in *In the Land of Dreamy Dreams* take place when Rhoda is a child, and half of the stories in this collection also focus on children (or more than half when one includes "Rich" and "The President of the Louisiana Live Oak Society," which have both child and adult protagonists), it is not surprising that a recurring plot line of these stories involves initiation. This unifying element is another significant point of comparison between *In the Land of Dreamy Dreams* and *In Our Time*, an exploration of which leads the Gilchrist reader to recognize the recurrent failure of her child characters to learn a lesson from their experiences. Susan Mann explains that "the process of initiation is so centrally important in *In Our Time* that it almost overshadows the knowledge that should result from the test" (72). She attributes this characteristic to the ironic handling of "the epiphanies or moments of recognition that end many of the . . . stories" (72). Mann calls these "parodies of Joycean epiphanies": "Nick at the conclusion of 'Indian Camp' comforts himself with the thought that he will never die. Similarly, at the end of 'Soldier's Home,' Harold Krebs convinces himself that he can escape his adjustment problems by leaving home for Kansas City" (72).

"Revenge" ends with an ironic epiphany much like the ones Susan Mann points to in the stories of *In Our Time*. As previously mentioned, at the end of this story, Rhoda accomplishes her desire to pole-vault like her brother and male cousins. Everyone is there to see it—including her brother, who earlier denied her access to their "broad jump pit" because of her sex. However, her triumph is paradoxically transformed into defeat by the last sentence of the story: "Sometimes I think whatever has happened since has been of no real interest to me" (*LDD* 124). This sentence foreshadows the stasis of Rhoda's character in later stories. She is only ten years old when this event occurs, and yet apparently at times she thinks of it as the highlight of her life. One gets the sense from this final comment that she has not had many such victories over the oppressive patriarchal society from which she comes. Reviewer Susan Wood suggests that "'Revenge' . . . would have been better without this last sentence" (13). Rather, it would have been *different*. Without the last sentence, the story would have ended with a sense of triumph. The last sentence undermines Rhoda's triumph, which is central to Gilchrist's point regarding the perpetual influence of the patriarchy.

The recurring initiation theme in both collections illuminates the fact that in the four Rhoda stories in this collection, as well as most of the Rhoda stories throughout Gilchrist's canon, Rhoda resists growth. Indeed, Mann's assessment of Hemingway's protagonists—that they "cannot tolerate too much truth . . . [and] often sidestep the difficulties that confront them at the ends of the stories" (72)—applies well to Gilchrist's initial prototype for her composite personality. Again, though, Gilchrist is not so ambiguous as Hemingway: her character may resist the truths facing her, but her readers can't miss them. In contrast, as Mann points out, Hemingway's stories "are riddled with ambiguity, because with Hemingway it is often impossible to distinguish between escapism and the kind of temporary retreat [which Hemingway seems to be suggesting] one *needs* in order to regain a sense of equilibrium" (72, emphasis added). In further contrast, the comic elements of Gilchrist's stories lead the reader to laugh with her at her character's foibles even as we sympathize with her dilemmas, while Hemingway's serious tone fails to suggest that any such mockery is due his character.

As Kenneth Johnston says of Nick Adams, "Nick will suffer through the painful lessons of boyhood and adolescence only to discover the even more terrifying insecurities of adult life" (58), so it will be for Rhoda Manning. Unfortunately, women are less likely to get away with acting according to the Hemingway code of conduct, and this compounds their alienation within and conflict with the patriarchal community. For ex-

ample, the southern lady is revered for enduring, not escaping, the conflicts she faces. Looking ahead only as far as Rhoda at nineteen, in "1957,
a Romance," one finds that she is considered more stubborn than stoic as
she resists her "duties" as wife and mother, and furthermore, although
she is able to get the abortion she seeks, Gilchrist's novel *Net of Jewels*,
which continues this episode in Rhoda's life, shows that this same act
may free her from having another child, but it also binds her more tightly
to her father, whom she tries unsuccessfully throughout the novel to escape.

"1957, a Romance," which concerns primarily Rhoda's abortion, can
be viewed as a deconstruction of Hemingway's "Hills Like White Elephants" (from *Men without Women*), at the center of which is also the
subject of abortion. In this first Rhoda story in Gilchrist's first book (thus
the story in which she introduces her prototype), Gilchrist establishes
Rhoda's connection with the Hemingway prototype. Rhoda's view of
her pregnancy is surprisingly similar to the male character's view in
"Hills Like White Elephants"—who, unnamed in the story, could easily
be Nick Adams; he shares, in any case, the composite personality of
which Nick is the prototype.[5] As Kenneth Johnston assesses him, he is an
"eternal adolescent who refuses to put down roots, or to shoulder the
responsibilities which are rightfully his" (129).

Like Hemingway's male character, Rhoda does not want to have the
baby, and one can infer, too, that, like the woman in Hemingway's story,
Rhoda's husband would have a different opinion on the subject, if he
knew about it. Thus, in her story, Gilchrist has reversed the attitudes of
her characters toward having a baby, thereby undermining any gendered
stereotype regarding distinctions between male and female responses to
pregnancy or babies. She is not retelling the worn-out story of a man
trying to convince a woman to get rid of a baby (found also, for example,
in Dreiser's *An American Tragedy*). Gilchrist recognizes that women are
often just as likely not to be enthusiastic about unplanned pregnancies as
their lovers and that many such women would willingly abort their unwanted babies if not for the the risks to their health. Her limited focus on
Rhoda, in contrast to the way Hemingway deals with this conflict from
both the man's and the woman's perspectives, suggests her belief, during the current period of so much conflict over the morality of abortion,
in a woman's rights regarding her own body. The morality of the issue
was not so much a social concern during the period in which Hemingway wrote his story. Hemingway alludes to the health risks merely in

order to develop the selfishness of his male character, who is willing to risk his lover's life in order to remain unencumbered by a child. His story takes no stand regarding whether abortion is murder. Although Gilchrist apparently does not consider abortion to be murder either, writing her story post–Roe v. Wade, she does propose the opposite view of abortion in contemporary times—that it is a woman's right to choose to terminate her pregnancy if she does not wish to have a baby.

In further contrast to Hemingway's story, from the beginning of Gilchrist's story the female protagonist is shown to be a strong-willed individual: she wants an abortion and goes to significant lengths to get one without concerning herself with her husband's wishes. Her characterization, however, may again put one in mind of the man in "Hills Like White Elephants," whose desire that his lover get an abortion reflects his wish to get rid of a problem rather than take responsibility for his actions. Later stories will reveal that this kind of action is typical of Rhoda, as it is of other Gilchrist female characters: more often than not, Gilchrist's heroines use their strengths to shirk rather than to take responsibility for their actions.

In spite of Rhoda's immaturity and irresponsibility, one does not totally blame her for her decision to terminate her pregnancy. Only nineteen years old, she already has two children, both of whom were delivered by cesarean section, a detail that, given the Hemingway connections already noted, might remind the reader of "Indian Camp," the first Nick Adams story in *In Our Time*. Rhoda's very difficult and terrifying first pregnancy is described in "Adoration," a Rhoda story in *Drunk with Love*.[6] In that story, Rhoda's husband Malcolm, like the husband of the woman suffering through labor in "Indian Camp," is unable to deal with the complications of her pregnancy: "He was scared to death of Rhoda's terrible blood" (*DL* 58). Although Malcolm does not commit suicide like the Indian husband, he does turn Rhoda over to the care of her parents by bringing her to a hospital in the town where they live; and he is not seen again in the story until after the crisis has passed.

The Indian father does not behave well, according to the Hemingway code. He is one of the negative examples from whom Nick should learn a lesson. Susan Mann notes of Hemingway's characters that "what is most important is the manner in which they are able to meet present challenges. Therefore, the actual test in the present tense—whether it is breaking off a relationship that isn't fun anymore or trying to maintain one's equilibrium as chaos threatens—is the heart of each story, its major plot and purpose" (72). Applying Mann's view of the important element in Hemingway's stories to Gilchrist's "1957, a Romance," one can see that Rhoda responds to her "test" by lying, which also goes against Hemingway's honor codes. In this way, Gilchrist uses her protagonist, rather than a minor character, as a negative example.

Here again Gilchrist's objectivity toward her characters is evident. She may limit her concern to Rhoda's dilemma, but she explores this dilemma from all sides. She risks losing the reader's sympathy for Rhoda by having her lie about and cast the blame elsewhere for her plight. For instance, Gilchrist's narrator reveals that the explanation for her pregnancy Rhoda gives her father—that her husband "got [her] pregnant on purpose . . . because he knew [she] was going to leave him"—is untrue: "She always believed her own stories as soon as she told them" (LDD 82). This narrative comment casts suspicion upon Rhoda's later stories about her husband's recent behavior, which, in essence, accuse him of raping her to produce this child. Furthermore, Rhoda's explanation to the doctor as to why she wants an abortion is different from the one she gives her father: to convince the doctor of the necessity of the abortion, she asks, "What would happen to my babies if I died?"—that is, if she were not to survive her next cesarean (LDD 90). Her stories explaining her pregnancy and telling of the problems with her marriage, including an accusation that her husband wants to kill her, become less believable as further evidence of her irresponsible behavior toward her husband and children is revealed by the narrator. The narrator explains, for example, that "this was the third time in two years that Rhoda had run away from her husband and come home to live" (LDD 84). Rhoda's mother attributes Rhoda's returns to her wanting someone to take care of her children rather than to problems in her marriage. Mrs. Manning says to Rhoda's father, "she has to learn to accept some responsibility for something" (LDD 84).[7] Further development of the story, however, brings the reader back around to Rhoda's side once the reader understands her past, including being spoiled by a Hemingway-like father and living in a patriarchal society, the limitations of which extend even to what she can and cannot do with her own body.

Rhoda's choice of accomplice in her plan to get an abortion—her father—reveals one condition of her background that somewhat lessens her responsibility for her actions in this story: her upbringing. Her father admits he has "spoiled her rotten" (LDD 82). His prayer promising "a stained-glass window with nobody's name on it, or a new roof for the vestry" if God will help them get through this ordeal successfully suggests that he believes, and has probably taught Rhoda, that money can buy anything (*LDD* 82). It also recalls one of the responses from Clinton Burhans's list of how Hemingway's characters deal with "harsh experience"—hypocritical prayer. This echo thereby supports my view that Gilchrist's protagonists were raised by Hemingway-like men who shaped their characters, which in turn explains their own likenesses to the Hemingway hero. Recall again the parallel between Rhoda's reaction to her pregnancy and that of the man to his lover's in "Hills Like White Elephants."

Applying Susan Mann's assessment of the Hemingway prototype unable to "tolerate too much truth" and "sidestep[ping] the difficulties that confront them at the end of the stories" (72), one can find another parallel between Rhoda and Nick in the ending to "1957, a Romance." Joseph DeFalco notes of "the infantile and illusory attitudes expressed" at the end of "Indian Camp," "This is not adjustment to the experience— a necessary step toward development; it is a direct denial of the implications of that experience. Poised on the threshold of illumination, Nick takes a step backward. He is not capable of crossing the threshold into more vital experiences as yet" (48). Neither does Rhoda, although several years older than Nick, gain insight from her ordeal in "1957, a Romance," in spite of its serious nature. Here, too, her father is partly to blame for her ability to dismiss so easily her experience: after her abortion, "whenever she woke up he was there beside her and nothing could harm her ever as long as he lived. No one could harm her or have power over her or make her do anything as long as he lived" (*LDD* 92). He takes such good care of her, in fact, that, feeling completely safe, Rhoda has "a dreamless sleep" (*LDD* 92). She suffers no nightmares from which one could infer subconscious guilt or regret for choosing to terminate her pregnancy. Furthermore, the next day, as she thinks about what she has accomplished, she reduces her abortion to the fact that she will not "have to have any more babies this year" (*LDD* 92). Regarding her future handling of possible pregnancies, she decides, "All I have to do is have one more and they'll give me a tubal ligation. . . . It would be worth having another baby for that. Oh well . . . at least I don't have to worry about it anymore for now" (*LDD* 92). She has just had an abortion and she is already thinking about having a baby, just so the doctor will tie her tubes and she will thereafter no longer have to worry about unplanned pregnancies. Rhoda misses the irony of her future plans entirely. She turns calmly to her book—a Hemingway novel—and falls asleep to dream, not of babies but of "leaning across a table staring into Ernest Hemingway's eyes" (*LDD* 93).

It is significant that Rhoda is reading a Hemingway novel during the time of her ordeal, not only because of her inability to gain insight about herself from her experiences but also because of her attitude toward pregnancy, which she would find corroborated in Hemingway's fiction. Debra A. Moddelmog traces Hemingway's depiction of pregnancy and childbirth throughout *In Our Time* and concludes that "nowhere . . . are the joys of pregnancy and young children described. Whenever mentioned, children and having babies are associated with suffering, unhappiness, an end of freedom and innocence, even death" ("Unifying" 28).[8] More recently, Nancy R. Comley and Robert Scholes have discussed the "number of [Hemingway's] finest early stories [with] a male protagonist . . . who resists fatherhood in one way or another" (13), the reason being, they argue, that "evidence in the larger Hemingway Text indicated that to father a son is to write your own death warrant" (15). With this characteristic of Hemingway's fiction in mind, one can see that, after her abortion and because of the memory of her first bloody pregnancy, Rhoda might find in Hemingway's books validation of the rightness of her choice to terminate her pregnancy.

It is also particularly appropriate that the Hemingway novel Rhoda is reading is *Across the River and into the Trees*, in which, as Richard B. Hovey puts it, "Hemingway . . . takes us into the dream world of adolescence" (179). Surprisingly, given this assessment, *Across the River and into the Trees* is a novel about an aging and dying American colonel who has never grown up—and neither will Rhoda have matured by the time she has reached the colonel's age (in Gilchrist's "Mexico" of *Light Can Be Both Wave and Particle*, in the preface and coda to her novel *Net of Jewels*, and in "A Statue of Aphrodite" of *The Age of Miracles*). Certainly her lightheartedness about having an abortion reflects her current immaturity. At the end of "1957, a Romance," looking at herself in a mirror, Rhoda exults in her appearance in her new bathing suit and laughs "clear abandoned laughter . . . at the wild excited face in the bright mirror" (*LDD* 95). One could use Joseph DeFalco's description of the final view of Nick given in "Indian Camp" to describe Rhoda's attitude here: "infantile optimism" (49). There is no mention of either any guilt for her actions or plans to divorce the husband whom she has described as being such a dangerous bully.[9] Rather, she luxuriates in the false sense of freedom that the abortion has given her and responds with generous goodwill to the members of her family gathered for Fourth of July festivities.

In another Rhoda story in *In the Land of Dreamy Dreams*, "Perils of the Nile," Rhoda is given another chance to learn a truth about life but rejects it by turning to one of humanity's sources of comfort: religion. Upon losing her new ring, Rhoda prays for its recovery—although "usually Rhoda wasn't much on praying" (*LDD* 133). She has earlier in her life associated religion with death and thus has not found the comfort in it that others do:

> When she said her prayers at night all she thought about was Jesus coming to get her in a chariot filled with angels. She didn't want Jesus to come get her. She didn't want to be lying in a box like Jerry Hollister, who was run over in his driveway. . . .
>
> Rhoda didn't want anything to do with that. She didn't want anything to do with Jesus or religion or little boys lying on their dining room tables with their eyes closed.
>
> . . . She didn't want anything to do with God and Jesus and dead people and people nailed up on crosses or eaten by lions or tortured by Romans. (*LDD* 133–34)

Rhoda is apparently repelled by the violence that has been directed historically toward those who profess to be Christians, and she has associated this violence with the death of her young friend. However, faced with personal "tragedy" (the loss of her ring), she seeks the comfort that faith provides—or at least the sense that she is doing something, praying in this case, toward rectifying the disagreeable situation. Therefore, as do many people—like her father in "1957, a Romance" and like the soldier (who might be Nick Adams) in the vignette of chapter 7 of *In Our Time*—Rhoda makes a deal with God: "If you will get it back to me I promise I'll start believing in you. . . . If you'll help me find it I'll be nice to everyone from now on. . . . I'll quit lying so much. . . . I'll do everything you want from now on. I'll even go overseas and be a missionary if that's what you want" (*LDD* 134–35).

Not only are such deals with God too common for the reader to entertain the idea that Rhoda will keep her promises after Bebber brings the ring back, but Rhoda also undermines her promise immediately by getting caught up in another egocentric fantasy, which she builds around the thought of herself as a missionary: "She could see herself standing on a distant seashore handing out bright fabrics to the childlike natives. Rhoda was beginning to feel quite holy. She was beginning to like talking to Jesus" (*LDD* 135). She concludes her prayer, then, by lying about her devotion and qualifying it at the same time: "To tell the truth I have always believed in you. And I'll be going to Sunday school all the time now *if* I get my ring back" (*LDD* 135, emphasis added). She is comforted by her prayer, since she has placed the responsibility for finding the ring in someone else's hands, and she is distracted from her misfortune by her fantasies. Since the reader knows by story's end that Rhoda's ring will be returned, one can see that once again Rhoda has evaded a harsh truth about life: that things do not always go one's way.

In the Hemingway vignette just mentioned, the soldier prays, "*Dear jesus please get me out. Christ please please please christ. If you'll only keep me from getting killed I'll do anything you say. I believe in you and I'll tell every one in the world that you are the only one that matters. Please please dear jesus*" (*IOT* 67). Like Rhoda's, the soldier's prayer is "answered": he is not killed. Using *In Our Time* as an intertext of *In the Land of Dreamy Dreams*, one can find in the soldier's actions support for the argument that Rhoda does not follow through on her promises to God: "*The next night back at Mestre he did not tell the girl he went upstairs with at the Villa Rossa about Jesus. And he never told anybody*" (67). If this young man's life has been spared and yet he fails to live up to his end of the bargain he made with God, then it is not difficult to surmise that Rhoda, too, who was never in such real danger, will not feel compelled to hold up her end of her bargain.

Although their situations are so completely different, one is reminded by the comparable response to "crisis" of the similarities between the prototypes, a result, perhaps, of the Gilchrist character's Hemingway-like father, who has had such a strong influence upon the development of his daughter's personality. Indeed, one might recall Dudley Manning's own bargain with God in "1957, a Romance." Rhoda resists her father's influence in the story "Music" in *Victory over Japan*, in which her father takes her on a trip to get her to stop smoking, to be more respectful to her parents, and to calm her overall demeanor and behavior. Furthermore, during their journey he tries to impress upon her an appreciation of the beauty and wonder of God's world; but Rhoda does not share her father's values. She does not believe in God and resists her father's attempts to force his cosmic view on her as much as she resists his social view. She is frustrated in her inability to support her theories of evolution against her father's creation theories and strikes out at him by trying to get another man's approval and thus a man's validation of her worth—the consequence of which is the loss of her virginity.

Like the Nick Adams story "Ten Indians" in *Men without Women*, "Music" centers on the protagonist's relationship with her father as well as her first sexual experience. However, in contrast, whereas Dr. Adams comforts Nick after his Indian girlfriend has been seen with another boy, Mr. Manning's harsh treatment of Rhoda drives her to her sexual encounter with a stranger. This time, the comparison has led to an analysis of the point of its ceasing, for the men react quite differently to their children's bittersweet introductions to sex. It should not be surprising that, while the young man's father would not be too upset by his son's emerging sexuality and thus can concentrate on his son's feelings about being cuckolded by his "first love," the young woman's father is so distressed by the idea of his daughter as a sexual being that he does not consider her probably tumultuous emotions after her sexual encounter as he rages about her affair.

"Music" also recalls the earlier Hemingway story "Indian Camp" in that both stories begin with the protagonist and his or her father setting off on a journey, during which the protagonist is initiated into adulthood: Nick observes both birth and death, and Rhoda participates in sexual relations. In "Indian Camp," the characterization of Dr. Adams is much less positive than in "Ten Indians": he is less nurturing of Nick, determined as he is to "make a man of" his son. In his reading of "Indian Camp," Kenneth Johnston argues that

> Nick's father must bear much of the blame for the failure of the initiation. In his attempt to educate Nick in the facts of life—the lesson will get out of hand and will include the facts of death, too—he thrusts his son into a situation, brutal and shocking, from which he can not escape. . . . As one recalls, the journey began with Dr. Adams' protecting Nick from the cold world with his cradling arm and his euphemistic language. Actually, Dr. Adams is not well prepared for his dual role of medicine man and moral guide. (53)

Comparably, one realizes that in "Music" Rhoda's father takes her to the site of her deflowering. This turn of events becomes even more ironic when one realizes that, as Nick's father intended to make a man out of his son, Rhoda's father's intention upon deciding to take her on this trip with him was to make her behave more in line with his concept of a young lady. Johnston's assessment of Nick's experience in "Indian Camp" can be applied to Rhoda's experience in "Music": "The initiation has miscarried. Nick Adams has not been matured by the experience; rather, he has regressed toward childhood, comforted by an illusion which the events of the night should have destroyed" (51).[10] After Rhoda's sexual encounter, she is seen lost in a fantasy in which some young man—either her current love interest back home or the young man who has just used her or the pilot who is, while Rhoda is fantasizing, flying her back home—stands at a bookstore window in which he sees her latest book, which is dedicated to him. In her fantasy, he is "crying and broken-hearted because Rhoda was lost to him forever, this famous author, who could have been his, lost to him forever" (*VJ* 50).

"Music" ends years later when Rhoda receives a letter from her father saying, *"Take my name off that book. . . . Imagine a girl with your advantages writing a book like that. Your mother is so ashamed of you"* (*VJ* 51). Like Nick Adams, Rhoda has become a writer. But a more interesting parallel between this Rhoda story and Hemingway himself can be found in Philip Young's report of Hemingway's father returning six copies of *in our time* (an earlier version of *In Our Time*) to his son. Young quotes Hemingway as saying that his own father "would not tolerate such filth in his home" (18). Young continues on the subject of Hemingway's father: "Later on when his son was becoming famous he is known to have answered sadly the question of how the boy was making out: 'Ernest's written another dirty book'" (18). I will leave it to the Hemingway scholars to analyze his father's influence upon his life, work, and apparently his death. Turning to Gilchrist, then, the reader will find that she, too, has commented outside her fiction upon her relationship with her own father: "There is an old gorgeous man living right here in Jackson, Mississippi, that I have been loving and fighting with and showing off for since I was born. . . . My father" (*FS* 155). Gilchrist's conflict with her father has influenced much of her fiction. Since this is not a biographical study, a discussion of the influence of this relationship upon her *life* is not appropriate, though I will add that she suggests in the same journal entry that the conflict is resolving itself—"My father and I have almost stopped arguing now that he is seventy-seven and I am fifty-one" (*FS* 155)—given its apparent effect on her writing. She has since allowed her prototype to experience a similar beginning of the end of her conflict with her father. In the first story of *The Age of Miracles*, "A Statue of Aphrodite," a "pushing sixty"-year-old Rhoda, who introduces herself as an established writer, explains that she decided to move to Jackson some years back (when she was around fifty) "to make my peace with my old man. 'The finest man I've ever known,' as I wrote in the dedication to a book of poems [which explains how his name got on her book, as indicated by the lines quoted from "Music"]. I don't think he ever read them" (*AM* 3). Even while perceiving the possibility of resolution, then, the reader is reminded of the earlier story, which suggests in turn that at some level the conflict will always be present. She can forgive and learn to get along with her father, but how can she forget his earlier rejection of her work?

Although several of Hemingway's stories do focus on father-son relationships, Richard Hovey notes that it is Hemingway's *mother* characters who "regularly appear as domineering over their families; as destroyers, actual or potential, of their children; as champions of respectability and defenders of cruel sentimentalities and false values" (43)—all of which roles are demonstrated in "Soldier's Home" of *In Our Time* and "A Canary for One" and "Now I Lay Me" of *Men without Women.* He calls the fathers "weak . . . men on whom sons dare not wholly rely" (43), as is also demonstrated in "Soldier's Home" and "Now I Lay Me," as well as in "The Doctor and the Doctor's Wife" and "My Old Man" of *In Our Time.* It is not surprising that a male author (Hemingway) would portray sons set against domineering mothers while a female author (Gilchrist) would portray daughters set against domineering fathers. Besides Rhoda, whose tumultuous relationship with her father is the central conflict of "1957, a Romance," "Music," and the novel *Net of Jewels,* Gilchrist's Anna Hand has a domineering father whom she loves and fights her whole life. Neither Gilchrist's female protagonists nor Hemingway's male protagonists receive much help from the parent of their own sex in their battles against the will of the other parent. Most of the mothers in Gilchrist's fiction support the patriarchy, as in "Revenge"; accept its double standards, as in "A Wedding in Jackson"; and do not understand their daughters who struggle for independence, as in "1957, a Romance."[11]

As the fathers in Hemingway's fiction are often employed as negative examples of dealing with confrontation, Gilchrist's mother-characters are certainly not role models for their daughters. Indeed, Gilchrist's little girls and young women have as much difficulty with their mothers as do Hemingway's boys and young men (though, again, these are not likely to be central conflicts in their lives as their mothers are easily ignored). These Hemingway and Gilchrist mothers are products of similar environments, the same environment that is trying to turn Gilchrist's characters into their mothers—and these girls and young women do not find their mothers any more likable than Nick or Krebs find theirs. Once the nature of the mother-daughter relationship is recognized, Rhoda's choice of parent—her father—to turn to for help with her abortion is less surprising. Rhoda knows who has the power in her society. Therefore, the reader should not be surprised to find that, like Nick Adams and Joe Butler, Gilchrist's young girl characters have more significant relationships with their fathers than with their mothers. Their fathers may not have the best characters, but they are more positive role models than their weak mothers.

Neither Hemingway nor Gilchrist heeds chronology in telling his or her prototype's story, although in *In Our Time* the stories are arranged almost chronologically. The first four Nick Adams stories proceed in order from his childhood to his adolescence.[12] The vignette of chapter 6, which takes place in the middle of battle, is the next time Nick is mentioned by name; and then the last two Nick Adams stories occur after the war. Similarly, in Gilchrist's second collection, *Victory over Japan*, the reader is given one story each, from Rhoda's childhood, adolescence, and adulthood. However, in *In the Land of Dreamy Dreams*, Gilchrist ignores chronology entirely in her arrangement of the Rhoda stories, introducing Rhoda in this first collection at the age of nineteen in "1957, a Romance," then portraying in the story "Revenge" a ten-year-old Rhoda. In the third Rhoda story, entitled "1944," she is eight, and in the last Rhoda story in this collection, "Perils of the Nile," she is twelve. Thus, Gilchrist has arranged the Rhoda Manning stories in her first collection more like Hemingway's arrangement of the Nick Adams stories in *Men without Women*, where Nick first appears as a soldier, then as a younger man, the next time as an adolescent, and finally as a soldier again (counting only the stories that refer to the protagonist by the name Nick Adams).

Noting the connection to this later Hemingway collection may lead one to ponder its significance and realize that many of the Rhoda stories in one way or another focus on "women without men." Although Rhoda's father plays a significant role in "1957, a Romance," she herself has left her husband; furthermore, she has made her decision to have an abortion without consulting him. In "Revenge" and "1944," Rhoda experiences and witnesses, respectively, part of the effects of her country's involvement in a world war: men like her father had to leave their families for a while, and their families had to get along without them during this period; some of these men, husbands of people she knew, did not return after the war was over, and their wives had to learn to get along without them forever. On the other hand, as these Gilchrist stories reveal, even in these situations of "women without men," the influence of the patriarchy continues. In "Revenge," for example, Rhoda's father writes to his son from Europe, where he is serving during World War II, "to take good care of [Rhoda] as [she] was [her] father's own dear sweet little girl" (*LDD* 112). Rhoda's brother, Dudley, Jr., interprets the letter to mean that Rhoda is not to participate in their "Olympic training" in spite of the fact that the Rhoda he is in conflict with throughout the story is no "dear sweet little girl." Surprisingly, no one on the plantation overrides young Dudley's edict that "this is only for boys" (*LDD* 112), even though Rhoda's grandmother is the voice of authority on the place at this time. Rather than admonish the boys for excluding Rhoda from their games and force them to let her play, their grandmother and the housekeeper suggest to Rhoda other forms of amusement that are more suitable for girls: playing with a little girl at a neighboring plantation and learning to dance.

More Echoes of Hemingway

Tom and Letty Wilson were rich in everything. They were rich in friends because Tom was a vice-president of the Whitney Bank of New Orleans and liked doing business with his friends, and because Letty was vice-president of the Junior League of New Orleans and had her picture in *Town and Country* every year at the Symphony Ball.

The Wilsons were rich in knowing exactly who they were because every year from Epiphany to Fat Tuesday they flew the beautiful green and gold and purple flag outside their house that meant that Letty had been queen of the Mardi Gras the year she was a debutante. Not that Letty was foolish enough to take the flag seriously. (*LDD* 3)

This passage, from Gilchrist's "Rich," unmistakably echoes the tone of the opening of Hemingway's "Mr. and Mrs. Elliot":

Mr. and Mrs. Elliot tried very hard to have a baby. They tried as often as Mrs. Elliot could stand it. They tried in Boston after they were married and they tried coming over on the boat. They did not try very often on the boat because Mrs. Elliot was quite sick. She was sick and when she was sick she was sick as Southern women are sick. That is women from the Southern part of the United States. Like all Southern women Mrs. Elliot disintegrated very quickly under sea sickness. (*IOT* 85)

Regarding the content of the Hemingway passage and the two stories as a whole, there are parallels as well. Both couples are southern, and the Wilsons have difficulty conceiving, too. In point of contrast, Gilchrist's female character is not a stereotypical swooning southern lady. In the course of this story she will withstand several tragedies, including the violent deaths of two of her children and her husband. Echoing the tone of this particular Hemingway story—reputed to be Hemingway's way of parodying T. S. Eliot, whom he supposedly did not consider much of a "man"—Gilchrist calls attention from the very first story in her first book of fiction to one of the accomplishments of her writing: her parodying and thereby re-visioning of Hemingway's depiction of women.

Gilchrist echoes "Mr. and Mrs. Elliot" again in *In the Land of Dreamy Dreams* within the story "Suicides." Comparing these stories, one finds that the two authors are more sympathetic toward the character of their own sex: Hemingway toward Mr. Elliot (even as he employs the character to mock the "unmanly man"), Gilchrist toward Janet Treadway. In both stories, a person of the opposite sex to these two characters intrudes upon the marriage: Mrs. Elliot's girlfriend and Philip Treadway's dead brother. Finally, in both stories a baby is seen as an answer to the couples' problems—but fails to be so: the Elliots are unsuccessful in their attempts to have a baby; Philip and Janet do have one, but, if anything, the baby serves to loosen further Philip's tenuous hold on his sanity. Given these parallels and Philip's suicide, Gilchrist's story seems once again to deconstruct Hemingway's promulgation, in his fiction and his life, of escaping life's "pressures" via any means necessary, even suicide if that is the only way. Indeed, Gilchrist emphasizes with her character's death that there is sometimes nothing "graceful" about suicide.

In contrast, in her story "Indignities," also in *In the Land of Dreamy Dreams*, Gilchrist seems to suggest that the Hemingway code of grace under pressure might in some situations be put to good use. In this story, too, she introduces a motif that will recur throughout her canon: cancer. Once characters are struck with the disease or face it in a loved one, the focus of their story is on their reactions, the grace and courage with which they deal with the situation. One might compare Gilchrist's development of this conflict with the recurrent war wounds suffered by

Hemingway's protagonists and his focus on how each man deals with the wound. However, although Gilchrist may make incredible heroes out of her cancer victims, she never romanticizes the disease the way that Hemingway romanticizes war. The victim of cancer in this story has just had a mastectomy when "Indignities" opens, and she dies before its close.

I mentioned previously the role of cancer in *The Anna Papers* as a much more real threat than the waiter's fear of the dark in Hemingway's "A Clean, Well-Lighted Place." Another parallel with Hemingway can be found in this novel. Like Hemingway, Gilchrist identifies very closely with her protagonists, and both writers often have their protagonists be writers. Speaking through the thoughts of his prototype in "On Writing," a Nick Adams sketch that at one time concluded "Big Two-Hearted River," Hemingway explains how he transforms fact into fiction: "Of course he'd never seen an Indian woman having a baby. . . . He'd seen a woman have a baby on the road to Karagatch and tried to help her. That was the way it was" (*NAS* 238). Gilchrist, too, speaks through a character to explain how she transforms fact into fiction. In *The Anna Papers*, Anna tells her lover that he has inspired her to write a love story and that he will "be in it" (*AP* 112). However, she explains, she will transform him into "a Chinese graduate student who meets a girl at dawn on a bridge" (*AP* 112). The story she is planning here appears in Gilchrist's next book of fiction, *Light Can Be Both Wave and Particle*. Also like Nick when he refers in his thoughts to Hemingway's "Indian Camp," Anna claims her creator's work as her own when she describes two other stories she will write, both of which appear in Gilchrist's collection of novellas, *I Cannot Get You Close Enough*.[13]

Indeed, Gilchrist's fiction is becoming increasingly metafictional in this way.[14] *Net of Jewels* begins with Rhoda introducing herself to the reader, comparing herself to Anna ("I'm not a great writer like my cousin Anna Hand, but I'm not bad either" [*NJ* 3]), and explaining how the novel came to be: "I meant this as a book of short stories and I started writing it that way. Then the stories started to bleed into each other and I decided to go on and let them bleed" (*NJ* 3). This explanation seems to sum up how Gilchrist's organic story cycle developed. Other metafictional instances of this type can be found in the Rhoda stories of *The Age of Miracles*. In "A Wedding in Jackson," Rhoda remarks that she "once killed a character in a novel on that road" and later "brought him back to life in a short story" (*AM* 37), which events can be found in

Gilchrist's *The Annunciation* and one of its sequel short stories in *Light Can Be Both Wave and Particle*. In "Joyce" (also in *The Age of Miracles*), she tells about the acceptance of her first stories for publication in *Prairie Schooner* and *Intro*, magazines in which Gilchrist also published early stories.

While the metafictional elements in Gilchrist's fiction remind the reader of her kinship with Hemingway—like him, she has difficulty divorcing her own ego from her fiction—two of the most interesting allusions to Hemingway in Gilchrist's fiction (in the short story "Traceleen, She's Still Talking" in *Victory over Japan* and in the novella "Mexico" in *Light Can Be Both Wave and Particle*) illuminate, perhaps best, how Gilchrist ultimately questions this model. In her essay on intertextual readings for Patrick O'Donnell and Robert Con Davis's *Intertextuality and Contemporary American Fiction*, Thaïs Morgan argues that Julia Kristeva's "most valuable contribution to the debate on intertextuality" is "the idea that an intertextual citation is never innocent or direct, but always *transformed, distorted, displaced, condensed,* or *edited* in some way *in order to suit the speaking subject's value system*" (Morgan 260, emphasis added). Reading Gilchrist intertextually with Hemingway, for example, shows how Gilchrist has both "transformed" Hemingway's masculine prototype into a quite feminine character type and "distorted" the reader's perception of the original Hemingway hero by refocusing the reader's attention onto the effects of the ultramacho character's actions upon the women around him. In the characterization of Rhoda, the prototype for all of Gilchrist's protagonists, the small detail that Hemingway is her favorite writer illuminates what is perhaps the central conflict for all of Gilchrist's female characters, most particularly Rhoda and her cousin Crystal. They have been raised by and alongside and are repeatedly attracted to men who would qualify as Hemingway heroes. Consequently, these women follow the examples of their fathers, brothers, and other male relatives to become Hemingway heroes themselves—"they can wisecrack and drink as hard as their male counterparts," as one reviewer says of Gilchrist's "New South heroines" (Carper 5)—while at the same time they strive to be less strong-willed and more dependent in order to be the kind of woman such men would find appealing. Their personalities are unable to reconcile with their desires, and therein lies the conflict of many of Gilchrist's stories.

Returning briefly to "Perils of the Nile," for example, one realizes that although Bebber Dyson seems to admire Rhoda's unique and brazen personality, he is more attracted to her soft-spoken, less self-centered mother: "Bebber thought about Rhoda's mother a lot. She was very beautiful and had looked straight at him out of sad blue eyes *while he talked about himself*" (*LDD* 131, emphasis added). Consequently, in spite of the anguish he knows Rhoda is experiencing over the loss of her ring, he withholds it from her to present it to her mother.

"Traceleen, She's Still Talking" reaches its climax during a parody of a Hemingwayesque safari, a sport Hemingway expects his reader to accept as a serious test of "manhood." Crystal's brother Phelan imports wild game from various countries and sets up "safaris" on his Texas ranch for businessmen too busy to go to Africa. In the course of the narration of this hilarious story, Gilchrist mocks the safaris in Hemingway's stories by emphasizing their falseness. One of the characters explains the way Phelan's "safari" works:

> "Now the boys will let 'em wait awhile and get all hot and bothered. Then they'll let one of the boars go. . . . Then Mr. Phelan'll let somebody shoot and he'll shoot too in case they miss and then they'll keep letting them loose till everybody that paid gets to shoot one. Then they'll be through and Rainey'll put the boars in a tarp and take them off to be stuffed unless somebody wants to drive home with it tied to the hood of the jeep." (*VJ* 270)

The reader might remember from Hemingway's "The Short Happy Life of Francis Macomber" the safari guide's various thoughts alluding to how the African safaris are similarly set up. Part of his job, too, is to back up the shooting of the paying participants, and there are natives on hand to take care of the kill for them. The description of the safari in Gilchrist's story also reminds the reader that although Francis Macomber supposedly finally behaves courageously when he hunts the buffalo, Robert Wilson was there to back him up. Thus, Gilchrist's story is not as much of a parody as it at first seems, recognition of which undermines Francis Macomber's achievement of "manhood" before his death.

In Gilchrist's story, no one is killed or even hurt and, not surprising, Gilchrist's female character is much more sympathetically drawn. Crystal's conflict with her macho brother does not end in her shooting him in order to maintain the power in their relationship. Indeed, she has no such power; their conflict, in fact, involves her desire to *share* power with him: to be allowed to control her half of their inheritance so that all of it is not thrown away on such schemes as this one. Instead of killing him, then, she drives his Mercedes Benz, only just imported from Germany, right into the middle of the set-up chase for a boar and then into the cages where other "wild" animals are kept. Here again, Gilchrist reminds the reader of the Hemingway story and undermines its protagonist's development, for Francis begins shooting at the buffalo from their car. Beneath this parody—or perhaps comic deconstruction—of Hemingway is a serious complaint against the macho hero he lauded, for this is the type of man Crystal grew up with and keeps marrying, according to the other Crystal stories of *Victory over Japan, Drunk with Love, The Age of Miracles,* and the novella "Summer in Maine" in *I Cannot Get You Close Enough.* Crystal is repeatedly hurt by such men. Unlike Amanda and Anna, Crystal does not develop beyond Rhoda in recognition of her abilities and in utilization of them for purposes other than attracting a man's attention.

Rhoda, the reader of Hemingway, not only finds herself confronted time and again with this same type of man but also admires such men. She marries her first husband because of his physical appeal to her, and in "Mexico," which takes place when she is fifty-three, she is still measuring her own value according to the opinions held of her by macho men. Even more Hemingwayesque than Rhoda's brother and cousin in this story is Rhoda's behavior at a bullfight. Her repeated reference to bullfighting as "Death in the afternoon" reflects her consciousness of her chance, finally, to live a Hemingway novel—as she dreamed of doing in "1957, a Romance" when she fell asleep after reading Hemingway's *Across the River and into the Trees.* At the bullfight in Mexico, she, like Lady Brett Ashley in *The Sun Also Rises,* attracts the attention of a young matador. She does not, however, possess the same scruples that keep Brett from continuing her affair and thus "ruining" the bullfighter's career. In order to keep Rhoda from her rendezvous, her brother and cousin must ply her with alcohol all afternoon so that she is too drunk to meet the young man. It is not that they are concerned with the bullfighter's career either, however. Rather, they are worried about Rhoda's meeting and having an affair with a strange Mexican. In this story, as in the Crystal story, then, Gilchrist finally mocks not safaris and bullfights but bored Americans—like Hemingway's heroes—who are chasing after such thrills because of their own empty lives.

Returning to *In the Land of Dreamy Dreams,* one finds, in the story "There's a Garden of Eden," another character seeking adventure to fill the boredom of her seemingly Edenic life: "Scores of men, including an ex-governor and the owner of a football team, consider Alisha Terrebone to be the most beautiful woman in the state of Louisiana. If she is unhappy what hope is there for ordinary mortals? Yet here is Alisha, cold and bored and lonely, smoking in bed" (*LDD* 38). The narrator's tone is clearly ironic, mocking those who presume that a beautiful, wealthy woman is without problems. But Alisha is dissatisfied with her empty life, not content to be a trophy wife or sex object. She longs for love, not just lovers, and her beauty and wealth apparently attract the wrong men.

The image of Alisha presented in this opening, together with the pouring rain outside, which emphasizes her entrapment, might call to mind the young woman in Hemingway's "Cat in the Rain." Alisha's story, then, provides the reader another focus on Hemingway's female character, a more fully developed view of the inner turmoil of this whiny woman who is seemingly close to becoming hysterical over a wet cat. Although this is one of Hemingway's more sympathetic depictions of women, his central concern is still the consequences of World War I. The woman's husband is apparently another member of the Lost Generation who is unable to face returning to the United States and starting a home and family.

To be fair, Hemingway does show in this story the consequential suffering of the veteran's wife as she must wander around with this man to whom she is committed. But reading the two stories together, one realizes more fully the woman's entrapment. As a middle-class American woman, she has been raised to one occupation, homemaker. Her value system and sense of social order has not been upset by firsthand experiences of a world war, so how is she to understand her husband's refusal to allow her to fulfill her role in life? And, given the time difference between this story and Alisha's, one realizes that she doesn't even really have the option, which Alisha has exercised repeatedly, of divorcing her husband in hopes of finding a more satisfying relationship.

Returning to Gilchrist's story, however, one realizes that although Alisha's options seem to be more open than this woman's, her chances of fulfillment are not much better.[15] She has had three disappointing marriages. Consequently, she has since insulated herself within her home, choosing tedium over the hurt of disappointment, until the day she takes a risk by having an affair with a young carpenter whom she has called to do some repairs around her home. Sexual relations with this man, whose occupation recalls that of Christ, seem to give Alisha new life, just when she "was going to stop dying [her] hair" (*LDD* 47)—that is, just when she was going to resign herself to old age. But his role in the story as an apparent savior is undermined by an earlier exchange between Alisha and her maid. When the maid reports that the carpenter has arrived, Alisha asks, "Which carpenter?" (*LDD* 39). The maid's answer, "Now it's going to be blue-collar workers," suggests that she knows why Alisha is asking—because Alisha will get up and dress to speak with the carpenter if he is "the young one"—and that this is not the first time that Alisha has taken a lover so spontaneously (*LDD* 39). The probability of other impulsive affairs deflates Alisha's later romantic idealizing of her affair with the carpenter. Looking back into the story provides a second point compromising its seemingly optimistic ending. Alisha's and her lover's thoughts reveal that they both fantasize during their lovemaking; thus, they are not making love to each other but rather to ideas they have of each other, and they are simultaneously creating false images of themselves: "Then Alisha closed her eyes and pretended she was an Indian princess lying in a tent deep in a forest, dressed in a long white deerskin robe, waiting for Jeff Chandler to come and claim her for his bride. . . . Then Michael closed his eyes and pretended he was a millionaire going to bed with a beautiful, sad old actress" (*LDD* 44). Not even Michael, who leads Alisha out of her false paradise at the end of the story, can rescue her if she chooses fantasy over reality. Furthermore, Michael's potential to be Alisha's savior is undermined by his desire for wealth, apparent in his fantasy; he seems to want to share Alisha's lifestyle rather than help her to escape it.

Also calling to mind the young wife of "Cat in the Rain," Margaret of "Generous Pieces" (and Rhoda in later stories) longs for a real home. Her family, like Hemingway's couple, moves around a lot. With their most recent move, the stability of Margaret's life has been further threatened by her friend's mother, with whom, Margaret has discovered, her father is having an affair. Still, Margaret clings to her father's promise that "this time we are going to stay put" (*LDD* 97). She tries "not to think about Christina's mother . . . how she leans over my father's chair handing him things when they have dinner at our house" (*LDD* 100); she concentrates, rather, on her friendship with Christina and the security it offers of being part of the popular crowd at school (another concern she shares with Rhoda, thus reminding the reader of Gilchrist's female composite personality).

The story's climax reveals that Margaret is finally unable to dispel completely her fears that her family, the one constant in her life, will be torn apart by her father's affair. Walking home late one day, she is chased by a group of boys who throw clods of dirt at her. This somewhat typical incident of boys trying to get a little girl's attention terrifies Margaret. Even after they are gone, she continues to run, feeling suddenly "afraid of falling down, afraid of every shadow, afraid to look up, afraid of the trees, afraid of the moon" (*LDD* 101). As is the case for the woman in "Cat in the Rain," who is unduly upset over not finding the cat she has seen outside her hotel window, the true reason for Margaret's seemingly exaggerated dismay over having dirt thrown at her by some strange boys is her precarious family life. With the cat, Hemingway's protagonist could pretend for a while that her hotel room is a home, which, one can see by the list of her desires, is what she really wants: "I want to eat at a table with my own silver and I want candles. . . . I want to brush my hair out in front of a mirror and I want a kitty" (*IOT* 94). Similarly, what Margaret is really afraid of is finding herself in another strange place, this time without both of her parents there to protect her. Both the young wife and Margaret are thwarted in their desire for a stable home by a dominating male—the woman's husband and Margaret's father.

Such a comparison serves to undermine somewhat Hemingway's reputation for being misogynous in his characterization of women, for reading "Cat in the Rain" intertextually with "Generous Pieces" can lead to an understanding of Hemingway's female character's desires. "Generous Pieces" concludes with no resolution to Margaret's terror, which is "watching [her] with cold eyes from the mirror on [her] father's dresser" (*LDD* 102). This lack of resolution, taken together with the connection between this story and Hemingway's "Cat in the Rain," emphasizes the absence of any resolution to that story's protagonist's problem: although the woman finally gets the cat, the reader knows that this temporary consolation will not solve her conflict. Thus, reading these works intertextually allows the reader a deeper sympathy for Hemingway's character than his characterization of her by itself might otherwise elicit.

Reading the two works together also brings up another point of contrast between the two writers—in the role of food in their works. In "Generous Pieces," Margaret refuses to try on the skirt Mrs. Carver has made for her, not because she is angry with Mrs. Carver for having an affair with her father but because of her own self-consciousness about "how big [her] waist is" (*LDD* 99). A concern with weight is expressed by several of the characters throughout Gilchrist's canon, young girls to middle-aged women, who share the composite personality. Eating is, according to Joseph Flora, "an important literary motif in most of the Nick Adams stories," too (*Hemingway's* 161).[16] In contrast to eating in Gilchrist's fiction, in Hemingway's it is not associated with guilt. Indeed, in a Hemingway scene involving food, the characters are most often enjoying their meal. Furthermore, Hemingway gives much more leisurely descriptions of the process of preparing meals and eating than does Gilchrist. Her characters are most often driven to food by frustration; thus, they are usually eating in a frenzy, sometimes right out of the refrigerator, as LeLe does in "Traveler" (also in *In the Land of Dreamy Dreams*).

One notable example of the contrasting role of food in the work of these two authors is that whereas Nick's father comforts his son with food in "Ten Indians" (*MWW* 102), Rhoda's mother insists that Rhoda go on a diet in *Net of Jewels* (*NJ* 21). This difference is not so surprising, of course, given the different sexes of their protagonists: Hemingway's protagonists are usually male and thus not as likely to be concerned about their weight as are Gilchrist's female protagonists. In this contrast one sees another instance of the double standard for men and women regarding weight, which Gilchrist alludes to directly in "Rich" when Letty Wilson attempts to help her daughter Helen curb her appetite, telling her, "You're so pretty . . . we don't want you to get too fat," while she says nothing to her husband about his weight gain (*LDD* 12). In "Traveler," LeLe's friend Fielding also mixes a compliment in with his *well-intentioned* advice about her weight: "You would be a really beautiful girl if you lost ten pounds" (*LDD* 147). The reader is thoroughly disgusted when he follows this statement up with "I'm only saying this because we've gotten to be such good friends" (*LDD* 147), but sadly, his rude comments do not diminish his appeal to LeLe. Instead of telling him off, she lies to him, offering a medical excuse for her weight: "I'm not really this fat. . . . I've been having a lot of trouble with my thyroid" (*LDD* 147).

The central plot of "Traveler" involves LeLe's desire to attract the attention of this young man in spite of his rude comment about her weight. Her attraction to an undeserving male is common in the characters who share the composite personality. LeLe ultimately swims five miles across a lake—quite an endeavor, though it is important to her only in that it involves "a first-rate boy . . . coming to take [her] somewhere" (*LDD* 85).

As in "Revenge," the climax of "Traveler" occurs when LeLe accomplishes this feat thus far allowed only to boys, for when LeLe suggests to Fielding that she swim across the lake with him, her cousin Baby Gwen says, "Girls don't ever swim across the lake" (*LDD* 149). In the water, though, LeLe feels empowered, "beautiful," "perfect," and thin (*LDD* 150). Her swim is a baptismal experience, a chance to start over and honestly *earn* the reputation she has sought via manipulation since arriving in Mississippi. Gilchrist uses water in this and other stories in much the same way that Hemingway does in such stories as "Out of Season" and "Big Two-Hearted River" in *In Our Time:* as representative of the source of life, of cleansing, rejuvenation, and second chances.

The ending to Hemingway's "Out of Season" is ambiguous; indeed, the whole story is. Many readers infer from the story's events that at issue is whether the young gentleman and his wife will have a child or abort their child, much as in "Hills Like White Elephants." The gentleman's apparent decision at the story's end not to fish out of season after all suggests that, just as he will not risk taking the life of a spawning fish, neither will he allow anyone to terminate his wife's pregnancy (or, if the issue is not abortion but merely whether they should have a child or not, not to do anything that would keep her from conceiving).

Just as "Out of Season" reminds the reader of "Hills Like White Elephants," but with a more positive, though ambiguous ending, so, too, does "Traveler" remind the reader of "Revenge." As in "Revenge," the ending of "Traveler" undermines somewhat the sense of LeLe's triumph. Although the reader does not know if LeLe's success remains as important to her as Rhoda's pole vault does to her (there are no final comments from an older LeLe), clearly it is a profound experience in her life, for she is striving to recall it in detail when the story closes: "I was dreaming of the lake, trying to remember how the water turned into diamonds in my hands" (*LDD* 153). Like Rhoda's triumph over gender roles, which the reader understands to be only a momentary one, LeLe's memory of her achievement is described in terms of illusion—the water as diamonds—which brings the reader back to the reality of LeLe's life: it is for the most part based on illusions she creates about herself. Consequently, she probably will not sustain the true empowerment she achieved in the water. Indeed, by the end of the story, her travels have come full circle, returning her to Indiana where she continues to tell exaggerated versions of the truth, if not outright lies. One is reminded by this falsely positive ending that Hemingway wrote "Hills Like White Elephants" after "Out of Season." He, too, seems to have had second thoughts about the positive ending to his earlier story—the young gentleman's decision to bring a new life into the world. In the later story, the young man is not yet ready for such a responsibility and encourages his lover to abort their baby.

Gilchrist again uses water as a central symbol in the last story of *In the Land of Dreamy Dreams*. "Summer, an Elegy" ends with Matille staring down into the river, calling to mind one last time the story cycle on which Gilchrist seems to have modeled her own first collection, Hemingway's *In Our Time*, which ends with Nick Adams staring into the swamp in "Big Two-Hearted River." Again, however, one cannot help but notice the differences between the two protagonists. Besides the obvious differences of sex, age, and recent experiences with death there is the distinct contrast in their attitudes toward the futures they are contemplating in these last scenes: Nick's one-day-at-a-time caution versus Matille's *joie de vivre* impatience. Of course this distinction is not surprising given the difference in kind between their recent tragic experiences—Nick has been to war while Matille has merely learned that her playmate/cousin has died—which is exactly why, although Hemingway's work serves well as a model of the craft of writing the short story and organizing the short story cycle, Gilchrist would have to turn to other writers to find someone *simpatico* with her subject matter.

3

The New Order

Picking Up Where Katherine Anne Porter Left Off

*Miranda persisted through her childhood in believing, in spite of her small-
ness, thinness, her little snubby nose saddled with freckles, her speckled gray
eyes and habitual tantrums, that by some miracle she would grow into a tall,
cream-colored brunette, like cousin Isabel; she decided always to wear a trail-
ing white satin gown. Maria, born sensible, had no such illusions. . . . "It's no
use . . . we'll never be beautiful, we'll always have freckles. And* you*", she told
Miranda, "haven't even a good disposition."*

Katherine Anne Porter, "Old Mortality"

*"It's a huge family, a network over five states. I love them but they don't have
any power over me anymore. Not that they ever did. I think I'm the first person
in my family to ever really escape from it. It's taken me a long time to do it. Now
I'm free."*

Ellen Gilchrist, *Victory over Japan*

Janis P. Stout calls Katherine Anne Porter's Miranda Gay, of "Pale Horse,
Pale Rider" in particular, "the Hemingway hero as woman" (138), an
appellation that prepares the reader to recognize parallels between
Porter's Miranda and Gilchrist's Rhoda.[1] In Rosemary Hennessy's discussion of the stories that comprise Porter's "The Old Order," she writes
that "in each epiphany story ['The Fig Tree,' 'The Circus,' and 'The
Grave'], Miranda briefly crosses the line between innocence and experience, but unable to integrate her revelation into action, she settles for the
'lies' and inadequate explanations of life which the adults in her world
offer" (308). Similarly, Darlene Harbour Unrue remarks that Porter's

"Old Mortality" "stops short of an epiphany" (*Understanding* 65). Thus, like Hemingway's Nick Adams and Gilchrist's Rhoda Manning, Porter's Miranda Gay has been perceived to be struggling against maturity.

After noting the "reaction to disillusionment that is visible all along in Miranda's rite of passage," Unrue connects it both to the reactions "of other [Porter] protagonists when their ideals prove to be imperfect" and "to the escape from a reality that is too much to bear" of still others "who create their own versions of reality in order to escape from truth" (*Understanding* 64–65), a description reminiscent of the chapter 2 discussion of the prototypes of Hemingway and Gilchrist. As with Hemingway and Gilchrist, at the center of Porter's canon is a composite personality. Jane Krause DeMouy alludes to the composite personality in Porter's fiction when she notes how "Violeta [of the story 'Virgin Violeta'] and the anonymous protagonist in 'Theft' seem to be early versions of a Miranda-like character" (16), when she regards the unnamed protagonist of "Hacienda" as "an implicit Miranda" (16), when she assumes that the un-named protagonist of "Holiday" is Miranda (166–76), and when she repeatedly compares other Porter characters to Laura of "Flowering Judas."[2] DeMouy links the protagonists of Porter's fiction by their shared conflict: "a desire, on the one hand, for the independence and freedom to pursue art or principle regardless of social convention, and, on the other, a desire for the love and security inherent in the traditional roles of wife and mother" (6). In this description alone, the reader can already see how Gilchrist's concerns are more compatible with Porter's than with Hemingway's.

With these readings of Porter's protagonists in mind and after seeing the connection between Gilchrist and Hemingway, the reader should not be surprised to find in Gilchrist's fiction several parallels to Porter's fiction.[3] Like Hemingway and Gilchrist, Porter has created a recurring character, Miranda Gay, who is both autobiographical and prototypical of the rest of her female protagonists. Furthermore, the suggestion that Gilchrist's canon as a whole is an evolving story cycle recalls Porter's remark in the preface to the 1940 Modern Library edition of *"Flowering Judas" and Other Stories* that her own collected stories "are fragments of a much larger plan which I am still engaged in carrying out" (*CE* 457). In fact, Gilchrist once made a similar comment in response to an interviewer who asked "whether the recurrence of . . . characters [in her first three collections of short stories] suggests a longer work": "The longer work is coming out piecemeal," she answered (T. Young 415, 418). Also like Porter—in the Miranda stories in particular—Gilchrist often writes of the upper middle class of the modern South. Indeed, one might argue that Gilchrist's stories and novels pick up where Porter's leave off: Porter's "Pale Horse, Pale Rider," which is chronologically the last Miranda story, is set during World War I, and her last work of fiction, *Ship of Fools*, anticipates World War II; Gilchrist's canon covers World War II to the present.

In still further comparison, both Gilchrist and Porter are superb short story writers who have also written novellas and novels, though both women's novels are considered by critics to be inferior to their short stories. Given her strength with the short story, Katherine Anne Porter is someone Gilchrist might seek out as an example of how women writers can make a place for themselves in the American short story tradition. Supporting the likelihood that Porter is another model to whom Gilchrist turned is the way that Gilchrist has organized her works into different volumes. For example, similar to Porter's *Pale Horse, Pale Rider: Three Short Novels*, she published a collection of three novellas in one volume called *I Cannot Get You Close Enough: Three Novellas;* Gilchrist's *In the Land of Dreamy Dreams*, with its several Rhoda stories surrounded by stories with Rhoda-like protagonists, is reminiscent of Porter's *"The Leaning Tower" and Other Stories*, which includes a series of Miranda stories followed by stories with Miranda-like protagonists; and finally, there is a similarity between the division and section titles of the two writers' first novels. *Ship of Fools* is divided into three parts: "Embarkation," "High Sea," and "The Harbors." Also in three parts, Gilchrist's *The Annunciation* has the section titles "Cargo," "Exile," and "The Annunciation."

In the examination of the two writers' works to follow, I am still following the intertextual practice of Nelly Furman and Nancy A. Walker, discussed in chapter 1, of making assumptions about texts Gilchrist has read and modeled her work upon. However, in contrast to intertextual studies by these two critics, my reading of Gilchrist with Porter in large part also employs intertextual theories that support reading works together for mutual and supportive, rather than corrective, illumination. In her list of what the intertextual critic should look for when examining two writers' works together, Susan Stanford Friedman, for example, includes not only how one writer "transform[s]" or "revise[s]" another, but also how the "successor" might have "adapted" and "assimilated" her precursor (155). Gilchrist's "assimilation" of Porter into her own stories shows the way that women writers' works—more particularly, the messages within their works—complement and corroborate each other's. The positive side to this "sisterhood" is that it often results in supportive relationships like those detailed in Rosemary M. Magee's collection of essays, *Friendship and Sympathy: Communities of Southern Women Writers*. The negative side to hearing the echoes of Porter in Gilchrist is the implication of both writers' concern with gender issues: that a generation later, conditions for women have not changed much.[4]

And neither have conditions for women writers, as one can see from a brief consideration of Porter's first novel, *Ship of Fools*, and Gilchrist's first Rhoda novel, *Net of Jewels*, which reveals how much pressure a woman writer faces to live up to readers' expectations, not only regarding her talent but also in her subject matter. Both works were eagerly anticipated by these authors' readers but then received mixed reviews. (Of course, Porter kept her readers waiting for her novel thirty years, whereas *Net of Jewels* was published only eleven years after Rhoda was introduced in *In the Land of Dreamy Dreams*.)[5] Although both novels are episodic and have numerous characters, a difference in grandeur must be noted: Porter attempted a much more epic novel than did Gilchrist, who fashioned a picaresque novel of Rhoda's college experiences and the early years of her first marriage. Neither satisfied her readers—in part, as an examination of the negative reviews shows, because neither novel is uplifting. In his response to the reviewers who criticized the bleak view in *Ship of Fools* of the evil of humanity, M. M. Liberman reminds the reader that "it is nowhere everlastingly written that literature must have a sanguine, optimistic, and uplifting effect" (16). Critics of Gilchrist's novel could learn a lesson from this statement. Like the characters of *Ship of Fools*, Rhoda does not develop very much in the course of her novel. She does not, by the novel's end, shake free of her father's domination over her, and for this reason some reviewers criticized the novel.[6] Such a reading misses Gilchrist's point that this lack of development is inevitable given the circumstances of Rhoda's life. Even a strong woman like Rhoda cannot escape the oppression of the southern patriarchy.

Before proceeding with more specific comparisons between stories by Porter and Gilchrist, one might note other parallels between these two writers' lives and careers, which might further account for some of the parallels between their works and provide additional insight into the inspiration for Gilchrist's writings (since the Gilchrist reader has very few of the biographical tools available to the Porter scholar).[7] According to Joan Givner, Porter's life was greatly influenced by her ambivalent relationship with her father (47–51). It is not surprising, then, that the central conflict in some of the Miranda stories is between Miranda and her father. Similarly, Gilchrist reports in her collected journal entries *Falling through Space* that she "ha[s] been loving and fighting with and showing off for [her father] since [she] was born" (*FS* 156), and she, too, recreates this volatile relationship in the thinly disguised biographical stories depicting the relationships between Rhoda Manning and Anna Hand and their fathers. Regarding the other men in their lives, both writers were married and divorced several times. Also no surprise, then, both women are published under their maiden names—perhaps an assertion of their independence in their common region of the country, the South, where women are too often identified in relation to their husbands—and both have written several stories centering on disturbing relationships between men and women, including husbands and wives.

Interestingly, Porter and Gilchrist were both journalists before breaking into fiction. The first edition of Porter's debut collection of short stories, *"Flowering Judas" and Other Stories*, was published in 1930 when Porter was forty years old. At forty-six, Gilchrist published her first volume of stories, *In the Land of Dreamy Dreams*. The opening stories of these two first collections, Porter's "María Concepción" and Gilchrist's "Rich," were also the first stories the two women had written.[8] Typical of first stories, both are based on actual events the authors had heard about while living in the locations in which the stories are set (Porter in Mexico, Gilchrist in New Orleans).[9] New Orleans has also provided Gilchrist with material for several other works, as Mexico did for Porter. Later on in their careers, both writers were to focus more closely on their own lives, their families, and the places of their birth and childhood for material for their stories. However, in spite of their being associated in many people's minds with particular areas of the South—Porter with Texas and Gilchrist with Mississippi—both writers have set their fiction in several different geographical locations. Besides Mexico and Texas, Porter has stories set in Denver, New Orleans, New York, Connecticut, and Germany. Besides New Orleans and Mississippi, Gilchrist sets her work in other parts of Louisiana, as well as Arkansas, Indiana, Illinois, Kentucky, Alabama, Tennessee, North Carolina, New York, Virginia, Oklahoma, Nebraska, Texas, California, Maine, Florida, Washington, Mexico, Europe, and even ancient Greece.

Enriching "Rich" with Parallels to Porter

The similarities between Gilchrist's "Rich" and Porter's "María Concepción" are not confined to the circumstances of their geneses. In both stories, the writers criticize the Catholic Church, exposing the weakness of its hold on its parishioners in times of crisis, along with its oppressive nature. The title character of "María Concepción" is proud of being a Catholic. This pride allows her to hold her head up when her husband runs off with another woman, but after the death of her baby and the birth of a healthy baby to her husband and his lover, perceiving that her religion has not served to protect her from such injustices, she breaks one of the Church's most serious commandments and murders her husband's lover.[10] Albeit in a much more satiric tone, Gilchrist, too, reveals how fragile are the laws of the Catholic Church, in particular the laws regarding birth control. After the Wilsons' fifth child is born, Letty decides to talk to their priest about allowing her to use birth control: "All her friends were getting dispensations so they could have time to do their work at the Symphony League and the Thrift Shop and the New Orleans Museum Association and the PTAs of the private school" (*LDD* 10).

Before the reader suggests that it is the superficiality of these women's dedication to their religion—María's is based on pride, Letty's on duty—rather than the ineffectiveness of their Church that leaves these women so powerless to ward off tragedy, one should note how Gilchrist's story exposes the human greed behind the Catholic Church. And certainly, too, this Church's history includes acts of premeditated and carefully calculated violence far worse than the murder María Concepción commits in a fit of grief and rage. Thus, both women writers have taken on this patriarchal institution, Porter against its role in colonialism and Gilchrist against its role in limiting women's reproductive rights.

Noting such parallels between these two works—as well as between "Rich" and "Noon Wine," "The Downward Path to Wisdom," and "He"—leads to a fuller understanding and appreciation of this strange opening story in Gilchrist's first book of fiction. Vincent Leitch explains this reason for recognizing intertextual relationships between books: "the critic reexamines [earlier texts] . . . in order to situate, decipher, and assess the new text" (123). In turn, Porter's stories are enhanced by a rereading in light of "Rich." As T. S. Eliot points out, "what happens when a new work of art is created is something that happens simultaneously to all works of art which preceded it" (38). This section demonstrates, then, how, in Eliot's words, "the past [is] altered by the present as much as the present is directed by the past" (39).

To continue this intertextual reading of "Rich" and "María Concepción," one finds that other issues explored in both include class consciousness and domestic violence. María Concepción is proud of how she has risen above her people by marrying in the church "instead of behind it" (CS 4), but her marriage does not turn out as she had planned. To expand upon the crisis already mentioned, while she is heavy with child, she spies her husband Juan in the arms of a younger woman named María Rosa, and soon thereafter the illicit lovers run away together. Then María Concepción's baby dies just after birth, whereas María Rosa bears a healthy baby boy soon after she and Juan return. In retaliation for her injuries, María Concepción kills María Rosa. Surprisingly, Juan and the townspeople protect her from incrimination. Finally, after the *gendarmes* investigating the murder leave, María Concepción takes María Rosa's son home with her to raise as her own, with the consent of her neighbors apparent in their silence.

Like "María Concepción," "Rich" begins with a description of a marriage and ends with a murder. In this case it is the husband, Tom Wilson, who has risen above his class through marriage, and it is he whose pride suffers as his life fails to measure up to his expectations. As it becomes less easy to laugh off his costly mistakes at work and as his oldest daughter Helen begins to show signs of psychological problems, Tom grows increasingly concerned about his social image. His concern escalates into obsession after Helen causes the death of his youngest child. One night Tom determines to put an end to his inner turmoil by killing Helen and himself. As in the wake of the tragedy in "María Concepción," Tom's wife Letty is protected from her husband's crime by her social circle, which closes in around her after the tragedy. Among the five one-sentence paragraphs that close the story is the statement, "No one believed a man would kill his own little illegitimate dyslexic daughter just because she was crazy" (LDD 23).[11] In this sentence the people of this New Orleans privileged class approach blaming the victim, as is the case as well in "María Concepción." Darlene Unrue notes how the scapegoat myth is employed in Porter's story: "As in ancient custom, María Rosa becomes the village scapegoat. She probably has done nothing worse than many village people, certainly nothing worse than Juan, but she becomes the object of their passionate rejection. . . . She is the sacrificial victim to their own guilts and sins, and the restorative effect of the 'offering' is confirmed when the departing gendarmes wish them all 'Good health!'" (*Truth* 23–24). Helen, too, is sacrificed so that the neighbors can feel better about themselves after such a tragedy has occurred. Rather than questioning themselves for having welcomed a murderer into their circle, they blame her for somehow provoking her own murder. Not only is there the implication in the labeling of Helen as "crazy" that the little girl must have done something to cause her father to murder her, but also believing that "she was crazy" is an attempt to undermine her sympathetic appeal. Only here does the social chorus that closes the story mention Helen, and it is neither a positive nor a regretful reference to her. Like María Rosa, Helen was not "of good reputation among [them]" (*CS* 19), and so the people's sympathy at the end of this story is directed exclusively toward the surviving wife.

The community protectively surrounding Letty at the end of "Rich" focuses the reader's attention upon who the survivor of the story is—not the male protagonist but his wife. Gilchrist's use of a male protagonist in "Rich" is atypical, the overwhelming majority of her protagonists being women. Jane DeMouy notes a similar point of contrast between Porter's "Noon Wine" and most of her other work, in that "Noon Wine" "is by no stretch of the imagination Mrs. Thompson's story" (6). Still, in "Noon Wine," as well as in "Rich," it is significant that it is the woman who survives in the end. These women are not destroyed, as their husbands are, by an obsession with public opinion. Like many, though not all, of their creators' other female characters, they have enough disregard for society's opinion to remain strong in the face of the destruction of their reputations.

A further comparison can be made between "Noon Wine" and "Rich" in that in neither story is the central character very much of a "hero." Upon noting this similarity, one then recognizes a significant difference between the two antiheroes. Harry J. Mooney, Jr., argues that "we do not begin to see [Thompson] in that role [the role of hero] until, after nine years have passed, he confronts an ambiguous but very real horror in the person of Mr. Homer T. Hatch" (40). In contrast, Gilchrist's Tom Wilson becomes *less* heroic as his story unfolds. The reader admires him at first for his seduction of and consequential acceptance by a usually closed society, but after his marriage, the charismatic personality that attracted this acceptance begins to deteriorate, along with his appeal to the reader. The story's central focus is on the destruction of this character.

Both stories end with the male protagonist's suicide after he has killed another person. In Porter's story, Thompson kills Hatch, whom he sees as a threat not only to Helton but also to his own present comfort and prosperity. Similarly, Tom Wilson kills his daughter Helen, whom he blames for the disruption of his Edenic lifestyle among the wealthy people of New Orleans. And, just as Thompson is driven to his suicide by his obsession with what people think about his having killed Hatch, Tom kills himself after killing Helen, knowing that his already tenuous position in society is now completely and finally destroyed.

Several critics of Porter's story have pointed out the similarities between killer and victim in "Noon Wine." Most recently, Janis Stout calls Hatch "Thompson writ large" (121). Perhaps the earliest to note the comparison, Frederick J. Hoffman remarks how Hatch's "every gesture, every remark, serves as a kind of grotesque parody of Thompson's own nature" (46). John Edward Hardy's similar reading of "Noon Wine" is most helpful in analyzing Gilchrist's "Rich." Hardy points to the passage in Porter's story in which Thompson begins to feel that Hatch "certainly did remind [him] of somebody" (*CS* 244) and argues that "the person Hatch reminds him of is himself. . . . All the things about Hatch that are most offensive to the farmer are a mockery, a wicked caricature, of Thompson's own prejudices and pretensions" (*Katherine* 103). In Gilchrist's story, too, Tom's daughter Helen can be viewed as a caricature of himself. *Washington Post* reviewer Susan Wood argues that "Helen embodies what Tom has tried so desperately to control in himself" (4).

As Hardy did with Porter's two characters, then, one can point to several similarities between these two Gilchrist characters. First of all, as Tom indirectly caused the death of a pledge whom his fraternity was hazing, Helen accidentally causes the death of her sister. Second, both Helen and her father are outsiders living among the New Orleans aristocracy: Tom married and Helen was adopted into this social circle.[12] Physically, father and daughter are both overweight and have vision-related problems: as already mentioned, Helen has been diagnosed as having dyslexia, and as Tom becomes obsessed with her, worrying that people believe she is actually his illegitimate daughter since she looks so much like him, "he began to have trouble with his vision" (*LDD* 17).[13]

Seeing the parallels between the two sets of characters, the reader can use Hardy's reading of "Noon Wine" to come to a deeper appreciation of the complexities of "Rich"—in particular, of Tom's motivation for killing his daughter. Hardy explains the mysterious events of "Noon Wine" just before Thompson kills Hatch: having noted how Thompson is made to recognize the similarity between his own exploitation of Helton and Hatch's bounty hunting, Hardy argues that Thompson "sees Helton knifed because he wants it to be so, wants to be rid of this living human evidence of his own mean-spiritedness" (*Katherine* 104). As already indicated, Helen's role in Gilchrist's story is comparable to Helton's as well as to Hatch's roles in "Noon Wine." However unwitting, her responsibility for her sister's death parallels Helton's murder of his brother, an act also unpremeditated. Since her sister's death, Helen has suffered at the hands of her father, just as Helton, a fugitive from his own home, has had to labor for Thompson.[14] Tom beats Helen at one point for playing with his pedigreed Labrador puppies. Her helplessness in the face of her father's insecurity is comparable to Helton's situation of having to endure Thompson's exploitation of his talents since he is in no position as an escapee from a mental institution to be selective about a job. Hardy contends that "it is himself, then, this intolerable image of himself that Thompson strikes at when he takes the axe to Hatch" (*Katherine* 104). Similarly, Tom kills, first of all, a "ruined" puppy, symbol of his now-tainted position in society, and second, Helen, who, like Thompson, is an "intolerable image of himself," before killing himself. But these deaths are not enough. Like Thompson, Tom "desires, and achieves, his own destruction" (Hardy, *Katherine* 104).

Finally, toward the end of Gilchrist's story is a scene quite similar to the one that closes "Noon Wine." Porter concludes with:

> Taking off his right shoe and sock, he set the butt of the shotgun along the ground with the twin barrels pointed toward his head. It was very awkward. He thought about this a little, leaning his head against the gun mouth. He was trembling and his head was drumming until he was deaf and blind, but he lay down flat on the earth on his side, drew the barrel under his chin and fumbled for the trigger with his great toe. That way he could work it. (*CS* 268)

Gilchrist describes her character's suicide more gruesomely but with no reference to his thoughts during the process: "Without removing his glasses or his hunting cap [Tom] stuck the .38 Smith and Wesson revolver against his palate and splattered his own head all over the new pier and the canvas covering the Boston Whaler. His body struck the boat going down and landed in eight feet of water beside a broken crab trap left over from the summer" (*LDD* 23).

In one significant respect "Rich" is different from "Noon Wine": that is, the manipulation of the reader's feelings toward the murderer and murdered. Porter's reader finds nothing sympathetic about Homer T. Hatch and thus, without condoning the violence, can pity Thompson even after he commits murder. In contrast, although Helen is not presented as a very likable child, Gilchrist's reader finds it difficult to pity a man who kills his own nine-year-old daughter. Still, given the negative development of Helen, the reader might find reading the story intertextually with two other Porter stories—"The Downward Path to Wisdom" and "He"—helpful in illuminating more clearly Helen's role as victim rather than mere catalyst, thereby eliciting deeper sympathy for the child.

First, Tom's physical abuse of Helen calls to mind "The Downward Path to Wisdom," in which the protagonist's father handles his son roughly in response to his own frustrations rather than to anything the boy has done to provoke him. Second, like the child Stephen in this Porter story, who passes balloons around to win friends, at one point in "Rich," Gilchrist digresses from the central events to show Helen bribing a schoolmate (with the promise of an icee) to come home with her after school. Finally, Stephen's singing at the end of his story, "I hate Papa, I hate Mama" (CS 387), is similar to Helen's singing, "The baby's dead. The baby's dead" (LDD 19). Both children are expressing their perceptions of the source of their unhappiness: for Stephen, his parents who seem to find him to be in their way; and for Helen, her siblings, who distract her parents'—and even the maids'—attention from her. These points of comparison between the two child characters help to make Gilchrist's somewhat unlikable child character more sympathetic to the reader. Helen's conflict in "Rich" is to some extent overshadowed by the story's predominant focus on Tom. The comparisons between Helen and Stephen illuminate Helen's position in the story as a lonely little girl whose parents are usually neglectful and whose father has suddenly become abusive.

Like Tom's treatment of Helen, Mrs. Whipple's treatment of her mentally handicapped son in Porter's story "He" is determined by her concern with her reputation. Comparing "Rich" and "He" provides further support for Debra A. Moddelmog's reading of Porter's story, which in turn can be used to aid Gilchrist's reader in recognizing the extent of Tom's deterioration in character as "Rich" proceeds. Moddelmog responds to the critics who do not quite know what to make of Porter's "He." Arguing convincingly that Mrs. Whipple actually hates her son, who is referred to in the story only as He and Him, and showing that this hate is "derived from the loss of comfort and prestige that Mrs. Whipple believes her retarded son has caused her," Moddelmog concludes that Mrs. Whipple's actions in the story can only be viewed as "despicable" ("Narrative" 125). Recognizing the similarity between Mrs. Whipple's treatment of Him and Tom's treatment of Helen (essentially his blaming her for his declining popularity, beating her in his frustration over his problems at work, and eventually killing her), the reader should find it difficult to sympathize with Tom, even though the story seems for the most part to be his. Looking back at Porter's story, then, the reader realizes that Moddelmog is right: it is only by chance that Mrs. Whipple's treatment of Him did not result in his death before the doctor instructs her to send him away.

Though in no way an excuse for Mrs. Whipple's treatment of her son, her neighbors' attitude toward this child is not much less despicable than her own: "Lord's pure mercy if He should die. . . . It's the sins of the fathers. . . . There's bad blood and bad doings somewhere," they say to each other (CS 49). The neighbors' declaration at the end of "Rich" that Helen was actually Tom's illegitimate daughter and their lack of sympathy for *her* suffering recall this callous attitude. In both stories, then, the neighbors' "chorus" reveals that neither Tom's nor Mrs. Whipple's concern about negative public opinion, due to these two mentally handicapped children, emerged solely from within themselves; rather, the two parents are revealed to be products of the society in which they live. Therefore, reading these two stories together also provides a rebuttal to a point made by Bruce W. Jorgensen about Porter's story. Jorgensen asks, "With a retarded child and *those* neighbors, how would we do?" (112). He, too, notes how the neighbors talk behind Mrs. Whipple's back and comments, "We can hardly blame Mrs. Whipple for not wanting to be looked down on by such neighbors" (112). I would argue instead that the reader wonders why Mrs. Whipple would care about the opinion of "such neighbors." Therefore, I would also contend that the purpose of the neighbors is not to excuse Mrs. Whipple's behavior but to show that she, like Tom Wilson, is not unique in her community.

And neither should Mrs. Whipple be considered unique in her seemingly unnatural reaction to her son. Porter presents in this story no stereotypical mother figure who loves her children equally, but a believable woman who, try as she might to love her afflicted son as she loves her other children, cannot help her very human reactions to this child—resentment, revulsion, but also guilt. It may take the reader some time to recognize himself or herself in this unlikable character and thereby come to sympathize with Mrs. Whipple's distress over this weakness in herself. Reading the story intertextually with "Rich," in which we meet and come to like Tom before seeing how he treats Helen, and noting the comparisons between the two stories and their protagonists allow the reader a quicker means toward recognizing Mrs. Whipple's humanity and thus toward sympathizing with her (even while condemning her actions, as advocated above).

In her introduction to a collection of essays on intertextuality, Jeanine Parisier Plottel explains how one identifies intertexts through the literary history suggested by "the context of a given work. The context may be the body of other texts in some way connected logically or culturally with the writing under consideration" (xviii)—as Ellen Gilchrist's "Rich" is connected to "sister" southern writer Katherine Anne Porter's "María Concepción," "Noon Wine," "The Downward Path to Wisdom," and "He." Plottel also explains the value to the literary critic of recognizing intertexts of a work: "Intertextuality is the recognition of a frame, a context that allows the reader *to make sense out of what he or she might otherwise perceive as senseless*" (xix). An intertextual reading of "Rich" with Porter's stories allows the reader to recognize the partial responsibility of the Wilsons' community for the murder and suicide that occur in Gilchrist's story, to perceive a significance in the survival of Letty, to understand more fully Tom's reason for killing his daughter, and to sympathize more with this unlikable victim of Tom's violence. In turn, the fresh perspective upon Porter's stories provided by a reexamination alongside Gilchrist's story leads to recognition of the ineffectiveness of María Concepción's dominating religion, the strength of Mrs. Thompson in "Noon Wine," the abusive neglect of Stephen in "Downward Path to Wisdom," and the humanity of Mrs. Whipple in "He."

Parallels between Prototypes

When Miranda's Cousin Eva Parrington meets her on the train in "Old Mortality," she recalls that Miranda was "a lively little girl . . . and very opinionated" (*CS* 207). She tells Miranda, "The last thing I heard about you, you were planning to be a tight-rope walker. You were going to play the violin and walk the tight rope at the same time" (*CS* 207). Similarly, in many of her stories, Rhoda daydreams about herself in the future, always in some incredible scenario: as Queen of the Nile, as a pilot on her way to Japan to drop the bomb, as a famous author who has left several broken-hearted men behind (to name just a few of Rhoda's fantasies). Her fantasy of being a missionary in "Perils of the Nile" leads one to more direct echoes of Miranda, who at one point in "Old Mortality" "expressed [her] ambition to be a nun" (CS 194). Just as the reader does not take Rhoda's fantasy seriously, given its egocentric rather than benevolent source, the nuns at Miranda's school do not believe that Miranda has any such calling. This same Miranda "had . . . given way to despair over arithmetic and had fallen flat on her face on the classroom floor, refusing to rise until she was carried out" (CS 195), an act which reminds the reader of the report in "1944" that Rhoda once "locked [her]self in a bathroom for six hours to keep from eating fruit cocktail" (LDD 126) as well as of a schoolmate's recollection in "Perils of the Nile" of the time she "faked a faint on the playground and was taken home in the principal's car without once opening her eyes or admitting she could hear" (LDD 131).

The parallels between these prototypes' personalities do not suggest that Gilchrist is not original. The similarities are between character types and themes; the plots are certainly distinctive. What the comparison does reveal is how very little has changed from one generation to another for little girls growing up in the South. Less discouraging, however, one also notes in the midst of these parallels several points of contrast that suggest that Porter's prototype has evolved—and is continuing to evolve—in Gilchrist's manifestations. In this development, one can find Gilchrist's belief that strong women are moving toward not only surviving but also thriving in spite of the limitations of southern gender roles and codes of conduct.

In Gilchrist's story "Revenge," ten-year-old Rhoda meets a positive female role model, her adult cousin Lauralee. Similarly, as a small child, Miranda meets her grandmother's sister Eliza (in "The Fig Tree"). Comparable details about these older women—that Eliza dips snuff and Lauralee smokes Camels—aid one in perceiving their similar characters. John Hardy's assessment—that "Eliza is a spirit of liberation for [Miranda], opening an unforeseen way of escape from the narrow, oppressive moral and intellectual authority of the Grandmother" (Katherine 18)—illuminates their similarity in character, for Lauralee's life since the death of her first husband is also unprecedented in Rhoda's experience of the lifestyles of southern women. Rather than stay home and grieve, "Lauralee dried her tears, joined the WAVES, and went off to avenge his death" (*LDD* 117). William Nance's assessment of Eliza as a "strong, self-sufficient woman, refreshingly different from the Grandmother" (113), is thus applicable to Rhoda's cousin.

After Lauralee's arrival, Rhoda has the courage to voice her determination never to marry and her ambition to become a lawyer. Both Miranda and Rhoda meet these women at a crucial time: when they are suffering from not being understood. Just as Eliza unwittingly soothes Miranda's guilt by telling her that the "weep, weep" she hears is the sound tree frogs make (therefore, the same sound she heard at home did not come from the chick she had just buried), Lauralee unintentionally gives Rhoda the courage to break social strictures and to go out, finally, to the broad jump pit to try to pole-vault. Recognition of the parallels between the two stories, then, brings to light Lauralee's role in Rhoda's feat. The alcohol she drinks during the wedding reception may give Rhoda the courage to face the dark, but it is Lauralee's example that inspires her to attempt this designated "male" stunt.

At later points in their lives, Miranda and Rhoda each encounter another female role model. In "Old Mortality," Miranda meets her cousin Eva on the train to her uncle's funeral, and Rhoda meets the young widow Doris Treadway at a restaurant in the story "1944." Rhoda is too young to recognize the kinship between herself and Doris and thereby realize that, in some respects, she is glancing into her own future. Like Rhoda, Doris is a person more concerned with her own needs than with what society thinks of her. This self-centeredness, with the help of alcohol, gives Doris the courage to defy social mores. Hence, she is out drinking alone in a restaurant bar when Rhoda meets her. The reader, however, knows that there will be consequences to her behavior: she will inevitably suffer from both a hangover and gossip.

When Miranda meets Eva on the train, she is ten years older than Rhoda is when she meets Doris Treadway. From the vantage point of eighteen, Miranda is able to see the connection between herself and her cousin. According to Janis Stout, Miranda "realizes that Cousin Eva's personal unpleasantness, or deformity, is somehow tied up with her very real strength of character and foresees a like duality in herself. [Thus,] she realizes that Cousin Eva, who denounces the tyranny of the family, is not only a pitiable person but a kindred spirit, a sister" (*CS* 136)—so much so that Eva seems to be able to read Miranda's mind: just after Miranda thinks to herself, "They didn't do you much good, those parties, dear Cousin Eva," Eva says aloud, "They didn't do me much good, those parties" (*CS* 208). Unlike Rhoda, who is fooled by Doris Treadway's glamour, Miranda is depressed by her cousin's appearance. Early in their conversation, Miranda notices how Eva, who "couldn't be much past fifty now, . . . looked so withered and tired, so famished and sunken in the cheeks, so *old*, somehow" and asks herself, "Oh, must I ever be like that?" (*CS* 208). And hearing Eva's later remark, "Beauty goes, character stays," she wonders, "why was a strong character so deforming?" (*CS* 215).[15]

The initial parallel between these two stories—a female protagonist meeting an older woman who is like her in character—might lead the reader to speculate about that which Rhoda is too young to realize about herself and Doris Treadway. When she thinks back upon this episode in her childhood, will Rhoda, too, come to view a strong character as "deforming"? Such questioning then leads to the recognition that Gilchrist, like Porter, does provide a view of her heroine at an older age in other stories and, indeed, that she depicts Rhoda struggling to suppress the forces within her that would lead her, in the patriarchal society of her upbringing, to drinking alone in a bar like Doris Treadway. In *Net of Jewels*, for example, the reader finds an older Rhoda repeatedly striving to suppress those qualities about herself that irritate her husband in order to keep him from leaving her. Ironically, her own desires often rise to the surface, and at these times the reader does find Rhoda drinking heavily, though not alone. She is usually with men, trying to forget about her marital troubles.

More specific parallels between Miranda and Gilchrist's characters—in particular Rhoda and, in *The Annunciation*, Amanda McCamey—include, first, the fact that all three are essentially motherless: Miranda's mother is dead; Amanda's mother spends all of her time mourning her deceased husband, which leaves her little time for her daughter; and Rhoda's mother is never more than a minor character in the stories in which she appears at all, reflecting her role in Rhoda's life. Like Miranda's, Rhoda's main parental influence, against which she repeatedly asserts herself, is her father. Yet, also like Miranda, whose grandmother fills in for her absent mother, both Amanda and Rhoda have strong female role models in their grandmothers, both of whom are "in charge" of their plantations.[16] In spite of—indeed, to a great extent because of—this strong feminine influence, Miranda, Amanda, and Rhoda are oppressed by the codes of their social orders: they come from Old South families with very definite ideas about the proper behavior of young ladies. These social codes are in large part disseminated by the women, who, both women writers reveal, participate in their own oppression. Again, then, Gilchrist's echoes of Porter express her lamentation that some things have not improved much since her mentor was crafting fiction that critiqued the South.

On a more positive note, all three of these young female characters are renegades of a sort: they all defy their families and their social orders at some point in their lives in order to establish their own identities. Like Miranda in "Old Mortality," Rhoda elopes at an early age to escape her family's (particularly her father's) oppression, and she later leaves her husband to escape his. She becomes a writer, and in her work she continues to defy her father. Like Miranda in "Pale Horse, Pale Rider," Amanda is busy through much of her novel establishing herself as a writer and experiencing life's blessings and hardships, like loving and losing love, away from the influence of her oppressive family.

An examination of the parallels between Gilchrist's novel *The Annunciation* and short stories "Revenge" and "Music" and Porter's "The Grave" supports the theory that these similarities between Porter's Miranda and Gilchrist's Amanda and Rhoda are more than coincidental, reflecting the like minds of these writers. To begin with, one hears similarity when saying these characters' names together: Mir*a*nda, Am*a*nda, and Rho*da*. More significantly, one might contend that "The Grave" provided Gilchrist with a couple of specific ideas (again, though, she employs these ideas in very fresh stories): first, the use of dead rabbits to represent the oppressive nature of motherhood; and second, the narrative technique of jumping forward in time at the end of a story to provide a backward glance at the events just narrated.

An early scene in *The Annunciation* echoes somewhat the scene in Porter's "The Grave" in which Miranda intuits the relationship between herself and a pregnant rabbit her brother has just killed. In *The Annunciation*, upon returning from hunting, Amanda's cousin Guy gives her a box of baby rabbits whose mother, it is implied, has been killed by one of the hunters. In "The Grave," Paul cuts into a pregnant rabbit he has shot and shows Miranda the fetal rabbits. Again there is an age difference between Porter's and Gilchrist's protagonists at these points in their stories: Amanda is only four years old, whereas Miranda is nine. Both, however, are precocious enough to recognize at some level the significant relationship between themselves and the baby rabbits. Miranda's first response is to be "excited but not frightened, for she was accustomed to the sight of animals killed in hunting" (*CS* 366). She then makes the connection between what she is gazing at and "where babies come from." This understanding is discomforting to her, and she tells her brother she no longer wants the mother's fur for her dolls. She does not want to profit from this death, perhaps because she has recognized subconsciously the connection between the dead mother and her own mother's death delivering her, as well as between the dead fetal rabbits and the babies she could someday bear.

Gilchrist's Amanda is also made uncomfortable by baby rabbits, although, as is also true for Miranda, it is not the idea of hunting and killing animals—like these rabbits' mother—that bothers her. Rather, she recognizes the helplessness of these orphaned rabbits, their dependence upon her, or someone, to keep them alive. Apparently, she does not want this responsibility: "Their little sucking noises bothered her, as though they might get on her and stick to her skin" (*A* 5). Like Miranda, she seems to intuit from these rabbits a presentiment of her own future as a mother, though she is too young to grasp the full significance of this impression. Her response to them, then, foreshadows her future unwillingness to find the child she had when she was a teenager—a baby girl who was immediately put up for adoption by her grandmother so that Amanda could "have her chance" (*A* 21).

After the parallel experiences with baby rabbits, events in *The Annunciation* continue to echo Porter's story. Upon realizing what he has inadvertently shown Miranda, Paul tells her, "Don't you ever tell a living soul that you saw this. . . . Don't tell Dad because I'll get into trouble. He'll say I'm leading you into things you ought not to do" (*CS* 367). Paul's anxiety is echoed by Amanda's cousin Guy later in Gilchrist's novel, though Guy has much more to be concerned about. He, too, has introduced his younger female playmate to sexual knowledge—and he has done so much less innocently. Amanda has adored Guy since he greeted her with such genuine welcome when she first arrived to live on her grandmother's plantation. From that moment on, Amanda receives from Guy the warmth that her deceased father and grieving mother are no longer capable of giving her. To prolong the sense of security Guy's presence provided in the daylight hours, she would often crawl into bed with her cousin at night, and at some point during her first four years with him, while they lay in bed together, Guy began to caress her intimately and then taught her how to reciprocate with him. When he is twelve, though, he puts a sudden stop to their sexual play for fear of being caught and punished and because he "want[s] God to let [him] be good at baseball" and he "want[s] to be on the football team next year" (*A* 12). He tells Amanda, "If I do this he isn't going to let me" (*A* 12). Like Miranda's brother Paul, Guy worries about Amanda telling someone about their actions. Intuiting Amanda's lack of concern for her own well-being in comparison to her concern for his, he warns her against telling with: "If you talk about it I'll tell grandmother. . . . I'll let them beat me to death" (*A* 12). Like Miranda, who recognizes that the "disorderly and unaccountably rude . . . [sexual] habits" of animals were "altogether natural" (*CS* 366), Amanda rejects Guy's attempts to convince her that sex is dirty and shameful. Still, also like Miranda, Amanda is left feeling rejected. She has allowed herself to depend upon someone, even though, as her earlier response to the rabbits shows, she despises dependence, having learned from her mother's experience the grief it can cause. From this point to almost the end of the novel, she fights against allowing herself to fall into this kind of situation again—first marrying someone "safe," someone she is not passionately in love with. Even when she does risk an affair with someone who stirs up passion in her, part of her resists falling in love with him. She tells this lover, "I can't love anyone. I don't know why other people can do that and I can't do it" (*A* 230).

Not surprisingly, given the differences between their relationships with their male playmates, Miranda is not as traumatically affected by the experience of her sexual awakening as is Amanda. The events of that day do trouble her, however. The reader is told that "Miranda never told, she did not even wish to tell anybody. She thought about the whole worrisome affair with confused unhappiness for a few days. Then it sank quietly into her mind and was heaped over by accumulated thousands of impressions, for nearly twenty years" (*CS* 367). In "The Grave," Porter leaves the child Miranda at the point at which she is being admonished by her brother to keep quiet about her discovery of her future role as mother. The narrator's report that she "never told" indicates an acceptance of her brother's authority over her, just as her desire for the ring Paul found in the empty grave indicates her acceptance, at that moment at least, of her proper role as woman in this society—to be a wife and mother.

For a while, Amanda tries to fulfill her "proper" role, too, but when both her endeavors to have children and her marriage fail, she abandons her husband and moves to Fayetteville, Arkansas, to develop a career translating poetry. In doing so, she is also renouncing her father's family, as Miranda does in "Old Mortality." The parallels between these two works might lead the reader to examine more closely Porter's Miranda stories to see if the comparison between these two characters continues to hold. Upon doing so, the reader will perceive more clearly the development of Miranda's character in the course of these works. Miranda, too, abandons a husband: in "Old Mortality," at the age of eighteen she privately decides that she will not return to her husband after the funeral, and evidence that she carries through with this decision is provided in "Pale Horse, Pale Rider," which takes place six years later and in which Miranda is single. However, in spite of her earlier conviction to "have no more bonds that smothered her in love and hatred" (CS 220), she does allow herself to fall in love in this later story—though her lover dies at the story's end, leaving her still single.

Porter ends "The Grave" by glancing even further into Miranda's future using a technique referred to by classical rhetoricians as *prolepsis*, "the anticipatory glimpse of what is going to happen in the future of the narrative" (Lodge 75). At twenty-nine, Miranda is wandering alone through a market street in Mexico when she experiences a Proustian moment: "It was a very hot day and the smell in the market, with its piles of raw flesh and wilting flowers, was like the mingled sweetness and corruption she had smelled that other day in the empty cemetery at home" (CS 367). Suddenly, she experiences a revelation that explains the discomfort of this memory: "the dreadful vision faded, and she saw clearly her brother, whose childhood face she had forgotten, standing again in the blazing sunshine, again twelve years old, a pleased sober smile in his eyes, turning the silver dove over and over in his hands" (CS 367–68). The dove, she now recognizes, was the superior treasure found in the grave, for as Jane DeMouy explains, the dove is associated "with the free flight of the bird and the hunt" (142), whereas the ring they found represents wife and motherhood, which was also represented by the hunted and killed rabbits. Furthermore, the hole in the dove's breast represents heartlessness—like the hunter's insensitivity to his prey—a trait Miranda might wish to achieve given her experiences with her family, marriage, and lost love.[17] DeMouy points out that "the image of Paul" in Miranda's memory is "full of potency and possibility," which Miranda "ignorantly traded . . . away" in her acceptance of her proper role, indicated both by the ring and by her desire to go home and change into a dress (144). Since that day, she has learned the possible consequences of the choice she made as a child at the grave site: death, both literal and figurative. Porter's focus at the end of the story, then, reveals the choice Miranda has since made: to be free, like her brother Paul, from the bonds of marriage and motherhood and to be "heartless," like the hunter, in order to avoid the pain of losing a loved one. Finally, the image of Paul, so vivid in Miranda's mind's eye, may reveal to her the power of imagination to recapture and illuminate the meaning of the past and thereby to remind her of the value of her choice to be a writer.

Gilchrist employs this same technique of jumping forward at the end of a story to a vision of the character at an age when she can perceive the significance of earlier events in her life. Again turning to David Lodge's explanation of prolepsis, employment of this technique "implies the existence of a narrator who knows the whole story" (75), in this case an older Rhoda who, at the end of the short story "Revenge," speaks from some point in her future: "Sometimes I think whatever has happened since has been of no real interest to me" (*LDD* 124). "Revenge" is also about gender roles and awakening sexuality. In "Revenge," Rhoda is just one year older than Miranda is in "The Grave." Also like Miranda, she has an older brother who plays a significant role in her awakening to gender difference. However, Gilchrist's story provides an even less accepting view of gender difference than does Porter's story, and there is no conciliatory ending for such a character in the South of Gilchrist's fiction.

In "The Grave" we are told that Miranda's overalls are causing "a scandal in the countryside, for the year was 1903, and in the back country the law of female decorum had teeth in it" (*CS* 364). Similarly, because of her sex, Rhoda is not allowed to participate in the "Olympic training" in which her brother and male cousins are engaging. The two girls' reactions to these forms of censorship differ, however: "Miranda, with her powerful social sense, which was like a fine set of antennae radiating from every pore of her skin, would feel ashamed" when neighbors commented on her attire, "though she . . . was perfectly comfortable in the clothes" (*CS* 365), whereas Rhoda is enraged by the injustice of the restrictions forced upon her. This difference does give the reader some hope that even if the limitations to "young ladies" are not slackening, at least some young ladies themselves are gaining the strength to struggle against their bonds.

Another not-so-encouraging difference between Miranda's and Rhoda's situations has to do with their fathers' stands on the subject of gender. In "The Grave," Miranda's father is surprisingly (given the conflicts between Miranda and her father in other stories) practical about the matter of her clothes. He tells his daughter that the overalls are "just what [she] need[s] . . . they'll save [her] dresses for school" (CS 365). In contrast, it is Rhoda's father who gives her brother Dudley the authority to forbid Rhoda to play with the boys. In a letter from Europe, where Dudley Sr. is stationed during World War II, he writes that "Dudley [Jr.] and Bunky and Philip and Saint John and Oliver were to begin training. The United States would need athletes now, not soldiers" (LDD 112). He does not include Rhoda in the list, and he ends the letter "admonish[ing] Dudley to take good care of" Rhoda as she is her father's "own dear sweet little girl" (LDD 112). Looking at the two stories together, one wonders if, in allowing Miranda to dress tomboyishly, Miranda's father is not also trying to protect his "dear sweet little girl"—in this case from becoming a woman too soon to suit him. Such a reading is confirmed by Paul's concern over their father's finding out about Miranda's seeing the fetal rabbits. Paul implies that their father would be angry about his "leading [her] into things [she] ought not to do," and he remarks, too, that their father "is always saying that" (CS 367). Like Mr. Manning, then, Miranda and Paul's father seems to want his son to participate in limiting rather than in broadening Miranda's experiences. This reading undermines the previously suggested inconsistency between Miranda's father as he appears in this story (more concerned about his daughter's comfort than social strictures) and his actions toward Miranda in other stories (distant and disapproving).

Ironically, in both works it is women who actually enforce the oppression of the young girls. Miranda is criticized by women for her outfit: "Ain't you ashamed of yoself, Missy? It's aginst the Scriptures to dress like that" (CS 365). And, although women are in charge at Esperanza Plantation while the men are overseas, no one overrules Dudley Jr.'s interdict against Rhoda's participation in their games. Rather, Rhoda's grandmother and the family servant Baby Doll try to distract her with more suitable activities for little girls. Although Rhoda is delighted with the attention she receives when she dances, the broad jump pit still looms in the back of her mind, for she will not be satisfied with succeeding only at "female" accomplishments.

Evidently, Rhoda does not have Miranda's "powerful social sense," the susceptibility to such embarrassment as that which Miranda suffers for "shocking" her community's women with her unladylike clothes.

Thus, Rhoda seems to have evolved from Miranda: she is, like her predecessor, a rebel, but in some instances, particularly in her tendency to be unself-conscious about making a scene, she is a stronger rebel. Still, the two girls remain to a greater extent alike, so that the reader is not encouraged that a rebellious nature will enable the next generation (Rhoda's) to succeed where the earlier generation (Miranda's) could not—namely, in defying sexist barriers. When Miranda puts the gold ring Paul found in the grave on her own "rather grubby thumb," she is all the more "turned . . . against her overalls and sockless feet. . . . She wanted to go back to the farmhouse, take a good cold bath, dust herself with plenty of Marie's violet talcum powder . . . put on the thinnest, most becoming dress she owned, with a big sash, and sit in a wicker chair under the trees" (*CS* 365). Similarly, when Rhoda's cousin asks her to be the maid of honor in her wedding and offers her the dress of her choice in which to appear in this role, Rhoda forgets for a while her desire to play with the boys. She, too, longs for a dress that "was dark and tall and thin as a reed" (*LDD* 121). Since Miranda's desire to put on a dress emerges after she puts on the ring, it reflects her acceptance at this point in her life of the roles society says she can play: wife (it is a wedding band) and mother (the leaves encircling the band represent fertility). Rhoda's wish for the perfect dress, then, is an acceptance of a third role allowed to women: the role of sex object. On the way home from the store, she anticipates the attention she will get from the boys when they see her wearing it: "Wait till they see me like this. . . . Wait till they see what I really look like" (*LDD* 121).

This view that her future role as a woman is to be a sex object is certainly not an attitude reflective of the evolution of Porter's prototype that one finds elsewhere in Gilchrist's development of her characters. Moreover, accepting such a role is potentially more destructive than Miranda's sudden awareness of her femininity. Indeed, the false sense of empowerment Rhoda feels here foreshadows the negative ending of Gilchrist's story, in spite of the girl's eventual defiance of her brother's rule against her participation in the boys' games. Feeling like an adult in her new dress, during the wedding reception Rhoda mixes herself an alcoholic ("grown-up") drink, which gives her the courage to wander out into the dark. She realizes suddenly that no one is there to stop her from going to the broad jump pit. Upon reaching it, she takes the dress off, once again rejecting constricting gender roles, and pole-vaults successfully.[18] The story then closes with Rhoda speaking from some time in her future. Her statement implies that, in spite of her success that night—both at pole-vaulting and at defying gender roles—Rhoda has apparently not gone on to greater and greater achievements. The view of "Revenge" as a success story is thus undermined by the notion that this accomplishment is sometimes perceived to be the highlight of her life.[19]

Gilchrist again employs the shift forward in time at the end of the later Rhoda story entitled "Music." In the events of this story about Rhoda's loss of virginity, as well as in the glimpse of an adult Rhoda at the end of the story, the view of her bleak future at the end of "Revenge" is further supported. In "Music," Rhoda is still using her capabilities as a sex object to fight patriarchal oppression. Her choice at fourteen years old to have sex with a stranger is, in large part, an act of defiance against her father, who, as related in chapter 2, has taken her on a business trip with him to get her to stop smoking, which in his mind is apparently a step toward making her behave in a more ladylike fashion. At one point during their trip, Rhoda has some time to herself and wanders into a pool hall to buy cigarettes. She flirts with the young clerk, hoping to fool him into believing she is older, since apparently he is not supposed to sell cigarettes to minors. Then, to add some excitement to her "vacation," she agrees to go for a ride with the young man and even follows him into some woods in order to impress him with her courage: "I'll bet he thinks at last he's met a girl who's not afraid of anything" (VJ 46). In truth, she is used by a man who "had set out to fuck the boss's daughter" (VJ 47) and who steals fifty dollars from her afterward to run off with someone else. Here again Rhoda has found that her sexuality is not empowering when she plays the role of sex object.

The narration jumps thirty years forward at the end of this story, and in this later scene the reader sees that Rhoda is still fighting oppression linked to her femininity. Like Miranda in Mexico in the closing scene of "The Grave," Rhoda has escaped her home by this time. She is a writer now, living in New York. However, she does not appear to be happy, and she is apparently still seeking her father's approval—which she is still not receiving. As also already noted, after dedicating a book to him, she receives a letter saying, *"Take my name off that book. . . . Imagine a girl with your advantages writing a book like that. Your mother is so ashamed of you"* (VJ 51). In her response to his rejection of her dedication, she rejects his religious and political codes and proclaims the rights of the female voice: *"Dear Father, You take my name off those checks you send those television preachers and those goddamn right-wing politicians. . . . Also, in the future let my mother speak for herself about my work" (VJ* 51). As in Porter's "The Old Order," in which work the reader recognizes the significance to Miranda's life of the history of her grandmother's oppression, Rhoda's reference to her mother in this letter alludes to the significance of her mother's silence to Rhoda's own oppression. Like her mother, Rhoda is expected to remain silent and to do as her father tells her. But, like Miranda, Rhoda has become a writer, a vocation that signifies her determination to exercise her voice.

During their trip together earlier in "Music," Rhoda's argument with her father about the existence of God also recalls Miranda's failure to understand her father's values. In spite of the autobiographical bases on which these plots are based, both authors create the father-daughter conflict quite objectively (a strength, then, of both writers)—that is, the two sides of the tension are treated almost equally. In the novella "Old Mortality," Miranda suffers from her father's neglect after he picks her up at the train station. He is clearly more pleased to see Cousin Eva than he is to see Miranda, and on their way home, "neither of them noticed [Miranda's] voice or her manner. They sat back and went on talking steadily in their friendly family voices, talking about their dead, their living, their affairs, their prospects, their common memories, interrupting each other, catching each other up on small points of dispute, with a gaiety and freshness which Miranda had not known they were capable of, going over old memories and finding new points of interest in them" (*CS* 220). Frustrated by her father's high regard for the past, Miranda contemplates the meaning of life, and here the narrator hints that her foolishness matches his: "Oh, what is life, she asked herself in desperate seriousness, in those *childish* unanswerable words" (*CS* 220, emphasis added). Her subsequent rejection of the past so valued by her father anticipates Rhoda's argument for evolution against her father's belief in creation, and Rhoda's foolishness, too, is revealed when she cannot follow her case against the existence of God all the way through:

[Dudley Manning, Sr., asks,] "Tell me this, who made the slate then? Who put the slate right on top of the coal everywhere it's found in the world? Who laid the slate down on top of the dinosaurs?"

"I don't know who put the slate there," [Rhoda] said. "We haven't got that far yet."

"You haven't got that far?" [her father] said. "You mean the scientists haven't got as far as the slate yet? Well, Sister, that's the problem with you folks that evolved out of monkeys. You're still half-baked. You aren't finished like us old dumb ones that God made." (*VJ* 40)

Later in the story, when Rhoda follows Johnny Hazard into the woods to a remarkable pond that "people come from all over the world to see" and beside which she will lose her virginity to him, her first question about this magnificent phenomenon is "Who made it?" (*VJ* 46), revealing a sub-conscious acceptance of or at least reflecting the influence of her father's beliefs in a divine source of life.

Similarly, the narrator of Porter's novella explains that Miranda's questioning about life comes from "*all her earliest training* [which] had argued that life was a substance, a material to be used, it took shape and direction and meaning only as the possessor guided and worked it; living was a progress of continuous and varied acts of the will directed toward a definite end. She had been assured that there were good and evil ends, one must make a choice" (*CS* 220, emphasis added).

Miranda, however, concludes these thoughts by again questioning "her earliest training": "But what was good and what was evil?" (*CS* 220). In addition, throughout "Old Mortality," she questions the truth of the memories her father values so highly, as do the rest of the members of his generation and the preceding one. The facts behind their romantic stories, particularly the story of Aunt Amy and Uncle Gabriel, belie the romance: first, Miranda does not perceive from a picture of Amy why she is considered to be so beautiful (*CS* 173); and second, the alcoholic Uncle Gabriel whom Miranda and her sister Maria meet just does not match their father and grandmother's description of Amy's ardent suitor. Furthermore, her father's assertion that "there were never any fat women in the family" is proved absolutely false by "great-aunt Eliza, who quite squeezed herself through doors," and by great-aunt Keziah, whose husband "had refused to allow her to ride his good horses after she had achieved two hundred and twenty pounds" (*CS* 174).

In like fashion, Rhoda more often questions than accepts her parents' assertions. For example, at the end of "The Expansion of the Universe," in which she is about the age she is in "Music," Rhoda is enraged by her father's decision to move his family again, and, when her mother tells her that "good comes of everything," she responds: "No, it doesn't. . . . That's a lie. Half the stuff you tell me is a lie" (*DL* 55). Another example can be found at the end of "The Time Capsule" when a younger Rhoda becomes suddenly afraid of dying and responds to her mother's comforting explanation of heaven with "That's a lie. None of it is true. Nothing you ever tell me is true" (*LWP* 24). Although these outbursts may sound like childish fits of temper, Rhoda's verbal rejection of her parents' "truths"—in contrast to Miranda's pensive (silent) rebellion—could instead confirm the view of Rhoda as an evolved descendant of the rebel-prototype created by Porter.

In defiance of her family, particularly her father it seems, Miranda elopes, in spite of her early recognition of the consequences of such romantic actions: Aunt Amy suffers from tuberculosis after her madcap ride to the Mexican border to see her brother off after he has defended her honor in a duel, and she dies soon after her marriage; and Uncle Gabriel lives his whole life in the past and is a complete failure in the present. Regardless of the not-so-romantic fates of Amy and Gabriel, Miranda's father has remained in awe of their love story. Perhaps, then, Miranda's elopement was motivated by a desire to attract her father's attention away from his romantic past to her romantic present. Such a view is supported, first, by Miranda's attitude toward her marriage: "It seemed very unreal . . . and seemed to have nothing at all to do with the future . . . and the only feeling she could rouse in herself about it was an immense weariness as if it were an illness that she might one day hope to recover from" (*CS* 213); and second, by her excitement upon seeing her father at the train station: "She rapped on the window to catch his attention, then ran out and threw herself upon him" (*CS* 218). But once again, she is to be disappointed by him. Apparently still angry with her for eloping, he treats her coldly while seeming pleased to see the unpopular Cousin Eva, who was, after all, another witness to the old romance. Finally, Miranda's wish to impress her father is supported, given the comparisons between her character and Rhoda's, by Rhoda's constant and less subtle attempts to get her father's attention.

In turn, the parallels between Miranda and Rhoda illuminate Rhoda's eventual insight about sex. Like Miranda, Rhoda elopes and, just as Miranda perceives the consequences of sexuality and womanhood from what she knows of the experiences of her mother, grandmother, and aunt Amy, Rhoda, soon after her marriage, discovers these consequences for herself. For Rhoda, then, the knowledge is much less ambiguous. Miranda can only guess at what might have happened to Amy, for example. The story "Adoration," in which Rhoda's elopement is first mentioned, focuses on her own experiences with pregnancy. Her first pregnancy begins with her confinement in bed while her body decides whether it will miscarry. This confinement reflects the limitations that her role as mother will place on her life. In spite of the difficulty of this first pregnancy, Rhoda chooses to "make another one" (*DL* 62) while her firstborn is still in a crib, and then carelessly allows herself to get pregnant with still another baby in the last section of the story. Like the young Miranda who traded for the ring in "The Grave," Rhoda has, for the time being, embraced her society's view of her role as woman, not yet realizing the oppressive nature of this view.

However, in the story "1957, a Romance," Rhoda does perceive the oppression effected by her pregnancies, and this time she refuses to have another baby.[20] In this story, too, it is revealed that Rhoda's marriage is not much happier than Miranda's apparently is, for also like Miranda, she recognizes her husband's role in her oppression. On her way to her family's home at the end of "Old Mortality," Miranda anticipates the crowd of people who will be there:

> She felt a vague distaste for seeing cousins. . . . Her blood rebelled against the ties of blood. . . . She did not want any more ties with this house, she was going to leave it, and she was not going back to her husband's family either. She would have no more bonds that smothered her in love and hatred. She knew now why she had run away to marriage, and she knew that she was going to run away from marriage, and she was not going to stay in any place, with anyone, that threatened to forbid her making her own discoveries. (*CS* 220)

Furthermore, she determines not to participate any longer in her family's stories about the past and to "know the truth about what happens to [her]" (*CS* 221). However, the mature narrative voice makes an evaluation of her pledge to herself by remarking that it reflects her "ignorance" (*CS* 221). Porter here mocks her protagonist for believing herself superior to her relatives.

Gilchrist also shows such objectivity toward her characters as she mocks their self-deceptions. "1957, a Romance" ends in similar fashion to "Old Mortality" as Rhoda and her father plan to stop at a Fourth of July family gathering on their way back from their trip to Texas where she had an abortion. In contrast to Miranda, Rhoda is excited about visiting with relatives. Indeed, she is in just the right mood for celebrating *Independence* Day. Surrounded by her family there, including her two sons,

Rhoda secretly revels in the freedom she has achieved by having an abortion, the control she has taken over her own body. However, like Miranda, who did not perceive the naiveté of believing that her own more realistic perception of life made her superior to her relatives, Rhoda does not recognize the flaw in her view of herself as being in control: she has had this abortion only with the help of her father's money. Although Gilchrist does not have her narrator step in with even the one-word illumination of Rhoda's "ignorance" (Porter's word for Miranda's similar attitude), she does end the story with Rhoda grinning foolishly at herself in the mirror, thereby leading the reader to a recognition of what a fool she is being.

There are several other parallels between Rhoda's adventures and Miranda's, reflecting the similar concerns of Gilchrist and Porter with the dilemma of the willful woman growing up in a patriarchal society. One can find, for example, in two of Gilchrist's stories with protagonists based on her prototype, the development of a conflict touched upon in Porter's "Pale Horse, Pale Rider"—the dilemma of the ambitious woman living in a man's world. "Looking over Jordan" in *Victory over Japan* and "First Manhattans" in *Drunk with Love* are both about women writers struggling to maintain their own ethics, particularly regarding the writer's responsibility for her words, while trying to establish a career in a man's world.

In "Pale Horse, Pale Rider," Miranda is a reporter assigned at present to cover local entertainment. Early in the story, she is confronted by "a little drab man in a derby hat" who asks her, "Are you the so-called drama critic of this hick newspaper?" (*CS* 288). He is there to complain about her review of his act. Miranda's answer—"You shouldn't pay any attention at all. What does it matter what I think?"—does not satisfy him (*CS* 288). He is evidently at the end of his career, though he tells her he is only worried about her review because if he "get[s] panned in the sticks . . . [people] think it's the same as getting panned in Chicago" (*CS* 288). Miranda is distressed by the pathetic little man, who has held her accountable for what she has written. The advice from the paper's sportswriter, who witnessed the incident, is not comforting to her: "You bring it on yourself. All you have to do is play up the headliners, and you needn't even mention the also-rans" (*CS* 289). Miranda "hopelessly" responds, "I seem to keep learning all the wrong things" (*CS* 289). While she has apparently tried to do her job as fully as possible, probably in hopes of career advancement, she might better have realized that all she had to do was fill her column, for the likelihood of a woman being promoted to reporter is slim at best. Porter does not develop this conflict far beyond this scene. It is mentioned only as one of many of Miranda's points of dissatisfaction with her life, all of which will eventually seem trivial in the triumph of defeating death herself only to have to face the death of a beloved. Death is the central concern of Porter's story.

In contrast, the issue of responsibility is at the center of Gilchrist's stories about dissatisfied career women. In "Looking over Jordan," Margaret Sarpie is, like Miranda, a (in her case, book) reviewer who aspires to more—to be a published author herself. Hence, Lady Margaret, as she is called, is another example of little progress from one generation to the next. Paralleling Miranda's dilemma, she, another of Gilchrist's Rhoda-based characters, is faced with the issue of responsibility when she meets the author of a book she has reviewed. It is a scathing review, and after its appearance in the newspaper, she thinks that the crank calls she is receiving are from the author's friends. Since whoever is calling hangs up without saying anything, Lady Margaret's connecting the calls with her review indicates that her conscience is troubling her for criticizing the book so harshly. She escapes the phone by driving to her family's lake house outside New Orleans, but there she comes face to face with the book's author, Anna Hand, who had coincidentally spent the night there with Lady Margaret's cousin.

Anna has not yet seen the review and is ingratiatingly friendly to Lady Margaret, feeling herself like an intruder on Lady Margaret's property. Lady Margaret does not know of Anna's ignorance, however, and thinks that, at any moment, she will be made to pay for her words: "She will throw it in my face. It will all be over, two thousand years of history, two thousand years of law" (VJ 92). The reference to "two thousand years" may allude to the beginning of Christianity, before which the "law" was "an eye for an eye." Lady Margaret apparently thinks she is about to receive from Anna just the kind of spiteful criticism she tendered in her review of Anna's novel. Suddenly, the significance of the earlier reference to a novel Lady Margaret is writing is clear. The passage she read to herself that morning from her own work-in-progress suggests that it is a popular romance. It is possible, then, that Lady Margaret's criticism came out of jealousy of an author whose work she recognizes as superior to her own. Lady Margaret's aspirations to be a writer herself and insecurities about her own writing compound her guilt, for now she realizes that Anna Hand is no longer just a name and a picture on the cover of a book. She is now, like herself, a flesh and blood person whose feelings might be hurt by a negative review of her novel.

When Lady Margaret is finally able to speak a coherent sentence to her unexpected guest, she blurts out, "I know about your work," to which Anna responds, "Well, now you know me instead. And I know you. The world is really quite astonishing, all the people you can meet" (*VJ* 92). Lady Margaret is only just beginning to grasp the significance of this fact and answers Anna's "Don't you find it so?" with "I don't know. . . . I don't think I do. Not really. Well, maybe I do. I don't know if I do or not" (*VJ* 93). She seems to realize that she has not, up to now, understood the world at all. Her puzzling fascination with Anna's story of how she and Lady Margaret's cousin broke the swing while he was singing "Swing Low, Sweet Chariot" may be explained by the relationship between this spiritual and her attempt now to come to such an understanding.

The subject of the spiritual is the individual's day of judgment, when she is to be held accountable to God for her actions. Lady Margaret thinks of the spiritual's lyrics: "*I looked over Jordan* [source of the story's title] *and what did I see, coming for to carry me home. A band of angels coming after me.* She shivered" (*VJ* 94). She then tries to convince herself that she "*didn't do anything wrong. I just wrote what I thought. . . . What difference does it make? She won't even see it until she gets on the plane and if Armand tells anyone about it I'll tell Momma never to let him have the house again. To hell with it. To hell with all of them. Swing low, sweet chariot. I'm going to quit thinking about it. I'm going to put it out of my mind and get to work on my tan. Oh, God, what a Sunday*" (*VJ* 95). In spite of not having been to church on this Sunday, Lady Margaret has clearly been exposed to a lesson on the Golden Rule. Still, as she leaves the lake house, she remains oblivious to the signs around her of other lessons from Christianity and the world at large: "She walked by a garter snake curled up in the roots of a tree [temptation], past a pair of grasshoppers mating on a leaf [love], beneath a mourning dove [peace] and the nest of a sleeping owl [wisdom]" (*VJ* 95). The last of these signs, a symbol of wisdom asleep, is most reflective of Lady Margaret's condition even at the end of this story. Rather than learn something from this discomforting experience, she is trying to put it out of her mind. Thus, "Looking over Jordan" is another Gilchrist story in which the protagonist resists maturation.

Gilchrist deals again with the theme of being held accountable for what one writes in her story "First Manhattans." The Rhoda-type character of this story, Annalisa Livingston, writes a column for the *New York*

Times called "Our Lady in Your Pew," in which she reports on and usually criticizes what is going on inside the city's churches. Like "Pale Horse, Pale Rider," "First Manhattans" begins with a nightmare that foreshadows the end of the story: "A huge choir robed in white fills the streets of New York City. They are singing her favorite hymn. . . . A lion appears among the people. He turns and sniffs the air, then looks at Annalisa. He starts her way. His jaws open wide" (*DL* 118). Just as Miranda's dream in "Pale Horse, Pale Rider" anticipates her fight with death when she is struck down by the flu, Annalisa's dream will come true when she is thrown to the lions on the Phil Donahue show and forced to justify her right to criticize churches. Annalisa does not heed her dream. Upon waking, she dismisses its effects by thinking about her position as "the hottest thing in town, the one everyone was reading" (*DL* 119). Unlike Miranda and Lady Margaret, Annalisa has been quite successful in her career, but the reader should recognize that her success has been based on sensational journalism. Apparently, even women can make it in the contemporary world that thrives on this kind of reporting, but the reader might question whether such an accomplishment is any indication that genuine talent has been recognized.

Annalisa herself introduces the idea of taking responsibility for one's words when she ends her criticism of a marriage sermon with "*Someone* must be held responsible when such statements are made in the presence of children" (*DL* 124). Her subconscious guilt over her own words is reflected in the fact that she apparently pays attention only to her hate mail. Although "the mail was running about three to one in her favor" (*DL* 129), the only letters she reads in the story are harsh criticisms of her column. Her need for affirmation, then, leads to her fall. She is not content with her friend Kenny's praise or her fame; however, she is thrilled by her recent rival's seemingly high regard for her and her work. When Kenny expresses his distrust of this man, Marvin Fannin, interspersing derogatory comments about Marvin's homosexuality within his criticism of the man's character, Annalisa answers, pointedly, that he (a black man) should "show a little Christian charity, not to mention broad-mindedness and lack of prejudice where other people's intimate lives are concerned. We are not on this earth to cast stones at glass houses, lest the house we break might be our own" (*DL* 134). In this admonishment, she foretells her own end after she lets Marvin talk her into appearing with him on the Phil Donahue show, and there Marvin discloses the dirt he has uncovered on her father.

Annalisa's guilt over her own right to criticize is reflected in the mirror on the night before the show as she looks at herself and thinks, "Yes, the camera would seek her out and know her. She would be laid bare before the whole United States. It would be all over, the small fame of which she had been so proud would be shattered by the cold light of the TV" (*DL* 137). She admits, then, that "her faith, which lately had been wavering like a candle in the wind, would be shown up for the tattered thing it was. Do you believe in what you're doing? The accusers would rise up around her like Valkyries. Do you believe in anything?" (*DL* 138). Without faith—in God, herself, or what she writes—what right has she to criticize? This is the conflict she struggles with before the show. On the air, Marvin further complicates the issue when he brings up her father. Marvin's disclosure reveals that Annalisa's motivation, like Lady Margaret's, is more personal than the reader has been led to believe. Apparently, she is actually getting even with all churches for one church's treatment of her father, formerly an Episcopal priest, who was apparently involved in some kind of church scandal several years before.

Once they are safe inside the cab after the show, Annalisa tells Kenny, "I'm quitting this job. . . . I'm not writing down what I think anymore for anyone to see or talk about or criticize. To hell with them. Love you one day, hate you the next. I'm going to work for a bank or a shoe store" (*DL* 144). Although she did not learn from her father's experience of being held accountable for what the newspapers said about him, she has learned now of one's accountability for what is printed. Therefore, although she echoes Lady Margaret in her "go to hell" attitude, she has learned a lesson from her experience. Like Lady Margaret, though, she will continue to shirk responsibility if she carries out her plans to quit writing. One can but hope she will listen to Kenny, who has answered her threat to quit the paper with "You'll change your mind You [sic] just burned out and mad" (*DL* 144).

Racism and More Gender-Related Conflicts in the Immutable South

Annalisa's relationship with Kenny is one of several interracial relationships in Gilchrist's fiction, only a few of which are as positive as this one—and even the positive relationships are all undermined in some way: Annalisa acts on her attraction to Kenny only after being publicly humiliated; the friendship between Robert and Gus in "The President of the Louisiana Live Oak Society" (in *In the Land of Dreamy Dreams*) centers around their experimentation with drugs; the close friendships between Amanda and Lavertis in *The Annunciation* and between Crystal and Traceleen, two of Gilchrist's major recurring characters, are undermined by the employer-employee hierarchy of each (Lavertis and Traceleen serve Amanda and Crystal, respectively, as maids); the relationship between a white woman and an Asian man in stories in *Light Can Be Both Wave and Particle* develops outside the woman's southern home in the more liberal state of California; similarly, the relationship between a white woman and black man (Katie and Clinton) in *The Annunciation* is accepted by an artists' community in Fayetteville, Arkansas, but not tested in a less liberal area of the South.

Sadly, Gilchrist's is a realistic, if not very optimistic, depiction of interracial relationships in the South, which, as she reveals repeatedly in her fiction, is still strongly characterized by racial prejudice. Particularly given Gilchrist's honesty about race relations, it is disturbing that Kenny is one of the few positive nonwhite characters in Gilchrist's canon, and only one of Gilchrist's Jewish characters—Alisha Terrebone of "There's a Garden of Eden"—is ultimately likable.[21] However, before condemning the author for her depiction of nonwhite and Jewish characters, one should realize that few of her white (non-Jewish) characters are developed very positively either. Gilchrist's fiction repeatedly presents the flawed human being—of various ethnicities. This balance can be illustrated with the title story of *In the Land of Dreamy Dreams*.

The antagonist in "In the Land of Dreamy Dreams" seems to be the story's Jewish character, "new-rich Yankee bitch" Roxanne Miller (*LDD* 60), who has "invaded" the Lawn Tennis Club of New Orleans. She is an unlikable grotesque in the tradition of Flannery O'Connor. One of her legs is shorter than the other, which gives her a slight limp but does not hurt her tennis game. The narrator's reference to her as "the crippled girl," then, points to more than this barely noticeable physical deformity (*LDD* 61). The narrator seems to share with the two central points of view, Claiborne Redding's and LaGrande McGruder's, a disparaging opinion of this intruder upon an Old South club. One of Roxanne's first disruptive actions after joining the club was "campaign[ing] for more court privileges for women" (*LDD* 65). The narrator's disapproval of such attempts to achieve equal rights for women at the club seems implicit in the description of Roxanne's "disconcerting habit of sticking the extra ball up the leg of her tights instead of keeping it in a pocket" (*LDD* 67). On the other hand, in spite of the narrator's satirical depiction of Roxanne, Claiborne and LaGrande ultimately reveal themselves and what they "stand for" as more despicable than Roxanne.

Perhaps this balance of satire is why reviewers of this volume failed to comment on the Jewish grotesque in this story, although the reviewers of her later collection *Drunk with Love* expressed discomfort with and/or criticized her development of two men of color within two of its stories: "The Emancipator" and "Memphis." The placement of these two stories together seems to suggest a xenophobia on the author's, rather than her characters' part, as it does not allow for the balance of satire that is found in "In the Land of Dreamy Dreams." Even D. D. Guttenplan, whose review notes the discomforting juxtaposition of these stories, in looking back to *In the Land of Dreamy Dreams* for Gilchrist's former depictions of race relations, considers only "The President of the Louisiana Live Oak Society." Guttenplan approves of the narrator's satirization of Lelia McLaurin's hypocritical racism in that story: "Robert's mother was a liberal. She never called black people niggers or Negroes even when she was mad at them" (*LDD* 27). Guttenplan admits that he "wince[s] with recognition" (of the false liberal, one assumes) when reading such a line (54). He also praises Gilchrist for "manag[ing] to put life into that stock figure of post-plantation fiction, the maid" with her character Traceleen of the Crystal stories in *Victory over Japan* (54). He fails to recognize that Traceleen's characterization is almost idealized and thus *does* comply with the "stock figure of post-plantation fiction, the maid," as well as with the stereotypical mammy in plantation fiction; nor does he comment on Nailor of "In the Land of Dreamy Dreams," another such stock figure straight out of ante- and postbellum plantation fiction—the happy darky whose prejudices are comparable to those of the white people he serves.

Any attempt to excuse this weakness in Gilchrist's characterization of the African Americans in her fiction would only sound like those who laud other white southern writers for their *efforts* to write of the "Black Experience" and to excuse the gaps in their narratives by saying how broad-minded they were "for their time period" (which implies that it is okay to be prejudiced as long as one is not *too* prejudiced). It would be more honest—and, it seems to me, less condemning of the writer—just to admit that the African-American experience is not a central concern in Gilchrist's fiction. She is more interested in telling the story of the white woman of the upper middle class in the South. African Americans, there-fore, as well as white males, are inevitably minor and hence underdevel-oped characters.

I bring this issue up here not to deconstruct this weakness of character-ization (as I have said, it is not "excusable") but to examine another reader response issue: that reviewers have failed to point out these some-what stereotypical character types in Gilchrist's fiction. They did not bring up Gilchrist's depiction of African Americans (or Jews) until the publication of *Drunk with Love,* in which nonwhite characters commit violent acts in consecutive stories.[22] Apparently, some stereotyping is viewed by reviewers as harmless and thus not a problem. Perhaps the most telling example of this attitude is that not one reviewer remarked upon Marvin Fannin of "First Manhattans," another story in *Drunk with Love,* the same collection that discomforted reviewers with its two stories of nonwhite characters committing murder. Marvin, the first gay charac-ter developed in Gilchrist's fiction, is as unlikable as Roxanne and per-haps more negatively stereotypical than any other character in Gil-christ's canon (though I would also point out that one of Gilchrist's most likable, most sympathetic characters to appear in her later works is Charles William Waters, Rhoda's gay friend in *Net of Jewels*). My point in mentioning Marvin is not that his characterization suggests homophobia but that reviewers have perhaps revealed their own prejudices via their selective view of which negative character development is deemed of-fensive. Although they are troubled by Gilchrist's depiction of men of color as violent, they do not seem to be disturbed by negative character-izations of Jews and gays.

This issue of reader response to Gilchrist may remind the reader of a debate that arose shortly after the publication of Porter's *Ship of Fools.* In contrast to Gilchrist's reviewers, who seem untroubled by her Jewish characters, after the first wave of reviews of Porter's *Ship of Fools* raved about it, critics began to look more closely at the novel everyone had awaited for thirty years, and one of the first things they noticed was Porter's negative portrait of the Jewish salesman Julius Lowenthal. Theodore Solotaroff argued that he was the most "wretched and repul-sive" of the German passengers and called him a "caricature of Jewish vulgarity" (283). Sybille Bedford asked, "Did the only Jew on board have to be such an utter wretch?" (764). In response to these remarks, Joan Givner comments at length on Porter's anti-Semitism and examines Porter's ambivalence toward African Americans, as both attitudes are expressed outside her fiction (450–53). Writing a biography, Givner must, of course, explore her author's attitudes in this way, though, admirably, she does not attempt to excuse Porter. She is introducing Porter to the reader, not seeking canonization into sainthood (just as one goal of my introduction to Gilchrist is to help establish a place for her in the *literary* canon, not to canonize her for sainthood). For her final word on the subject, then, Givner turns to Porter's novel and shows Porter to be no hypocrite about her inherent prejudices even while recognizing them as wrong and consequential: "*Ship of Fools* is perhaps the accurate expression of the ambivalence of her attitudes. She could not depict a likable Jewish character and yet the book consciously shows the irrational, mindless, dangerous nature of such prejudice and, by implication, its devastating course toward the Holocaust" (453). In other words, in spite of her own apparent prejudices, Porter recognizes and exhibits in her fiction the ultimate consequences of prejudice.[23]

The critic can follow the example of Givner to determine what to do with the two Gilchrist stories that have been specifically criticized by her reviewers for their negative development of nonwhite characters. As indicated, reviewers did not begin to take note of seemingly xenophobic attitudes in Gilchrist's fiction until her fourth book, *Drunk with Love*, in which, as Guttenplan points out, she "put two stories together, back-to-back, which seem to say: 'Cross the line and you're dead. Sleep with a black man and he'll kill you for thanks'" (54). Again, the two stories are "The Emancipator," about a blond midwestern American woman's courtship and marriage to a Lebanese student who physically abuses her and eventually murders her, and "Memphis," about a similarly idealistic southern woman's marriage to a black man who is also physically abusive and who also eventually murders her. As Givner considers the overall message about the evil consequences of prejudice in *Ship of Fools* in her response to Porter's critics, Gilchrist's readers should examine the ultimate message of these two stories before condemning her absolutely for her depiction of these two men of color. Like Porter's novel, these Gilchrist stories end by showing the possible violent consequences of the racial prejudice and oppression depicted in the course of their narration.

"Memphis" is not, in that light, a story confirming taboos against miscegenation.[24] The blame for the black man's murder of his white wife ultimately falls back upon the white patriarchy. The story's narrator, who is the victim's aunt, assesses the situation: "We brought them here [as slaves]. Someone did. Not me. We are being punished forever, the bringers and the brought. Tautologies, old clichés, pray for us all. Pray for the world" (*DL* 105). In this summation, Allie both accepts and rejects responsibility for her niece's murder and recognizes the suffering of both races due to the past system of slavery and the continuing oppression that results from it.[25] Allie's ambivalence regarding her own responsibility for the situation is a result of the other theme of oppression running through the story: the oppression of women. Earlier Allie had remarked, "Anybody in my family could tell a version of this. This is the real story. Of whiskey and slaves and bored women and death. Two hundred years of slavery and still going on and still paying for it" (*DL* 100). Actually, it is the "bored women" who are Gilchrist's main concern in this story. Through Allie, she is not merely telling the story of a white woman murdered by her black husband. This story is about the woman's conflict with her father, a man who "wrote all those books about man's inhumanity to man," worked for integration, lost "family and friends and inheritance" for his ideals, and was a revered scholar and teacher as a result of it all (*DL* 93). However, due in large part to his lack of attention, his wife drank herself to death and, to attract his attention, his daughter Baby Kate brings home a black man. Ironically, Baby Kate is thrown out of the house by her reputedly liberal father. She then marries her black lover Franke—who knows he is being used. Franke's subsequent violence against Baby Kate, though not condoned in any way by the narrator or author, is understood in light of the preceding events. He is lashing out at his wife for using him—as members of his race have been used by whites since "we brought them here," recalling Allie's recognition of even her own complicity in Baby Kate's murder. Baby Kate's childless aunt/surrogate mother seeks the reason for her niece's death and does not blame the black hand that committed the act. White patriarchal oppression and hypocrisy, exhibited by the father who drove his daughter to use another human being in order to attract his attention if not his love, are condemned in this story.

The other disturbing story in this collection, "The Emancipator," has no first-person, emotionally involved narrator rationalizing the events. Since it precedes "Memphis" and parallels it in many ways—idealistic white woman marries man of color, is physically abused and then murdered—the reader may consider how Allie's insight at the end of "Memphis" might apply to the former story as well. In "The Emancipator," the abusive husband Hadi is also at the mercy of a system, and he reacts with violence against his wife, the person he thought might be able to save him (hence the title) but who is ultimately as powerless against the system as she is against him.

Hadi has come to the United States from Lebanon to attend school. Once here, he wants to stay, but as a result of participating in—or perhaps even merely attending—"a meeting on campus . . . for the problem of voting in student elections" (*DL* 70), his request to renew his visa is turned down. The reader may be suspicious that Hadi is not telling the whole story behind his presence at or even the nature of this seemingly minor political rally; however, regardless of how insignificant the rally actually was, getting together to complain about and perhaps devise a plan to fight the system is supposed to be allowed on an American campus. When Mae, the foreign student advisor, inquires into the matter, she is told that "they don't fool around with the ones from the Middle East" (*DL* 72). In other words, Hadi is not allowed all of the freedoms enjoyed by the American college student.

Although the discrimination is evident, the reader might not feel the full injustice of the treatment of Hadi because, like Porter's Jewish Lowenthal, he is not likable in any way—much less so even than Baby Kate's husband Franke. He uses Mae, rather than the other way around as in "Memphis." While she works on helping him in one way, he seduces her so that, should her efforts to renew his visa fail, which they do, he can (sweet)talk her into marrying him. If the reader had been ready to believe his stories about how dangerous it would be for him to return to Lebanon, he loses the reader's pity when he boasts proudly to a friend of his manipulation of Mae.

Once he is legally married to Mae and thus safe from deportation, Hadi begins physically abusing his wife: he is unhappy both with "the system," because of some course requirement mix-up that is delaying his graduation, and with his American wife, who does not share his priorities (that the coffee be made in the painstaking manner he taught her even if she is running late) or values (that she put him first in all matters). In no way does the narration condone his abusive behavior; yet, after reading the two stories together, the reader understands Gilchrist's message about oppression in this one. Those who feel themselves discriminated against are more likely to seek out a weaker group over whom they can assert their rights than to join forces with that group and retaliate against their common oppressor.

It is made apparent by the incredibly negative characterization of Hadi that Gilchrist's central concern in this story is not with him. Rather,

"The Emancipator" is another story about a white middle-class woman seeking love. In Mae's case, the consequences are much more violent than the results of, for example, Nora Jane's plan to follow her lover to California in "The Famous Poll at Jody's Bar" in *In the Land of Dreamy Dreams*. Nora Jane is not caught for robbing a bar to finance her trip; she merely learns (in stories in *Victory over Japan*), by the time she finds Sandy, that this man for whose sake she committed robbery had already replaced her with another woman. In marked contrast, enraged by Mae's innocent friendliness toward another man, Hadi violently murders her.

Gilchrist also deals with domestic violence in her narratives about Crystal Manning Mallison Weiss. During one altercation between Crystal and her husband Manny, Crystal falls down a staircase, and it is suggested that Manny pushed her. This incident haunts the reader throughout the Crystal stories even when one finds oneself siding with Manny against Crystal's sometimes unreasonable demands or outrageous behavior. Still, Crystal's numerous affairs do not justify physical violence. Rather, the physical violence, though it is a single incident, reflects one motivation for Crystal's affairs. She is seeking a gentler love than Manny is capable of giving.

Although born in quite different time periods, Porter's Sophia Jane, Miranda's grandmother, is surprisingly comparable to Gilchrist's Crystal. In this case, there is a time difference of a century separating the two characters, revealing perhaps most poignantly how little has changed for the upper-class white woman in the South. Both women have disappointing relationships with men—fathers, brothers, husbands, and sons, and in Crystal's case, extramarital lovers as well. Most devastating to them both, their marriages do not fulfill their romantic expectations. Even their sons run away from them at one point in each character's life. Consequently, Sophia Jane and Crystal both spoil these sons to keep them home and thereby make certain that the next generation of men will be as demanding and thus as disappointing to their wives as the mothers' own husbands have been.

The person closest to each of these women is a black woman, significantly, a subordinate in the household and thus someone who can relate to their own oppression. Nannie is bought by Sophia Jane's father when they are both little girls and is given to her when she marries. To set up a similar arrangement, Crystal's mother-in-law telephones Traceleen, whose aunt works for the Weiss family, just after Crystal marries into the family: "Traceleen, Mr. Manny has taken himself a bride and I would like you to go around and see if you can be the maid" (*VJ* 215–16). As Nannie chooses to stay with Sophia Jane after emancipation, Traceleen remains maid to the Weiss family and companion to Crystal. A genuine bond seems to develop between the women in each pair. One could argue, however, that Porter's depiction of the relationship between Sophia Jane and Nannie, which culminates in Nannie's choice to stay with Sophia Jane after emancipation, is an example of stereotypical romanticizing of the mistress-mammy relationship. And one might find Traceleen's explanation of her devotion to Crystal similarly romantic: "Ever since the first day I went to work for her I have loved Miss Crystal as if she was my sister or my child. I have spread out my love around her like a net and I catch whatever I have to catch. That is my decision and the job I have picked out for myself" (*DL* 216).

Regardless of Traceleen's *choice* of occupation and her rejection of the opinion of another black woman who "call[s] her a slave" (*DL* 216), the reader recognizes how reminiscent her position in the Weiss household is to Nannie's role in Sophia Jane's house. Just as it is Nannie who nurses most of Sophia Jane's children, in many ways Traceleen is more of a mother to Crystal's daughter than Crystal is.[26] Traceleen is called upon in the first place in part because Mrs. Weiss believes Crystal will need help with the son she already has from her first marriage. Later, just as Nannie is indispensable to the family she works for, as is evidenced in "The Last Leaf" when, after she "retires" into her own house, "everything slackened" and work "did not accomplish itself as it once had" (*CS* 35), Traceleen is the one who, in Betty Matthews's words, "manag[es] to hold together the Weiss household when all the occupants (and most of the guests) are regularly falling apart" (78). Matthews calls her "the voice of common sense and order . . . the most stable" (78).

Though Gilchrist places Traceleen in the Crystal stories by way of a traditional occupation in the Weiss household, she does not use her major black female character to support any depiction of the strong black matriarch having to compensate in her own home for a worthless or absent man. In contrast to Sophia Jane and Nannie's similarly unpleasant experiences with marriage, Traceleen does not share Crystal's disappointment in marriage. Like Crystal, Traceleen has been married twice, but unlike Crystal, she has been happy with both husbands. Her present husband Mark loves her and encourages her to take advantage of the opportunities her employment offers her. Then, when she gets home from her adventures he is there waiting for her, eager to listen to her stories, except when they involve some danger to herself. His support comforts her with the assurance that love is not, indeed, a myth, as Crystal's experiences would otherwise seem to prove.

Porter's description of Nannie's marriage to Uncle Jimbilly, in contrast, serves to illuminate the double oppression of the southern black woman. Nannie had not chosen her husband; she had been "mated" to him by their owners "with an eye to the blood and family stability" (CS 350). After she is past childbearing, the two drift apart, but later he shows up at the house she has been given to pass her last years in, asking her, "Whut you doin with all this big house to yoself?" (CS 351). Seeing the threat of being oppressed into further servitude, this time by her husband, Nannie sends him away: "I don' aim to pass my las' days waitin' on no man. . . . I've served my time" (CS 351).

Gilchrist's positive portrayal of Traceleen's marriage highlights instead the continued oppression of the women of the formerly slave-holding class, which continues to be Gilchrist's key concern even in these stories with a central black character. Traceleen may play a major role in the Crystal stories, but her conflicts are never the issue. As Betty Matthews points out, "Of all Gilchrist's women, only Traceleen appears to be undamaged by her relationships with men" (78). In these stories, Gilchrist continues to explore the conflict of a woman with a record of disappointing relationships with men. Twice Crystal marries "suitable" men—powerful wealthy businessmen—and twice she is disappointed. Although they can give her any*thing* she wants, love still eludes her. The stories about her marriage to her second husband Manny Weiss are in large part about control: his efforts to control her and her efforts to maintain her independence.[27]

Although the Crystal/Traceleen stories focus on Crystal's unhappy relationships with men, and in contrast the reader is repeatedly reminded of Traceleen's happy marriage, this is not to say that Traceleen does not suffer at all as a black woman in a society dominated by the white race. She still has to deal with people like Crystal's brother, who is outraged that Crystal "let the nigger maid drive" his new Mercedes Benz, even though Traceleen was the only sober adult at the time (VJ 261). However, her strong sense of self and the confirmation of her worth that she gets at work from Crystal and Crystal's friends and at home from her husband enable Traceleen to recognize such small-mindedness for what it is: a statement on the character of the speaker rather than a reflection of her own.

In this story in which Crystal's brother Phelan plays a part ("Traceleen, She's Still Talking" in *Victory over Japan*), yet another connection can be seen between Crystal and Sophia Jane. Both women have to stand helplessly by while the men in their families waste their money. Crystal complains repeatedly that her brother is wasting what is supposed to be their shared inheritance on such far-fetched schemes as his safari ranch. Similarly, it is reported in Porter's "The Journey" that much of Sophia Jane's frustration in her early life came from the fact that "she despised [men] and was ruled by them. Her husband threw away her dowry and her property in wild investments in strange territories: Louisiana, Texas; and without protest she watched him play away her substance like a gambler. She felt that she could have managed her affairs profitably. But her natural activities lay elsewhere, it was the business of a man to make all decisions and dispose of all financial matters" (*CS* 337). It is not surprising, though no less unfair, that in the nineteenth century Sophia Jane is not allowed to voice her own better judgments about financial investments to her husband. More disturbing, then, are Gilchrist's similar scenarios set in the twentieth century. Crystal is not the only woman in Gilchrist's canon who is kept from handling her own money while her brother is allowed to invest recklessly. This incident echoes Letty Wilson's situation in the story "Rich." Unlike Crystal, however, Letty appears unconcerned about this injustice; rather, it is her husband Tom who, like Sophia Jane, seethes inwardly over the fact that his wife's brothers "controlled their own money while Letty's was tied up in some mysterious trust" (*LDD* 8). Letty's lack of response to this situation does not differ much from Sophia Jane's silent anger, for both women ultimately support their oppression through silent acceptance of it as the way of their world and with their view of their world as superior to others.

In spite of their subordinate positions in their society, Sophia Jane and Nannie complain about the changing times, and they contend that each new generation is increasingly inferior to their own. This attitude is echoed in the focus of Gilchrist's story "In the Land of Dreamy Dreams." Not only does old Claiborne Redding lament the changing times (and with reason, given his position of power), but (like Nannie) so does Nailor, the black man in charge of tennis court maintenance. Porter's narrator of "The Journey" remarks upon Sophia Jane and Nannie's constant talk about the past and their regret over the changing times and then asks, "Who knows why they loved their past? It had been bitter for them both, they had questioned the burdensome rule they lived by every day of their lives, but without rebellion and without expecting an answer" (*CS* 327). One might ask a similar question regarding Nailor's devotion to a tennis club that he *served* rather than belonged to, as well as regarding LaGrande McGruder's willingness to cheat at tennis in order to beat Roxanne Miller, a *woman* not so very unlike herself in that both suffer under the patriarchy that rules this club; a woman, furthermore, who has won more court privileges for women club members and who worked to change the symbolically oppressive all-white dress code.

This story's focus on the conflict between LaGrande and the new Jewish club member also illuminates the paradox both Porter and Gilchrist explore of women supporting the patriarchy that oppresses them. Once again, then, the reader sees how Gilchrist's works show that, with respect to women's oppression, little has changed in the South since the time when Porter and William Faulkner were writing, a subject developed further in the next chapter.

4

The Annunciation as a Dialogue with William Faulkner

Giving Caddy Compson a Fighting Chance

> *"The past is never dead. It's not even past."*
>
> William Faulkner, *Requiem for a Nun*

> *"I used to believe the past was the present, that we could never live it down, never leave it behind. Bullshit. The past is the past. You can dwell in it or you can move forward."*
>
> Ellen Gilchrist, *The Annunciation*

In his review of Ellen Gilchrist's *The Annunciation*, Charles Stubblefield confirms the unfortunate realization of the South's immutability that one reaches through comparisons between Gilchrist's work and the writings of Katherine Anne Porter, William Faulkner, and even, as is shown in the next chapter, Kate Chopin:

> Gilchrist is a southern writer in the tradition of Faulkner, O'Connor, and Welty. She knows the New South, its institutions, its mores, and its people as [they] knew their earlier South. And although [*The Annunciation*] is a contemporary story about a modern woman, and although there are changes on the surface of southern society, little has changed in the way family and the land—the institutions, myths, and traditions which the family and land perpetuate—hang like shadows over the lives of these people. They are all the victims (and the price is a terrible one) of the society they inherit and of the society they blindly support. (107)

The characters in Gilchrist's novel may indeed all be "victims," as Stubblefield suggests, but the victimization of women in particular in the South is illuminated by an intertextual reading of Faulkner's *The Sound and the Fury* and Gilchrist's *The Annunciation*. Gilchrist's repetition in this novel of events that occur in *The Sound and the Fury* reveals that the South is still filled with people who have a false and often destructive sense of themselves and reinforces the bitter irony that those who suffer the consequences most unjustly are those who strive to expose rather than promote the hypocrisy. Two such victims are Faulkner's Caddy Compson and Gilchrist's Amanda McCamey.

Both of these characters are strong women who choose to live according to their own values, rather than their families' hypocritical codes of honor and morality. Sadly, the love and courage of Faulkner's Caddy Compson are ultimately broken down by her family, leaving her with a destructive self-image, which in turn provides the reader with a sense of her ultimate doom. For much of her life, Gilchrist's Amanda McCamey also responds self-destructively to her family's similar treatment of her; however, she is eventually able to save herself by recognizing and recollecting her early strengths. Armed with a restored ability to love, she takes what Caddy was first denied and then herself refused—a second chance. As summarized by Rosellen Brown in her review of the novel, Amanda "ris[es] above genes, memory, and money to try motherhood again in a more receptive, even joyous state of mind" (53). The reader who examines the parallels between the lives of these two characters and notes the differences in their fates will realize that the fortitude of people like Amanda, who do not break under the pressure of discrimination and hypocrisy, allows them to survive the traditionally rigid codes of the South, even to flourish in spite of these codes. Therefore, although reading *The Annunciation* intertextually with Faulkner's *The Sound and the Fury* confirms the notion that the South has not changed much since Faulkner wrote his novel, it also reveals how Gilchrist transforms the character of Caddy Compson into a more positive, less doomed figure. Gilchrist thereby subverts Faulkner's depiction of women even as she agrees with his depiction of the South.[1]

To prepare for her subversion of Faulkner's novel, Gilchrist mocks acceptance of his view of the South as representative rather than romantic. Close to the beginning of the novel the narrator reports sardonically that Amanda's husband Malcolm Ashe "married [her] to be part of this world [the South] he liked to read about in books. He had been a Faulkner scholar at Yale and it had a big effect on his life" (*A* 47). Like so many readers of Faulkner, Malcolm does not realize that Faulkner has provided only a limited perspective on the South. Having not heard—and apparently not missed hearing—Caddy Compson's voice, her side of the story, Malcolm is not prepared for Amanda's refusal to be silent.

Indeed, Gilchrist begins the empowerment of her protagonist by making the novel truly Amanda's story: it is not told from the perspective of the men in her life, as Caddy Compson's story is told by her brothers. Caddy's silence may be more dignified than her brothers' ravings, but it does not allow her to control her own story. To appreciate Gilchrist's various achievements through giving "Caddy" a voice in her novel, one might here apply to Faulkner's female *character* Patricia Yaeger's deconstruction of the notion that silence is empowering to women *writers*. In *Honey-Mad Women*, Yaeger counters "the assumption that women's speech can only be represented by an 'absence'" through a reevaluation of "the use of 'silence' as metaphor to describe women's relation to speech" (152). Yaeger criticizes the view that the silence in women's texts is "an essential part of women's plots" in that it "emphasize[s] the vulnerabilities, fragilities, [and] interruptions" of the woman writer's life—or, when applying Yaeger's view to Faulkner's novel, the female character's life (154). Yaeger illustrates her point by analyzing the criticism of Wollstonecraft's *A Vindication of the Rights of Women* that focuses on "the ways in which Wollstonecraft has either been silenced by her culture or else been complicitous in its values" (155). Yaeger then proposes that, rather than focus on women's silence, one should "examine women's noise and articulateness in inventing emancipatory strategies to empower themselves in relation to a tradition that restricts their right to speak" (156). Her method is to view *A Vindication* as a response to and as operating as a dialogue with Rousseau's writings. In doing so, Yaeger is also rejecting "the assumption that dialogue with the dominant tradition is useless to the woman writer as an emancipatory strategy [since] it always involves representations of a complicitous or oppressive discourse, and such representation inevitably reenacts this oppression" (152). Yaeger believes that the woman writer who creates a dialogue within her text with a text by a member of the dominant tradition takes the position of power, for she is then in control of this other writer's words:

Writing . . . gives the woman writer a space in which she can expro-
priate men's texts and treat these texts as bodies. These embodied
texts are mortal, penetrable, excitable; they become imperfect sites
of that sometime thing we call "patriarchal discourse." Thus male
bodies and texts can be made to circulate through women's texts—
breaking that circuit of meaning in which women have been the
objects of circulation. Wollstonecraft's dialogue with Rousseau in
the *Vindications* serves double ends. First, she quotes his texts liber-
ally—in order to decontextualize his misogyny, to place it in a context she can control. Then she draws Rousseau into a conversation
that . . . he would prefer to resist. But since Wollstonecraft is controlling his words, she can change their import by revealing their violence. Finally, Wollstonecraft corrects this violence with her own
ideas. (161)

With *The Annunciation*, Gilchrist engages in such a dialogue with
Faulkner's *The Sound and the Fury*, within which she exposes the misogyny that created, destroyed, and all the while revered Caddy Compson. No less than the Compson family, Faulkner has objectified Caddy,
not only by having her brothers do so in their respective sections of the
novel but also in his own response to the question of why he did not give
Caddy a section in the novel: "Caddy was . . . to me too beautiful and too
moving to reduce her to telling what was going on. . . . It would be more
passionate to see her through somebody else's eyes" (Gwynn and
Blotner 1). The absence of her voice, however, emphasizes (using
Yaeger's words) Caddy's "vulnerabilit[y]" and "fragilit[y]" (154). It reflects, according to Karen Kaivola, "women's absence in patriarchal discourse and culture" (29). Kaivola remarks of Caddy, "Silent and absent,
she remains a mystery: alien, other, unknowable. . . . While Caddy's silence does give the text much of its power, and her brothers the power to
speak her, it deprives her of power" (29). On the other hand, Gilchrist's
novel, the plot and characters of which parallel in many ways those of
Faulkner's novel, is told from the perspective of her female central character, Amanda McCamey, and thus the silences are filled in, the woman is
empowered. In this way, Gilchrist, as Yaeger advises, resists the practice
of "represent[ing women] as objects who circulate through culture and
through men's texts," seeming to realize, as Yaeger argues, "that, as cir-
culating 'objects,' women are outside culture—they give social texts the
marks of coherence at the price of their own alienation" (152). In direct
contrast to Faulkner's placement of Caddy in his novel, the female pro-

tagonist of Gilchrist's novel is physically present throughout her story. Though temporarily alienated from her family, she is never alienated from society. She makes a place for herself in a less oppressive community and refuses, rather than is forbidden, to return home.

In his review, Charles Stubblefield praises Gilchrist's novel for being if "not a 'feminist' novel, [then] an ardently pro-woman, pro-human novel . . . a story of the human heart and the way it is twisted and wrenched by the loves that are fostered there" (107). He therefore approves of "the quest of a woman to understand and repudiate the loves that do not sustain and regenerate her, and to understand and develop the personal freedoms that do" (107). Stubblefield's positive opinion of *The Annunciation* is not typical of reviewers; this first novel by Ellen Gilchrist was not as well received as were her preceding and following collections of short stories. For example, Rosellen Brown's review of the novel finds fault with Amanda's ultimate triumph against the kind of oppression suffered by Caddy: "When things go well for Amanda—as when she remembers where she begins and the cursed McCameys end, and so escapes the narcissistic seductiveness of her family—*The Annunciation* becomes a fairly ordinary story, and its heroine yet another of the bumper crop of lively and admirable women finding themselves" (53–54). Brown's assessment suggests that she is, surprisingly and disappointingly, bored with a triumphant heroine.[2] I would contend, in contrast, that unfortunately Amanda's story is not "ordinary" enough and thus is a welcome respite from stories of victimized women who come to tragic ends.

Many reviewers of the novel simply suggest that Gilchrist's medium of expertise is the short story rather than the novel. This opinion, too, might be rethought when one re-views this novel intertextually with Faulkner's novel in light of what Yaeger believes such readings reflect of the woman writer's achievements. Yaeger applauds the choice of women writers since Jane Austen to write novels, a genre that "allow[s] them both to disrupt a dominant literary tradition and to interrogate their surroundings" (183). Such "interrogation" is exactly what Gilchrist does. She examines the role that Amanda's family and society play in her conflicts, thereby also illuminating the role of family and society in Caddy's conflict, and she does so without the distraction of Faulkner's focus on Caddy's role in her family's conflicts.

As Jeanie Thompson and Anita Miller Garner point out, "Amanda is the central focus of the novel, most of which is narrated in a close third person through her perceptions, though occasionally Gilchrist . . . dips into the consciousnesses of other characters for a balancing effect. Still, it is Amanda's story, her quest to know who she is and how to live her life that is the main theme of the novel" (105). The inner turmoils of Amanda's cousin Guy McCamey, in particular, while present in the novel, are never central. The reader is so much in Amanda's consciousness that the omniscient narrator's occasional visits into Guy's consciousness are not enough to divide one's loyalty. Indeed, in order not to condemn him too harshly for his part in Amanda's troubles (which begin with an illegitimate pregnancy with Guy's child), one must strive for objectivity—call to mind, for example, the fact that Guy was only eighteen and had put a stop to his and Amanda's sexual play (which had only involved fondling) when *Amanda* seduced *him* into consummating their relationship.

Such attempts at objectivity, however, might only lead the reader back to recognizing Guy's role in Amanda's problems as opposed to pitying him for his own. First, the reader will recall that Guy is the one who initiated the sexual intimacy with Amanda, when she was only a little girl. Second, as earlier noted, he puts a stop to their fondling each other for selfish reasons: "I want God to let me be good at baseball, Sissy. I want to be on the football team next year. If I do this he isn't going to let me" (*A* 12). And finally, consciously or not, Guy, who receives his family's adoration and thus attention, had taken advantage of Amanda's recent losses (the death of her father and her grieving mother's neglect) and consequential need for someone to love her when he initiated their sexual fondling. One might understand that the family spoiled Guy and is thus responsible for his needy personality, but one becomes impatient with his failure to make something of his life and his tendency to hold Amanda responsible for making things right for him. When his loveless marriage does not result in a family, for example, he turns to Amanda: "I'll leave Maria. We'll go somewhere together. We'll be happy" (*A* 59). Amanda completes "the scenario" for him—"And we'll find our little girl [who by this time is a grown woman] and live happily ever after" (*A* 60)—annoyed that he was not listening to her as she tried to explain her excitement about her new studies. He had merely responded to her desire to find "some purpose" with "You could have me for a purpose" (*A* 60).

One cannot deny that both characters operate with their own interests in mind, but since Guy's egocentric nature is condoned, even supported by their patriarchal society, the reader is more apt to forgive Amanda's, which goes against her society's view that the woman's role in life is to nurture and support the man at the expense of herself. Therefore, though the reader realizes that, like Guy, Amanda married for money, one is more understanding of her seemingly shallow motivation, considering that as a woman she had few career opportunities, and considering her past experience, when economic security was all her family offered her when she was in trouble. Furthermore, one can see that she married a man who was "safe," in that she did not have with him the volatile relationship that she had with Guy. She could therefore remain in control and thus not risk being hurt again. In contrast, Guy, a man, a former football star, is in a position to support himself quite easily and well. The reader is therefore not so tolerant of his choice of an easy route to wealth by marrying for money.

Nor is the reader very sympathetic when Guy realizes several years into the marriage that he is unhappy. When Amanda finds that she is unhappy, she changes her lifestyle. To start, she quits drinking. To fill her time, she goes back to school and pursues her talent with languages. Then, when their grandmother dies and leaves them (Amanda and Guy) with an inheritance, Amanda, now having the means to support herself, leaves Malcolm to try her hand at being a translator; certainly not a paying career, but now that she has the pension that Virginia Woolf says the woman writer in particular needs, she can take the risk. Whereas Amanda is going forward, Guy wants to return to Esperanza with Amanda, their daughter, and grandchild. He is unconcerned with whether or not Amanda wants the same things or with how the sudden appearance of her natural parents might affect their daughter. Repeatedly, Amanda must reject Guy's wish to turn back the clock. So, when Guy calls her in Fayetteville, Arkansas, his voice bringing the past into her new home where she is pursuing love as well as a career, she threatens his backward vision, rejects its source, and asserts her right to live as she chooses: "I'm going to sell Esperanza . . . to the Arabs or the blacks or anyone who wants it. I'm going to have my own money and live my own way and never have to ask anyone for anything. . . . I'm through with the past and the terrible decadent south and everything it represents" (*A* 206).

Perhaps the most striking similarity between *The Sound and the Fury* and *The Annunciation* is the parallel relationships between Gilchrist's cousins, Amanda and Guy, and Faulkner's siblings, Caddy and Quentin.[3] Analysis of this point of comparison emphasizes the role these weak young men play in the destruction or near-destruction of these strong young women.[4] It is clear from the time of the Compsons' childhood that Caddy is strong-willed and courageous, while Quentin is ruled by manners and mores. For example, Caddy risks punishment by climbing a tree in order to look into a window to find out if it is true that their grandmother is dead. Her older brother Quentin remains on the ground, afraid both of being punished and of what he might see: his deceased grandmother's body. In a similarly telling incident from the childhood of Amanda and Guy McCamey, Gilchrist establishes their comparability to these two Compson children. Amanda finds Guy cleaning some birds killed on a hunting trip. "One of the birds was so warm Guy thought it was still alive. His thumb hit a tendon and it moved in his hands. He leaned over and vomited. . . . Amanda stood beside a rocker watching him" (A 6). She is not sickened by the dead birds; her only response is concern for Guy.

Surprisingly, in spite of this episode, Amanda believes that "Guy could do anything . . . [and] was afraid of nothing in the world" (A 9) and that "there was nothing to fear when Guy was there" (A 11). Guy maintains his power over Amanda for as long as she remains blind to his weaknesses. Whenever she sees him, she falls under the spell he cast upon her the first time she saw him, just after the death of her father, when she and her grieving mother arrived at Esperanza and "Guy [came] down the hall holding out his hands to her" (A 3), seeming to promise with that gesture the love that her parents could no longer provide. She will only be able to resist him much later in the novel, forty years later in time, when she is finally able to see him as he really is: "He turned her face up to his with his hands and all the pain and longing of his life was there for her to see. It seemed to Amanda that all her life Guy had been turning that lonely face up to her, asking her to get him warm with the light that was in her" (A 289). After this insight, Amanda berates Guy for coming back into her life and dredging up the past. When he apologizes to her, she asserts, "No, you aren't. You aren't sorry or you wouldn't have done this to me. You're just sorry I won't give in to you. You've figured out a way to be miserable and you want me to keep you company" (A 291).

In this aspect of Amanda's development, Gilchrist reverses the pattern of Faulkner's more romantic heroine's paradoxical behavior. Caddy's loyalty to Quentin increases simultaneously with her recognition of his weaknesses. Thus, Quentin's control of Caddy increases as her respect for him decreases. When they are children, Caddy acts against her brother's directions, denying his right to tell her what to do. Besides climbing the forbidden tree, she also takes off her dress in front of her brothers and the black children they play with, in spite of, indeed seemingly inspired by Quentin's challenge, "I bet you won't" (*SF* 18). When he slaps her, she hits back. She fights back again a few years later when Quentin catches her kissing a boy, reminding him that she had recently caught him engaging in some kind of sexual play with Natalie and arguing against his double standard. The older they get, however, the more Caddy gives in to Quentin's will, ultimately accepting his opinion that she is damned.

The turning point toward this surrender may be the period of Caddy's involvement with Dalton Ames. As she has in the past, she defies Quentin's objections to her meeting with Dalton, during which rendezvous she gains knowledge that Quentin is afraid to seek. Whereas Quentin apparently never consummated his relationship with Natalie, Caddy does engage in sexual relations with Dalton. After losing her virginity, however, she is ready to surrender to her brother's demands, in part, it seems, because she pities him for his lack of sexual experience. "Poor Quentin . . . youve [sic] never done that have you" (*SF* 151), she remarks just before agreeing to either a double suicide or sex.

I refer here to Quentin's veiled suggestion, when he takes out his knife at the branch, that, if Caddy must engage in sexual activity, then why not do so with him, which brings up the next point of comparison between the central relationships in these two novels: the issue of incest.[5] Paradoxically, one could argue that incest does or does not occur in either novel. Regardless of which conclusion the reader reaches with each novel, what remains unarguable in either case is the absence of parental guidance and the consequences of this void. The parents' refusal in both novels to acknowledge such a possibility as incest, or their blindness to it, reflects their negligence and, perhaps, their fear of scandal, both of which contribute to the destruction of the novels' women.

The incest in *The Annunciation* is a physically irrefutable fact: Amanda and Guy are first cousins (raised, in fact, more like brother and sister—Guy even calls Amanda "Sissy"), and they are lovers.[6] This latter fact cannot be denied with any fanciful reading of the text since Amanda conceives and bears a child as a result of her sexual relations with Guy. With Caddy and Quentin, however, the question of incest has been debated since the earliest criticism of the novel. In support of the presence of incest, many critics give explanations similar to that of Lee Clinton Jenkins, who contends, "Good Puritan that Quentin is, he feels the prohibition and allure of the forbidden act so strongly that the admission [to his father] of it as a possibility constitutes its enactment" (136). John Arthos suggests that Quentin feels as responsible for Caddy's sexual activity as if he had been her partner: "He is extremely fond of [Caddy], and her situation thrusts upon him a burden of responsibility he accepts. . . . He comes to believe that his own love has failed her, and in something like adolescent self-torment he thinks his guilt is equivalent to the betrayal itself. He extends his torment to the point where it is as if he himself had betrayed her through incest" (22). To this line of thinking can be added the argument that Quentin becomes more of a father to Caddy's child than whoever the natural father may be. Indeed, Caddy, in a way, establishes Quentin as the father, according to Lawrance Thompson, when she names the child after him. Thompson concludes from this naming that although "in the literal sense, Quentin did not father her child, . . . in some figurative sense he did" (43).[7] In the same figurative sense, then, he also committed incest.

More easily argued is the contention that incest is at least propositioned. Although Quentin never overtly broaches the subject with Caddy for fear that she would accept (as he explains to his father [SF 177]), many critics interpret his suggestion that they commit a double suicide as a thinly disguised sexual proposition. John T. Irwin, for example, explains the presence of an incestuous impulse in Quentin's fumblings with the knife: "When Quentin puts his knife to his sister's throat, he is placing his knife at the throat of someone who is an image of himself, thereby evoking the threat of castration—the traditional punishment for incest. The brother seducer with the phallic knife at his sister's throat is as well the brother avenger with the castrating knife at the brother seducer's throat—the father with the castrating knife at the son's penis" (Doubling 46).

In spite of symbolic and psychoanalytical readings, there is still the fact that Caddy and Quentin do not actually have sexual intercourse with each other and therefore do not technically commit incest. One can also argue reasonably that Quentin does not even *want* to do so. Quentin's reasons for contemplating and admitting to incest have little if anything to do with desire for his sister's body. Susan Gallagher notes that his recollection of his conversations with his father on the subject "is really the only textual indication of a prurient interest. In fact, Quentin seems more concerned with denying his physical nature" (215). He certainly seems to turn down a veiled offer of sex from Caddy shortly after his own veiled offer at the branch. Caddy returns from her tryst with Dalton and, in response to Quentin's command that she go home, seems to offer herself to her brother again, as the passage below suggests (though in contrast to the critical analysis of the sexual nature of Quentin's request in the knife scene, critics have overlooked Caddy's sexual innuendo in this one):

> [Caddy:] yes I will if you want me to I will
> . . .
> [Quentin:] go on to the house like I told you
> [Caddy:] yes Ill do anything you want me to anything yes
> she didn't even look at me I caught her shoulder and shook her hard
> [Quentin:] you shut up (*SF* 156)

Furthermore, Faulkner's description of Quentin in the appendix to the novel, which he wrote for Malcolm Cowley's *Portable Faulkner*, reveals the author's support of the notion that Quentin did not desire Caddy sexually: "Who *loved not his sister's body* but some concept of Compson honor precariously and . . . only temporarily supported by the minute fragile membrane of her maidenhead. . . . Who loved *not the idea of the incest* which he would not commit, but some presbyterian concept of its eternal punishment" (*PF* 709–10, emphasis added).

Finally, one can view any desires on Quentin's part as more narcissistic than incestuous.[8] Quentin sees Caddy as his other half. She has many of the positive qualities he lacks—courage, for example, as previously illustrated—and she lacks qualities important to him, such as respect for certain codes of behavior. Thus, union of the two, in Quentin's eyes, is necessary; without such they are each incomplete and thus weak. Lee Jenkins explains this "narcissistic self love" as that which "seeks others only to the extent that they can be used to fortify the ego against its sense of underlying vulnerability, satisfy its self-justifying needs, and stave off the threat of its own dissolution" (149). As future head of his family, Quentin will need Caddy's strength and authority; and, he believes, if their family name is to maintain its respectability, Caddy must adopt his codes of morality.

In relation to this idea, Quentin's reasons for contemplating a sexual relationship with Caddy may go back to some primitive reasons for incest, as listed by Constance Hill Hall in her book *Incest in Faulkner: A*

Metaphor for the Fall: first, "to stabilize and unify the dynasty by limiting the peripheries of a clan"; second, "a privilege that . . . was reserved for royalty"; and third, an act "necessary to the survival of a race" (6). In theories similar to Hall's, Warwick Wadlington describes "Quentin's desperate fantasy of incest" as "a rigorous extension of the inbreeding attitude of a household that feels itself surrounded by relative nonentities" (416), and André Bleikasten explains that "in sociohistorical terms, [Quentin's] obsession with incest may reflect the panic of a declining social class which struggles for survival but refuses any influx of outside blood" (227). Quentin is concerned with the survival of his family, a family he views as "royal" in the sense that they are descendants of the aristocracy of the Old South. This elevated perception of his family allows Quentin to contemplate incest in spite of his puritanical nature. In this light, he would view the notion of Caddy committing incest with him as more acceptable than her philanderous behavior with "unsuitable" partners, which could result in "unsuitable" descendants. Thus again, his reasons have nothing to do with sexual desire, and his impulse is more narcissistic than incestuous.

One can repudiate the occurrence of incest in Gilchrist's novel on similar grounds—despite the existence of the child Barrett Clare, whom the reader knows to be the indisputable offspring of first cousins Amanda and Guy. Thus, the criticism of Faulkner's novel on the subject of incest illuminates the ambiguity of the nature of the relationship between Guy and Amanda—which might otherwise not seem so ambiguous. Whether or not sexual intercourse took place is again not really the issue. As in Faulkner's novel, the issue is more complicated. The question in this case is: was it *incest*? From Amanda's perception, the answer is no. First of all, the narrator notes early in the novel that when Amanda was a child "no one minded when they found her in [Guy's] bed" (*A* 6); and later, the narrator remarks that "everyone on Esperanza watched it [the growing love between Amanda and Guy] but only the black people knew what they were watching. Only the black people knew what it meant" (*A* 12). One can deduce, too, from the position of African Americans on a southern plantation, that these servants would not have spoken up about their understanding of this developing "situation."

Given both of the above narrative comments, one can also say that, to Amanda, sexual relations with Guy were a *natural* development of their relationship and therefore not incest, for incest is a taboo, and none of the authority figures on the plantation had intimated to her any such prohibitions regarding her *unconcealed* feelings for Guy.[9] Rather, they had encouraged her love by their silence. Moreover, when Amanda does deliver her baby, it is immediately taken from her and she is told *by a nun*, "Now you can be a girl again" and "put it out of your mind" (*A* 20). In addition to this negation of Amanda's sexual relationship and pregnancy, the matriarch of her family, her grandmother, welcomes her back into the fold—if not back into their home—as if nothing has happened. Further, the ugly word *incest* is never mentioned in the novel. Both the Catholic Church and her family choose to deny Amanda's actions, and the reader recognizes that Amanda did not knowingly commit a crime or sin.

It is only later that Amanda expresses any shame for her relations with Guy. Shortly after arriving at a Virginia college, where she is sent by her family after the baby is born, she must see a doctor about painful menstrual cramps. On the way to his office, she thinks about what she will tell him in lieu of the truth, suggesting that she is ashamed of having had her cousin's baby: "I'll tell him I got raped. I'll tell him it happened while I was asleep. . . . I'll tell him the boy I did it with had cancer. . . . I'll say I did it because he was going to die" (*A* 37). Significantly, these thoughts come after Guy visits her at school and refuses to resume relations because of a deal he made with God in hopes of being forgiven for getting Amanda pregnant. Although Amanda starts to deny God's existence (as she had done when Guy had years earlier called a stop to their sexual play), and only stops herself out of fear that Guy will get mad and not even touch her (as he is still surprisingly willing to do in spite of his deal with God), one might wonder if Guy's belief in a vindictive God has gotten through to her subconscious and if she is now associating her painful cramps with Guy's belief in divine wrath.[10]

Though on the way to the doctor's office Amanda does seem to feel shame about her relationship with Guy, this feeling does not last. She easily resumes relations when she next sees Guy almost thirty years later, when they meet in Mississippi for their grandmother's funeral.[11] And she has sex with him again when he visits her in Fayetteville toward the end of the novel. In the first instance of resumed relations, Amanda makes fun of stereotypes of incestuous southern families—"you're supposed to fuck your cousins at your grandmother's funeral" (*A* 58)—her mockery reflecting her lack of genuine concern about the issue. There is no shame; in both instances, she feels merely sad after their lovemaking because of the futility of their attempts to recapture the past with each other. Amanda cannot go back. It is shortly after their first reunion that she leaves Malcolm, but not to return to Guy. Rather, she starts her new life in Fayetteville, Arkansas, significantly moving into her new home there on Christmas day. Her lifestyle in Fayetteville, which includes an affair with a younger man, reveals that she has left behind the Old Testament sensibilities of the Deep South. Her second reunion with Guy, which takes place in her Arkansas home, is instigated by Amanda when she is feeling insecure after this young man, Will Lyons, leaves and she finds herself pregnant. When she first sees Guy, she asks him to "take care of me. I'm tired of taking care of myself" (*A* 284). Her later announcement of her pregnancy, however, reveals that she has changed her mind, that she will not again turn herself and her child over to the will of others: "I don't know what I'm going to do about all this. I might just have an abortion and forget it. Then I might not" (*A* 291). She continues asserting her possible plans for the future, at no point asking Guy what she should do or for his opinion of these plans.

Returning briefly to the subject of incest, the way that Gilchrist simplifies the issue (making clear that her characters have sex with each other) while keeping it ambiguous (their relations being questionably incestuous) leads her reader to recognize that which causes the trouble in both cases. The confusion of these four adolescents regarding the morality or immorality of their desires is in large part a consequence of the failure of their parents to counsel them on the matter. The intense relationships between siblings and cousins, respectively, develop as a result of parental neglect. As Constance Hall explains in the introduction to *Incest in Faulkner*, "In cases of sibling incest, the brother and sister are likely to be . . . the children of weak and neglectful parents who fail to provide a strong and positive influence" (4). Of the mother in particular (of siblings involved in incest), Hall writes, "typically she is either passive and dependent or else rigid and puritanical . . . not present to her family, often relinquishing her responsibilities to her daughter and sometimes abandoning her children altogether" (4). It is easy to see that this passage is an accurate description of Mrs. Compson.[12] The notorious image of the hypochondriac Mrs. Compson doing little else besides whining about being punished by God for her family's transgressions reflects her neglect of her children, as does Amanda's mother's persistent mourning for her deceased husband, which leaves her little time to see to her daughter's emotional needs.[13]

Caddy fills in for her mother's inattentiveness to her children's emotional needs by being a good mother herself to Benjy. In Sally Page's explanation of "the role of motherhood," one can see how Caddy's maternal instinct can be viewed as a positive reaction to her own motherlessness: "The role of motherhood fosters communication and self-transcendence, for child-bearing unites the woman with the ultimate purpose of nature and enables her to defy her own isolation and to create relation through the establishment of the family. The ideal of self-sacrifice on which effective motherhood is based provides mankind with an ethic that can bring moral order to the chaos of existence" (46). Caddy's ability to love enough for both herself and her mother is quite admirable, given her circumstances. Such a positive reaction to motherlessness may be viewed as part of Faulkner's idealization of his character. Amanda, in direct contrast and perhaps more credibly, responds to her mother's rejection with comparable rejection, as is evident in her discomfort with the baby rabbits discussed in chapter 3: "Their little sucking noises bothered her, as though they might get on her and stick to her skin" (*A* 5).

For a while, with the help of their individual methods of compensation—Caddy's nurturance and Amanda's rejection of others—and the care they receive from other members of their families, neither girl suffers excessively from being essentially motherless. However, the love of other family members, particularly Quentin and Guy, eventually fails them, and when this happens, their own personal responses to being motherless cause certain consequences to ensue; hence, the betrayal from outside causes a betrayal from within the self. That both girls' reactions to motherlessness do lead them toward doom, despite the disparity between these reactions, is largely the responsibility of Quentin and Guy, who remain undeviating in their similarity. Whereas Gilchrist has taken pains to empower her female protagonist through point of view and a less romanticized character (heroines of romances being so often inevitably doomed), she changes little in the characterization and behavior of her central male character. At the same time, the change in the characterization of her female protagonist—from romantic heroic ideal to a more realistic woman—illuminates the role that Faulkner plays in Caddy's doom, in turn revealing how closely akin Faulkner's ideals are to Quentin's and how equally destructive.

Catherine Baum's description of the factors that lead to Caddy's fall illuminates how Faulkner's idealization of his character dooms her: "Ironically enough, those qualities in her character that are admirable are the ones which lead to her fall: her complete selflessness, which leads her to be indifferent to her virginity and to what happens to her; her willingness to put the other person's interests first; and her great desire to communicate love" (38). Such a desire leads Caddy to sexual activity. The sacrificing nature of her relationship with Dalton is poignantly evident in the words she uses to admit to Quentin that she has had sexual relations with Dalton: "I would die for him Ive already died for him I die for him over and over again" (*SF* 151).

Caddy is more self-destructively self-sacrificing in her relations with her brother Quentin. Once Caddy becomes sexually active, Quentin betrays her love as he breaks down her strong self-image in his attempts to make her see the immorality of her actions. Seeing her brother's distress over her loss of virginity, she tells him, "dont cry Im bad anyway you cant help it" (*SF* 158). She later essentially gives up Dalton Ames for Quentin, staying with her brother after his altercation with Dalton instead of going to her lover to apologize for mistakenly thinking he had shot Quentin and for sending him away.[14]

Quentin's desire to force his convictions on Caddy consequently backfires. As Peter Swiggart explains, "Caddy becomes a helpless victim both of her capacity for love and of her brother's efforts to pervert that love into abstract morality. Her promiscuity reflects the self-hatred which Quentin has helped to force upon her" (92). Once Caddy looks at her sexuality through Quentin's eyes, she perceives it as sinful, accepts her damnation, and behaves accordingly. After Dalton's departure, she becomes promiscuous, the result being pregnancy with no knowledge of the father's identity.

Caddy then gives up her desire for love in order to comply with Quentin's ethics of respectability. She goes along with Mrs. Compson's plan to marry her to a man she does not love in order to "legitimize" the child she carries: "I've got to marry somebody," she tells her brother (*SF* 113). Here again Quentin betrays his sister: he voices his objections to her fiancé Herbert Head only to her, rather than standing up for her against a deceitful and loveless marriage. Then he kills himself, and although Caddy's feelings about his death are not given, the reader can imagine that his suicide only compounds her guilt and negative self-image. Furthermore, since Quentin is dead, when Caddy's husband perceives his wife's condition too early for him to be the father and consequently kicks her out, she has no ally at home. Thus, when Mrs. Compson agrees to take in the baby but not the mother, Caddy has little choice but to comply.

Her family's rejection reinforces Caddy's acceptance of Quentin's belief in her sinful nature, and she loses confidence in her capability of being a good mother to her child. She apparently believes, rather, that she would be a harmful influence upon her daughter and therefore allows her family first to take and then to keep her child from her, despite her justified misgivings about their treatment of the innocent baby as a symbol of her mother's sin, not to mention her own firsthand experience of her family's destructiveness. According to Lawrence E. Bowling, this act—abandoning her child—is what truly dooms Caddy: "She is 'damned,' not because she committed fornication and bore an illegitimate child but because, living in a state of perpetual sin, she has neither desire nor hope for redemption; but, most of all, she is damned because, instead of accepting her duty to her child and being the best mother she could, she abandoned the child to the same household which had been her own ruin" (476). I will return to the injustice of the judgmental tone of this assessment in a moment. For the issue at hand, I would point out that for their participation in Caddy's doom, the Compsons are punished, for the Compson family is doomed as well. Sally Page writes, "Had Caddy been allowed to return home to care for [Miss] Quentin and Benjy and thus to fulfill the destiny of her nature, the Compson history might have been different. Instead, the tragedy of Caddy's life is repeated by her child" (66). Both Caddy and her daughter are lost to the Compsons, and since the girl Quentin is the only progeny of this generation of Compsons, this loss means the end of the family line as far as they will ever know.

Parallel to these circumstances of Caddy's decline and destruction in *The Sound and the Fury* are the circumstances of Amanda's decline and near-destruction in *The Annunciation*. As long as Amanda has Guy's attention and affection and hands-on care from the people at Esperanza Plantation, the negative implications of her fear of attachment are not so apparent, for hers is not an all-encompassing attitude against bonding: she does allow herself to love Guy. Then, fearing the loss of Guy, before he leaves for college Amanda seduces him into consummating their relationship, apparently hoping the memory will seal their bond and thus bring him back to her. Thus, like Caddy, she uses sex as a means of getting the love she craves but which has been denied her in the past.

Just as Quentin fails Caddy, Guy ultimately fails Amanda. He is significantly absent from the narrative when their family sends Amanda away to have his baby, and he does not contact her while she is at the home for unwed mothers or even after the baby is born. Rather, again like Quentin, Guy silently condones the family's decisions about Amanda's life and goes on with his own life at college. When he does come to see her at school (only after she summons him), he blames her pregnancy on the sinfulness of their actions: "It happened because we did things we weren't supposed to do" (*A* 32). Clearly, Guy's God, like Quentin's, is the punishing God of the Old Testament. As Amos N. Wilder explains it, Quentin believes in a "truncated Christian conception of guilt and retribution, severed from all ideas of grace" (125). Like Quentin, Guy needs a God who will punish him since his family fails to do so. He wants to pay for his sin in order to purge his guilt, but Amanda is tired of paying for an act she does not regard as sinful. She does not want to give Guy up as she did her child. When he tells Amanda, "I ask God all the time to forgive us" (*A* 32), he is coercing her to acknowledge their guilt. Amanda refuses to do any such thing; rather, she lashes out blasphemously, knowing that her words will terrify her God-fearing cousin: "There isn't any God. . . . Only idiots believe in God. If there was a God I'd hate his guts" (*A* 32).

When Guy refuses to have sexual intercourse with Amanda, she fights back with the same tools that Caddy has, but in Amanda's case she is consciously using them. Caddy only inadvertently avenges herself against Quentin, whose interference has contributed to the departure of Dalton Ames, by becoming promiscuous—as far as the reader of the novel can tell, that is, since Faulkner does not provide her point of view and thus her reason for behaving as she does. Gilchrist has Amanda threaten Guy directly with her own future promiscuity if he does not have sex with her: "If you don't do it to me I'll start doing it with every boy I see. I'll go over to VMI and do it with the whole football team" (*A* 35). Later in the novel, the reader finds that to some extent she has gone through with her threat, but not so much to punish Guy. Like Caddy, she is still seeking love. Unlike Faulkner, Gilchrist allows her to find at least joy with a man and then to learn to love herself, the first step to being able to establish a healthy relationship with another. Before this self-love is attained, however, Amanda admits to the lover with whom she finds such pleasure, "I don't know what happened to me, Will. I don't know why I can't love anyone. I don't know why other people can do that and I can't do it" (*A* 230).

Returning to this earlier juncture, when Guy visits Amanda at college, the reader can see that he is oblivious to her suffering, and he remains so consistently throughout the novel. Even when she breaks down and cries in front of him during their last encounter, he responds, "Please stop doing this *to me*" (*A* 290, emphasis added). Earlier, when he sees her for the first time since she had the baby, typical of him—and again, reminiscent of Quentin—he can only focus on his own guilt and suffering, his desire to pay for their sin. Regardless of Guy's perpetual angst, the reader is more concerned for Amanda, who clearly suffers the harshest "punishment" for their actions, while Guy goes off to college and becomes a football star, thereby adding all Ole Miss fans to his list of admirers. Upon learning of Amanda's pregnancy, the McCameys reveal their perception of her condition as sinful by sending her away to have the baby. Significantly, although they are Episcopalians, they send her to a Catholic home for unwed mothers. Once she atones for her sin—by giving up her child to "ma[k]e a barren woman happy" (*A* 20)—she is absolved, according to Catholic beliefs in penance and forgiveness. Her family can (conveniently) forget her shame then, so that "she will have her chance" (*A* 21), as her grandmother selfishly desires since Amanda is necessary for the continuation of her father's line, her father having been another of the adored McCamey men.

One of the most obvious echoes of *The Sound and the Fury* occurs at this point in Gilchrist's novel, and again Gilchrist transforms the original provocatively. Just as the Compsons sell Benjy's pasture to send Quentin to Harvard and pay for Caddy's wedding, Amanda's grandmother sells "a sixty-acre stand of wooded land, and puts the money into an account for the next six years of Amanda's life" (*A* 21), during which she will attend school away from home and thus away from Guy, whose future they are really investing in. In Faulkner's novel, the money is of course wasted: Caddy's marriage does not work out, and Quentin commits suicide after his first year at Harvard. By having the McCameys provide continued economic if not emotional support for Amanda, Gilchrist allows her protagonist a chance at a better future. Amanda does not have to concern herself with the question of how she will fulfill such basic needs as food and shelter, as Caddy does when her family bars her from home after her husband kicks her out. By this contrast, critics like Lawrence Bowling, who associate Caddy's doom with apparently becoming a prostitute ("living in a state of perpetual sin") and deserting her child to the family who destroyed her life, might be reminded of how little choice she had: what few respectable paying occupations a woman might find and how little chance a "fallen" woman had of fulfilling the traditional woman's role of wife and mother and thus being supported and having her child supported by a man.

Of course, the brighter future for Amanda is some time in coming.

Forgetting or denying her past is not as easy for Amanda as it is for her family. Since she is given money rather than therapy, she continues to be haunted by the memory of her baby. Hence, for much of her life, she refuses to allow herself to want another child or to find and make amends with the one she had. Furthermore, from the time that the baby was born, "the scar was there, and debilitating cramps when she menstruated" (*A* 37), and the doctor she sees at the college reports that "she'll probably never conceive again" (*A* 41) because of her early pregnancy (although he, too, contributes to the fictions fed to Amanda at this time by not telling her so). Consequently, when she allows herself to think of having another baby, she and Malcolm are repeatedly disappointed when they mistake her irregular menstrual cycle for pregnancy. Amanda eventually gives up again, announcing to Malcolm that she refuses to suffer any more such disappointments and therefore plans to "get an IUD to regulate [her] periods," which will, of course, also prevent conception (*A* 71). Thus, her family's cover-up actually almost ensures its sterility and ultimate extinction, for Guy has thus far produced no more children either— *almost* in this case, since Amanda eventually regroups her strengths, rejects the negative self-image she has been fostering, and decides to keep the baby she conceives when she is forty-four and then to find her first child, who by that time has a child of her own.

Again, though, this is all a while in coming, and when Guy, who has not committed suicide as Quentin does but has not been able to get on with his life either, asks Amanda to go with him to claim their daughter and grandson, she rejects his pastoral idealization of how their future together might be: "I know you've got this scenario all worked out where you and I go live on Esperanza and no one ever gets old and your dick never gets soft because I'm the magic elixir and my face never gets wrinkled and the black people all come back from Detroit and bring coffee around on trays" (*A* 293). This passage is reminiscent both of Quentin's desire that he, Caddy, and Benjy run off together (a plan Caddy, like Amanda, rejects) and of his longing for a revitalization of the Old South. Amanda further rebukes Guy for repeatedly breaking her heart, and she remarks upon her survival in spite of him, the family, and the child they took from her: "I have walked through my life for thirty years dealing with this every day. . . . And I didn't give in to it. I didn't die. I didn't end up a drunk or a suicide. I made it. And now you bring me this. . . . You make me want to go out and get drunk. You make me want to cry forever. You make me want to die" (*A* 290). In this passage,

Amanda reveals that Guy has a power over her self-image similar to that which Quentin has over Caddy's. However, unlike Caddy, Amanda finally rejects this power; she refuses to "pay out [her] life for something that happened when [she] was fourteen years old" (*A* 291). To that effect, she tells Guy that she is finally pregnant again (with another, a younger man's child) and that, whatever she decides to do about this fact, she is "going to live in the present, *and in the future*" (*A* 291).

In further contrast to Caddy, who, the novel suggests, becomes a prostitute, Amanda relies on her empowering, rather than further subjugating, profession to help her face this future. She is a writer. By the end of the novel her translation of the poems of an eighteenth-century Italian woman, who was also oppressed by her society, is accepted for publication. She plans to start immediately on a novel for which she has "been making notes for ages.... A novel about love ... everything [she] know[s] about love and everything [she] can find out" (*A* 349).

This book plan is certainly a sign of positive development that supports the view that Gilchrist's novel ends in triumph. Earlier, Amanda had planned to write a novel based on the life of Helene Renoir, the Italian poet whose work she is translating. The novel idea seems inspired by Amanda's anger toward this woman for allowing the Catholic Church to take away her baby and then committing suicide. Frustrated that the poems are so "depressing," Amanda asks, "What good did she do anyone by killing herself? Why didn't she run away and look for her child instead? Or poison the nuns" (*A* 281). When her mentor later asks her why she is "so down on Helene all of a sudden," she responds: "When I first heard about the manuscript I thought it was all so romantic and exciting. Then, the more I worked on them the worse I thought the poems were. Now I think it's her life I object to as much as the poems" (*A* 297). In this answer, one can trace Amanda's handling of her own past, so similar to Helene's experience. On the night she met Malcolm, she announced (falsely) to some people at a piano bar that the two of them had just gotten married: "Had to do it.... Got to give this baby a name. Can't have babies running around without daddies to fight off tigers" (*A* 63). Clearly, her subconscious is rewriting her earlier illegitimate pregnancy so that it ends romantically. Amanda's initial reasoning that her negative reaction to Helene's poetry is due to its being bad is evidence of an attempt not to see the connection between Helene's life and her own; she has repressed her past and is not yet ready to deal with it. But, after finding herself pregnant at forty-four, she can no longer repress the memory of her previous pregnancy. The anger toward Helene is actually toward those who did not allow her—Amanda, that is—a voice in the decisions made about her first child: "She should have gone and found the baby instead of killing herself. She was twenty-one years old.... If I'd been that old no one could have taken my child from me" (A 297–98). She is unable to take into consideration, as Jordon reminds her, "what things were like that long ago" (A 298) because she is not really talking about Helene. She is expressing her anger toward herself for allowing her own will to be so ignored, toward those who took away her child when she was too young to stop them or to know how it would affect her life, and toward a world in which treatment of women has not changed much in the past two hundred years. It is not surprising, then, that she soon determines that whatever she does about her current pregnancy will be her decision alone and that she will make that decision without regard for social views of unmarried middle-aged women having babies.

Another striking parallel between these two southern novels involves an issue that has incurred further division among the critics of *The Sound and the Fury*. Since its four sections correspond to the four days of the Easter weekend, it is inevitable that critics will speculate on which character is the novel's Christ figure. Although many see Benjy as the logical choice, given his age and his suffering, John Edward Hardy argues a more compelling case for Caddy's daughter ("William" 151–52).[15] It has already been mentioned that the girl Quentin is paying for her mother's sin. Additionally, Lyall Powers calls this Quentin "a second chance for the Compson family" (35), but in keeping with the story of Christ's crucifixion, the Compsons are not responsive to this gift of being allowed to make up somewhat for their actions toward Caddy. On the contrary, Miss Quentin is, in Hardy's words, "betrayed ... to her doom of ostracism and exile ... [and] denied the love of her people" ("William" 152).[16] Finally, Miss Quentin's departure is, in a sense, a "resurrection" from the corrupt microcosm of the Compson home, as illustrated by Doreen Fowler: "Just as on Easter morning the disciples and Mary Magdalene find the rock rolled away from Christ's tomb, the body gone, and Christ's shroud left behind, so Dilsey, Jason, and Mrs. Compson find Quentin's window open, Quentin vanished, and a soiled undergarment left behind" (147–48). However, as John Earl Bassett notes, her "flight from the tomb of her house is a parodic Easter resurrection," for she "does not rise; she descends down a tree" (17). Furthermore, no glimpse is given of her new life to provide assurance that she has gone on to a better world. Without such knowledge of Miss Quentin's fate, the reader cannot be sure that Caddy is ever released from her guilt. One finds no evidence that she gains from her daughter a sense of her own potential for salvation or discontinues her belief in her impending damnation.

In Gilchrist's novel there is less inversion of the Christian mythology alluded to in its title. Events do not lead to a parodic resurrection because of a family's rigid Old Testament focus on punishment and retribution that does not allow for forgiveness and salvation. Rather, the novel progresses from Guy's Old Testament sensibilities, which would doom Amanda, to a sense of the potential for her emotional salvation.

This novel's Christ figure appears to be Amanda's second child, a son born on her second Christmas in Fayetteville. The massage therapist who tells Amanda she is pregnant remarks, too, "It's a special case . . . Perhaps it will be a very special child" (*A* 278). On her way home, Amanda alludes to her view of this child as a second chance and a means of salvation from the past when she remarks to herself, "Fateville. . . . Land of dreams. . . . I was blind. Now I can see. Water, I have found water" (*A* 279). She then asks herself, "Is he [the massage therapist] to be the angel of the Annunciation?"—hence the novel's title—and notes that she is "wearing blue and white, the virgin's colors" (*A* 279). She continues playfully, "*A special case. A very special child.* And Will Lyons [the baby's father], is he my Joseph leading the donkey?" (*A* 279). Even her friends contribute to this perception of the baby's miraculous conception: "It doesn't have a father. She willed it into being, all by herself, out of light and air" (*A* 315).

More seriously, Amanda's son is certainly the catalyst for the transition from Old to New Testament morality—that is, to belief in forgiveness and second chances. It is after learning of her pregnancy that she is able to reject Guy's and the past's hold over her and look forward to the future: "I'm going to do the hardest and most exciting things there are to do in the world. Because I'm not afraid of life anymore. I'm not afraid of my power or intelligence or energy. The only thing left in the world that scares me is being afraid of things. I used to believe the past was the present, that we could never live it down, never leave it behind. Bullshit. The past is the past. You can dwell in it or you can move forward" (*A* 293). After this rejection of the "presence of the past" mentality that makes Faulkner's characters such fatalists, Amanda remarks upon her resolution not to allow the past to control her behavior any more: "I figured out that what I loved about being drunk was that it made the tapes from the past quit playing in my head. I'm going to learn to do that sober" (*A* 293).

Indeed, knowledge of her pregnancy seems to empower Amanda and give her the courage to face the future in spite of past mistakes. She even decides shortly after giving birth that part of that future will involve the product of her first pregnancy. It seems, therefore, that the possibility of her "salvation" also involves the daughter she gave up for adoption. Thus, Amanda's abandoned first child, a young woman by this time, is comparable to Caddy's abandoned daughter Quentin in that she has the potential of releasing her mother from guilt. Hence, like Miss Quentin, she plays a Christ-like role in the novel, a role supported by the McCameys' complete disregard of her paternity, the suffering she endures, and the fact that Amanda does not find peace until she makes the decision to acknowledge her daughter.

The last time Guy reappears in Amanda's life, the nature of her attraction to him is revealed, within which one can discern further support for their child as a Christ figure: "He was the same old Guy, direct, *impenetrable*, true. *How could [she] have been expected to love an ordinary man . . . after loving a man like this? . . .* Now, because she had touched him, she came within the circle of his *power*, forgetting as she always did when she was near him where she began or he began" (*A* 287, emphasis added). In this passage, not only is Guy described in divine terms, but also the reader recognizes an element of narcissism (again, a major motivation for incest) in Amanda's attraction to him. Her earlier admission of Guy into the realm of her protected self can now be viewed not as an ability to bond with another human being, as was posited previously, but rather as further rejection of others. To her he is not a separate entity but part of her own self. Hence, taking him as a mate reinforces her aversion to relationships with other human beings. She even tells Guy during this reunion, "I love you as I have always loved you. Like I was loving my own self" (*A* 289). Returning to the issue of the novel's Christ figure, if Amanda and Guy are two halves of the same person, then the child is the product of this unity and therefore not of a union of two people—she is another miracle child of one parent. It should be remembered here, as well, that a nun told Amanda she was as good as new after the birth of this child; hence, the notion of a virgin birth is confirmed by an "authority" on the subject.

In still further support of this child as the novel's parallel (to Miss Quentin) Christ figure, as Jeanie Thompson and Anita Garner point out, "Barrett Clare has suffered from feelings of neglect, isolation, abandonment, and despair" (114).[17] Amanda apparently "made a barren woman [*so*] happy" by giving her a baby that the woman was able to conceive, the consequence of which was that Barrett has never felt the love from her parents that she detects directed toward their natural children. Of course, the reader has no way of knowing if Barrett is correct in her assumption that they regret adopting her or if her insecurities are a result of not knowing why her own natural mother gave her away. Whatever the case, Barrett feels unloved and cast aside. Aggravating her insecurity, her husband is unfaithful to her.

But Amanda does not know of Barrett's suffering. In fact, in contrast to Caddy, who knows exactly who is raising Quentin and thus what kind of home her daughter is growing up in, Amanda is told by the nuns: "She's in a wonderful home. The people who took her are very special, very devout. She'll have everything the world has to offer" (*A* 20). While Amanda may not be able to guess the actuality of her daughter's life as well as Caddy can, she still carries for thirty years a "cargo" (the title of the novel's first section) of guilt for giving up her child. Although her second child gives her a second chance to be a good mother, that would be only a partial atonement for her past. Her decision after her son is born to seek out her lost daughter in order to make amends finally puts Amanda at peace with herself, and the novel ends with a positive, uplifting sense of hope. Therefore, Amanda's parody of the Lord's Prayer, which closes the novel, is not more blasphemy. Rather, it is an assertion of self-worth and an acceptance, finally, of the value of relationships. "My will be done" (*A* 353), she begins, reminding the reader that she once complied with others' will to take away her baby and has suffered for it ever since. The reader is reminded, too, that this second baby is an exercise of her free will, her right to choose, that she had gone to get an abortion and, upon changing her mind in the abortionist's office, told him that her decision had nothing to do with there being "anything wrong with what you're doing" (*A* 306). "My life on my terms," she continues her revision of the Lord's Prayer, adding "my daughter, my son," reflecting a willingness to bond with others (*A* 353). "My life leading to my lands forever and ever and ever, hallowed be my name, goddammit, my kingdom come, my will be done, amen, so be it, Amanda" (*A* 353). Although one might at first be concerned about the egocentricity of this pronouncement, considering it along with the self-abnegation of Caddy Compson reminds the reader that it is certainly a more productive attitude. Whereas Caddy, after giving up her free will to others' attitudes and commands, loses her belief in her right to receive or give love, Amanda allows herself in the end to do both.

This prayer to herself may also be viewed positively when one recalls her earlier mixture of fear and fascination regarding the myth of Narcissus. When Amanda was a child, "the bayou was a place of endless fascination for [her]. She would stand on the bank or lie on the pier looking down at her reflection in the water, thinking about the story of Narcissus, who was turned into a flower for liking to look at himself too much. She would stare down into the water hating and fearing the gods who had such powers, wondering how far she dared go to challenge them" (A 11). This passage reveals Amanda's spirit of rebellion, which promises an ability to overcome southern mores that support women's self-deprecation; and indeed, she ultimately does overcome such attitudes, as reflected in this prayer in praise of herself as well as in her earlier profession to Will of her belief in "loving yourself, not letting your self-esteem be in the hands of other people" (A 230). A connection between the myth of Narcissus and self-denial can also be discerned in Amanda's memory of her grandmother's story of "an old dog [that] . . . lost his bone by trying to bite the reflection of it in the water" (A 52). When Amanda recalls the story as an adult, she says to herself, "Old greedy yellow dog. . . . Poor old dumb thing" (A 52).

What she had previously failed to recognize from these stories is that their warnings against vanity and greed could be taken too far and used to support women's subjugation. With this aspect of her past in mind— that she grew up in a region where women are not supposed to think too highly of themselves or want too much for themselves—the reader should realize that her closing prayer, while extreme, is a victorious pendulum swing away from such attitudes. When she awakens from her nap and finds that while she can assert her will and control her own life, she cannot control any other lives (Will has a car accident on his way back to her and the baby), the pendulum should swing back toward a healthy compromise between Narcissus-behavior/God-complex and self-sacrificing, self-loathing southern woman. Recalling that inserted within her prayer of self-adulation was the reference to "My life leading to my lands forever and ever," the reader should realize that Amanda is finally more *comparable* to Scarlett O'Hara than to Caddy Compson (to whom she has been *contrasted*). Scarlett, one will recall, is planning to return to Tara, "her lands," at the end of her novel to gather together her strengths in order to face her most recent tragedy: the loss of Rhett, who has just announced that he is leaving her. With this comparison in mind, one is further assured that Amanda has the strength to overcome as many losses as Scarlett does, even while the Ashleys and Rhetts in her life are destroyed.[18]

The reader senses, then, the possibility of a positive future for Amanda and for both of her children, which contrasts distinctly with the picture Faulkner provides in the appendix to his novel of Caddy as the mistress of a Nazi officer and with the lack of specific information in this appendix about her daughter Quentin's fate. Faulkner ends his entry on Miss Quentin with the night she "ran away with the pitchman," which is narrated in the novel; however, he adds a detail not provided in the original novel—that this man "was already under sentence for bigamy"—which does not bode well for the young woman (*PF* 720). He then concludes, "And so [Miss Quentin] vanished; whatever occupation overtook her would have arrived in no chromium Mercedes [alluding to the photograph of Caddy]; whatever snapshot would have contained no general staff" (*PF* 721). This hint as to Miss Quentin's fate suggests that her "occupation" is similar to Caddy's, though not so "luxurious" as being the mistress of a Nazi general. Faulkner may not have idealized Miss Quentin in the way that he has Caddy, but he has certainly as effectively damned her. Although the reader is to understand that the circumstances of Miss Quentin's life are to blame for her actions, the character must still be punished (as so many fallen women in literary history have been punished by their creators)—apparently for not rising above those circumstances and remaining uncorrupted and undefiled in spite of them.

In contrast, regardless of Amanda's "corruption" and early "defilement," Gilchrist does not damn her protagonist. At the end of her novel Amanda is preparing to start over, which gives the reader the sense of a happier future for her daughter as well. Interestingly, Gilchrist also wrote a kind of appendix to her novel. In her fourth collection of short fiction, *Light Can Be Both Wave and Particle*, published six years after *The Annunciation*, she includes two additional chapters to *The Annunciation*. The first of these shows the reunion between Amanda and her daughter, to which Barrett brings Amanda's grandson; thus, in direct contrast to Faulkner's appendix, the reader is given a sense of the continuation of the family line. At the end of the original novel, as well as in these two added chapters, Amanda realizes not only that it is never too late to begin anew but also that one can make up for past mistakes; second chances can be taken to improve one's lot; and the individual's role in life is not as immutable as are the defined roles within a southern community. Furthermore, God has not punished her after all for her earlier behavior: in the second additional chapter to the novel it is revealed that Will survived the car accident. Indeed, Gilchrist unmistakably provides the reader with a more optimistic view of the future of the nonconforming southern woman than Faulkner chose to offer.

5

The Reincarnation of Kate Chopin's Edna Pontellier in *The Anna Papers*

We drown in the first chapter. I worry about the sexual doom of womanhood, its sad inheritance.

Margaret Drabble, *The Waterfall*

This above all, to refuse to be a victim.

Margaret Atwood, *Surfacing*

As *The Annunciation* evokes recollections of *The Sound and the Fury*, it illuminates what is left out of Faulkner's novel. When Gilchrist evokes memories of Kate Chopin's *The Awakening*, in contrast, the reader does not sense that she is filling in a gap in the author's focus on the South. In developing a character reminiscent of Caddy Compson, Gilchrist reveals how the creator of the earlier incarnation of this nonconforming southern woman participates in her inevitable destruction. In contrast again, when she develops a character who seems to have evolved from Chopin's characterization of Edna Pontellier, Gilchrist confirms the heroic potential of the earlier character, potential that is thwarted by society rather than by the author's idealization of the character. *The Anna Papers*, then, is a sequel to and a contemporary recasting of *The Awakening* rather than a revision. Sadly, again the reader will find when reading the novels together that Gilchrist's protagonist, as well as her novel itself, faced almost as much social censure in the 1980s as Chopin's protagonist and novel faced in the 1890s.

Before proceeding to an intertextual reading of these two novels, one might note the many similarities between the lives of Ellen Gilchrist and this nineteenth-century southern woman writer, as well as other parallels between their earlier works, which serve together to suggest why Chopin is a likely model for Gilchrist. Earlier it was mentioned that, like Katherine Anne Porter, Ellen Gilchrist did not begin to publish her fiction until she was in her forties. Kate Chopin, too, was over forty when her first collection of short fiction was published. And, as Gilchrist might have turned to Porter's short stories as she developed her own talents in that genre, so, too, might she have turned to Chopin's, particularly since many of them are set in Louisiana, which would be the setting of several stories in Gilchrist's first collection and a recurrent setting in later works.

In fact, Louisiana plays a significant role in both writers' careers, for it is their Louisiana stories that are in large part responsible for the public's initial attention to these budding fiction writers. Furthermore, Gilchrist's New Orleans stories remain among her strongest works, and Chopin's "Désirée's Baby," set in Louisiana, continued to be anthologized even after the author fell out of favor because of her scandalous novel. One can even see similarities between Gilchrist's New Orleans story "Rich" and Chopin's "Désirée's Baby," as well as "Doctor Chevalier's Lie," that would corroborate the possibility that Gilchrist read Chopin and learned from her predecessor's technique.

"Rich" treats the unknown past of an adopted child not unlike the way Chopin handles Désirée's past. Chopin never discloses Désirée's origins, and only hints are dropped that the child Helen in Gilchrist's story might actually be the illegitimate daughter of the man who adopted her. If the reader cannot know for certain where these children come from, then their parentage must not be the stories' issue. Like Chopin, then, Gilchrist therefore distracts her reader with this mystery even while leading her reader to the real source of conflict: not whether or not the characters are biological father and daughter but, rather, that Helen's father, like Désirée's husband, is afraid of the world discovering through her the truth about himself. Gilchrist's use of this Chopin technique allows for a shocking ending—not some revelation about Helen but a murder and suicide—that reminds the reader of Chopin's surprise revelation—not about Désirée but about Armand. The shocking discovery that it is Armand who is of African descent almost certainly prompts the reader to a rereading, perhaps several rereadings, ultimately revealing the real villain in the story to be the society that created Armand Aubigny.[1] Gilchrist's powerful ending—the murder/suicide as well as the sardonic statements regarding the community's reaction to the tragedy—leads the reader to a similar recognition that Tom is also a product of his society.

The plot of "Rich" and its ending's direct focus on the community's response to the deaths is also reminiscent of Chopin's "Doctor Chevalier's Lie." Evidently, both authors, though a century apart in time, had perceived the destructiveness of this city's closed society. In each of these stories, a character from a poor family has moved to New Orleans to make his or her way in the world and eventually kills himself or herself after life has not turned out as the character wished. As discussed with regard to the similarities between plot lines in the fiction of Gilchrist and Porter, this point of comparison is not meant to suggest that Gilchrist's work merely resets and updates the works of earlier writers. The parallels are noted, rather, to reveal the similar concerns of these three southern women writers, which then leads the reader to recognize the lack of significant improvement over time of the situations that cause the writers anxiety. Like "Rich," "Doctor Chevalier's Lie" is based on actual events (Rankin 134). In this case, then, the reader recognizes that, like Chopin, Gilchrist is struck by what it is about a tragedy that upsets the community—not the loss of life so much as what the violence that took that life reflects about members of the community.

In the case of other comparable stories, Chopin's "A Pair of Silk Stockings" and Gilchrist's "Revenge" and "Traveler," the reader sees the authors' shared concern about the limits to a woman's possible triumph over the oppression of gender roles predominant in her community. The final view of Chopin's Mrs. Sommers wishing the streetcar would never stop after her day of shopping and pampering herself in "A Pair of Silk Stockings" is vocalized in Rhoda's comment at the close of "Revenge" about the rest of her life not measuring up to the moment she polevaulted and is echoed in LeLe's efforts at the end of "Traveler" to recall her sense of empowerment in the lake she swam across. These endings rob the reader of the sense of each heroine's triumph, to which the stories seemed to be moving. Both authors evidently realized that such moments of transcending one's oppression are only temporary.

Some people might argue that, in spite of such feminist themes in some of their works, neither woman can accurately be called a feminist—and the writers themselves would in all likelihood not disagree. As pointed out by Elaine Showalter,

Despite her identification with the New Women, . . . Chopin was not an activist. She never joined the women's suffrage movement or belonged to a female literary community. Indeed, her celebrated St.

Louis literary salon attracted mostly male journalists, editors, and writers. Chopin resigned after only two years from a St. Louis women's literary and charitable society. When her children identified her close friends to be interviewed by her first biographer, Daniel Rankin, there were no women on the list. (42)

According to Showalter, Chopin criticized didacticism in any fiction, including "the rhetoric of such feminist bestsellers as Sarah Grand's *The Heavenly Twins*" (42). Showalter believes, therefore, that "Chopin certainly did not wish to write a didactic feminist novel" (42) when she wrote *The Awakening*. Martha Fodaski Black points out, however, that "even though [Chopin] was not an advocate or unequivocal reformer, *The Awakening* reveals the influence of late-nineteenth-century feminists and their search for a new kind of heroine on whom women could model their lives" (95). Furthermore, regardless of whether or not Chopin considered herself a feminist and what her intentions were when she wrote her novel, *The Awakening* can be and is read as a feminist text.

Comparable to Chopin, Gilchrist, too, enjoys the company of men, as she attests in her collection of journal entries, *Falling through Space* (*FS* 152–53), and she responds herself to those "who read my books and decide that I am a feminist" (*FS* 152). Believing that such readers are "bas[ing] this assumption on the stories that deal with an intense sibling rivalry between a little redheaded girl named Rhoda and her brother, Dudley," she explains, first of all, that these characters are "poorly disguised versions of my brother Dooley and myself" and then contends that "my problem with [Dooley] . . . had nothing to do with male and female roles. It was pure sibling rivalry, a bitter battle for the minds and hearts of our parents" (*FS* 152). In spite of what Gilchrist may say about *her* conflict with *Dooley*, the conflicts within the *stories* between *Rhoda* and *Dudley* can, indeed, be read as resulting from the double standards for boys and girls, which are supported by Dudley and resisted by Rhoda. Thus, these stories are feminist in nature whatever Gilchrist's intentions may be. They are not, however, didactic or propagandistic, perhaps because the author did not have a feminist agenda in mind when she wrote them. One might say the same of Chopin's novel and thus recognize that feminism is not an agenda as much as it is a state of mind.

Like Chopin, Gilchrist ultimately developed a "new kind of heroine," one for the late twentieth century, "on whom women [can] model their lives," to use Martha Black's description of Edna. In preparation for the proposition that Gilchrist's character Anna Hand is an evolution of Chopin's Edna Pontellier, one might note similarities between characters who appear in each writer's earlier fiction and who may be viewed as prototypes for the central characters of these novels. The title character in Chopin's story "Charlie," for example, may remind some readers of Gilchrist's Rhoda Manning, although Charlie has a much more positive relationship with her father than does Rhoda.[2] Both girls are tomboys who (like Porter's Miranda, too) suddenly decide to put on a dress and concentrate on their femininity for a change. They also both write poetry and win the favor of their schoolmates upon disclosing their writing talents.[3]

Patricia Hopkins Lattin's description of Chopin's Athénaïse, "a hard-to-handle young girl [who] ran away from the convent and whose rebellious streak continues when, after two months of marriage, she slips away from her husband's Cane River home" ("Childbirth" 40), also recalls Gilchrist's Rhoda, as well as Porter's Miranda, reflecting again the sense that Gilchrist's fiction is part of a particular tradition within a broader canon of southern women writers. Like Athénaïse, Miranda longs to escape her convent school in New Orleans, where she and her sister feel themselves "immured" (CS 193) and, at the end of "Old Mortality," determines that she will leave her husband. Also a rebel, Rhoda does leave at least three husbands.[4]

Like Athénaïse's, Rhoda's marriages do not live up to her expectations. In contrast, however, Athénaïse finds sex distasteful, whereas Rhoda's sexual relationship with her first husband Malcolm is the only part of her marriage she does enjoy. She does not enjoy her sexual relationship with her husband Eric, but the problem is that she finds relations with him unsatisfying rather than distasteful. The difference between these women's reactions to sex can be seen again between the similar characters Edna Pontellier and Anna Hand. In fact, Lattin suggests that Chopin's Athénaïse is a prototype for her later creation, Edna Pontellier ("Childbirth" 40–41).[5] Similarly, Rhoda is the prototype for all of Gilchrist's female protagonists, including Anna Hand of the short stories "Looking over Jordan" in *Victory over Japan* and "Anna, Part I" in *Drunk with Love*, the novel *The Anna Papers*, and the three novellas collected in *I Cannot Get You Close Enough*.

However, just as Lattin illustrates how ultimately "the educated, sophisticated Edna is quite different from the simple, provincial Athénaïse" ("Childbirth" 41), Anna is an *evolution* of Rhoda, not the same character with a different name. As noted in chapter 2, some of Gilchrist's characters, most notably Margaret of "Generous Pieces," LeLe of "Traveler," and the recurrent Crystal Manning, are separate manifestations of the same composite personality for which Rhoda is the prototype. Anna, in contrast, has Rhoda's strength of character but has overcome many of Rhoda's weaknesses. For example, she does not concentrate all of her energies toward attracting the attention of a man, and she does not find herself repeatedly being used by men. Rather, men fall in love with her, and she usually ends up leaving them. Also, Anna does not repeatedly run home to the father who does not understand her. She loves him but does not need his approval, as Rhoda needs her father's. Perhaps most significant, unlike Rhoda, Anna is quite satisfied with her life. And her generous nature, which the completely self-centered Rhoda lacks entirely, drives her to try to teach those around her to enjoy life, too.

Other parallels might be noted between Chopin's and Gilchrist's stories, but the most comparable works from the canons of these women are Chopin's magnum opus, *The Awakening*, and Gilchrist's second novel, *The Anna Papers*. Like *The Awakening*, *The Anna Papers* received mainly negative reviews. Gilchrist is accused of self-aggrandizement and unbelievable dialogue, character development, and plot. Reviewing for *Mother Jones*, Georgia Brown argues that Anna Hand, the central character of this novel, sounds too much like Gilchrist herself; consequently, "having Anna die early on reminds [Brown] of the way a child fantasizes his or her own death and thinks how awfully sorry everyone will be" (46–47). Maggie Paley, writing for the *New York Times Book Review*, sums up the novel's weakness as follows: "we can only see Anna through a haze of adoration" (16). The reviewer for *Publishers Weekly* finds an inconsistency between Anna's view of herself as "lucky" and "her doomed marriages, inconclusive affairs and aching unhappiness over her 'empty troubled womb'" (rev. of *Anna* 439). One might recall here that Chopin's critics raged against Edna Pontellier's adulterous affair, neglect of her children, and choice to end her life. Anna, too, commits adultery, though in the 1980s that did not seem to offend those who criticized the character and her creator (although they do seem to be bothered by Anna's sexual appetite). What most irritates them is the high opinion Anna holds of herself in spite of the disappointments she has suffered in her life. No reviewer praises Anna's ability to rise above these failures. It seems that they feel, rather, that she should be crushed by her inability to bear children or to maintain interest in one man; and they do not see her art either as valuable in its own right or as compensation for her dysfunctional uterus and fickle heart. In short, the tone of the criticism of this 1988 novel is not much different from the conservative views reflected in the contemporary reviews of Chopin's 1899 novel.

Reviewers also took issue with Anna's choice to end her own life shortly after learning that she has cancer. Georgia Brown seems to condemn Anna for ending her life "to avoid pain" (47), and in a remarkably similar comment, Pat Taylor sees her reason for committing suicide as "fear of pain" (8). Also critical is the tone of the reviewer for *Kirkus Reviews* in writing that "because Anna . . . is addicted to gracious living and pleasure, particularly sexual pleasure, she chooses not to live when she contracts breast cancer" (rev. of *Anna* 1176). Such criticism sounds disconcertingly like Edna's critics, who felt that rather than end her life, Edna—upon realizing that she would eventually get over Robert, fall in love again, and repeat the cycle—should have given up the new desires she was feeling and returned to her life as it was (regardless of the "painfulness" of doing so). The implication in such criticism of both characters is that living at all is what is important. Such a view misses one of the central themes of both novels: that the quality of life is what is important, not how long one lives.[6] Gilchrist goes so far as to suggest that the comedy that was Anna's life overshadows the tragedy of her premature death. Should this death have come after her incredible life force had been beaten down, *that* would have been a tragedy. Anna did not live at the mercy of society; nor should she have died in its care. As A. Alvarez points out in his *The Savage God: A Study of Suicide,* in the modern world "without an after-life . . . how you die . . . sums up and somehow passes judgement on how you have lived" (182).

After recognizing the similarities between *The Anna Papers* and *The Awakening* and recalling reviewers who criticized Edna Pontellier's hedonistic behavior, critics of Gilchrist's heroine may wish to reevaluate their responses to this novel. Indeed, it becomes clear that although Gilchrist's heroine is an evolution of Edna Pontellier as well as of Gilchrist's own prototype, the society that greets this heroine—both the reading public and the other characters in the novel—has not itself evolved much since the publication of Chopin's novel. The attitudes toward women reflected in these reviews of Gilchrist's novel have not progressed far beyond those of the society that rejected Chopin's heroine— also including Chopin's reading audience and her character's social circle.

The prelude that opens *The Anna Papers* ends with a description of Anna's suicide, part of which reads as follows:

> On a cold November morning . . . she stuck a cyanide tablet in her mouth and walked off a pier into the Atlantic Ocean wearing a fur-lined Valentino jacket with a hood and a pair of knee-high leather boots, leaving behind a man she could finally really love and leaving behind the Pap smears and blood tests and tissue cultures that said that she was going to die anyway and soon and in plenty of endless disgraceful boring cruel pain. (*AP* 9)

After this prelude, in section one of the novel, the narration backs up two years and tells of the events in Anna's life leading up to her suicide. This first section also ends, then, with Anna's death. Still, this is only the half-way point of the novel, and Anna is as present in the remaining four sections of the novel, as her family and friends mourn her death, as she is in the prelude and first section.[7]

Given the manner in which Anna Hand has chosen to die, one cannot miss the connection between her suicide and that of Edna Pontellier. By *opening* her novel with a suicide by drowning, however, Gilchrist picks up where Chopin's novel, which *closes* with Edna's fatal swim, leaves off. It is interesting to recall here Per Seyersted's contention that, similarly, Chopin used *Madame Bovary* "as a point of departure, giving the story an entirely new emphasis"—that is, her "focus . . . on the truly fundamental problem of what it means to be a woman, particularly in a patriarchy" (138). He concludes, then, that "it is possible to see *The Awakening* as a woman's reply to a man's *Madame Bovary*" (138). One can view *The Anna Papers* similarly: as a twentieth-century woman's sequel to a nineteenth-century woman's *The Awakening*, as well as to *Madame Bovary*, since Anna takes poison before walking into the water.

In *Illness as Metaphor*, Susan Sontag discusses how cancer is perceived as "a disease of middle-class life, a disease associated with affluence, with excess" (15). It is not surprising, then, that Gilchrist chooses this disease to threaten the life of her exuberant Anna Hand. On the other hand, according to Sontag, cancer is also traditionally depicted in literature as a disease caused by "the repression of emotion" and is thus evidence of one's "failure of expressiveness" (48), yet Anna certainly does not repress her desires, and she is a successful artist. Therefore, Gilchrist obviously does not go along with such a view of the symbolic source of cancer in literature, which, as Sontag points out, is especially problematic because it blames the victim for her illness. Sontag illustrates with W. H. Auden's "Miss Gee" how, in literature, cancer is the disease of "life's losers" who did not achieve their ambitions (48). One stanza of this poem, in which a doctor is the speaker, both applies to Anna and reveals how Gilchrist's characterization of her cancer victim does not go along with the myth:

"Childless women get it,
    And men when they retire;
It's as if there had to be some outlet
    For their foiled creative fire."

Anna was indeed childless, but she does not suppress her "creative fire"; instead, she turns it toward writing. Thus, in contrast to the traditional depictions of cancer, Anna's cancer symbolizes the times in her life when she was not able to maintain the control she valued so highly, such as her inability to bring a pregnancy to term or when she falls in love with a married man.[8] Instead of giving in to despair in each case, Anna ponders the situation in order to determine what to do about it. In the case of her childlessness, she devotes herself to her nieces and nephews. Regarding her married lover, she decides to appreciate and enjoy their love, rather than feel guilty about it. One's death, too, is often an event one cannot control. But, upon learning that she has cancer, Anna determines to end her life before the quality of it is diminished.

Edna's story ends with her suicide, but Anna's has just begun; hence, the reader is not left in the end with the image of the heroine swimming toward death. As a result, her suicide can be viewed more positively than Edna's or the similar suicides of such literary figures as Emma Bovary, Anna Karenina, and Maggie Johnson. Whereas Edna is physically sound when she swims out into the gulf, Anna "was going to die anyway and soon and in plenty of endless disgraceful boring cruel pain." Therefore, Anna's choice to end her own life before her body succumbs to the cancer invading it is ultimately a victory over the oppressive forces of this world, which would restrict her in her illness as they were unable to before. To her doctor's remark that "there are lots of things to do" toward recovery, Anna answers, "Like be a cripple, an invalid, have my breasts cut off, have my hair fall out. Go to the hospital all the time, have people feel sorry for me. . . . I won't do it" (AP 142). Rather, she bravely takes her own life while it is whole to avoid having it taken from her piece by piece. Anna takes control of her death, as she has always taken control of her life, and she dies as wholly as she has lived. In contrast, as Carolyn G. Heilbrun notes, for women like Edna, "death becomes the *only* part of their lives they can control. They can at least choose to die" (183, emphasis added); and, as Eleanor B. Wymard argues in the conclusion of her article on *The Awakening*, it is not until "the moment of her sea-walk [that] Edna is whole" (384).[9] Thus, regardless of the similarity between their deaths, Anna can be viewed as an evolved Edna.

And in spite of the *differences* between the motivations behind Edna's and Anna's deaths, reading *The Anna Papers* intertextually with *The Awakening* allows the reader to re-view Edna's suicide, focusing more on what triumph there is in her death than on the waste of her life in the end. Edna, too, one realizes, dies at a point in her life when she is living most fully and before social conventions will force her to curb her appetites and actions. Such a reading also links Edna with the heroes and heroines of ancient Greek literature whose suicides were viewed as "an honourable way out of an insufferable situation" (Alvarez 51). Not quite the rebel that Anna is, Edna finally cannot go completely against social strictures. However, she cannot go along with them any longer either; so she ends her brief life.[10] Although her death can be viewed as a waste of potential, still, when the difference is noted between the healthy Edna and the cancer-stricken Anna, a similarity can also be seen between the society that drives Edna to the decision to end her life and Anna's cancer. In *Illness as Metaphor,* Sontag describes how cancer is perceived from its depiction in literature: "Cancer is thought to cripple vitality, make eating an ordeal, deaden desire, . . . [and] to be de-sexualizing" (13), all of which is what society attempts to do to Edna in *The Awakening*, and Edna, like Anna, will not allow her vitality or her appetites to be suppressed. Thus, if one turns to pre-Christian views of suicide as heroic and recalls, as A. Alvarez reminds his readers, that in ancient Greek literature and philosophy, "painful disease *or intolerable constraint* were sufficient reasons to depart" (53, emphasis added), Edna's suicide, like Anna's, should not be condemned. Judging Edna's actions from a non-Christian perspective is appropriate, for, as Sandra M. Gilbert argues, in the course of *The Awakening,* beginning with Edna's departure from the church she has found oppressive, Edna "abandon[s] the suffocation of traditional Christian (that is, traditional patriarchal) theology" (54).[11]

Interestingly, Anna, too, abandons her Christian upbringing. Her suicide is her most poignant statement against the teachings of her family's religion, Catholicism, which preaches that suicide is a mortal sin. Just as

Edna "r[an] away from prayers, from the Presbyterian service, read in a spirit of gloom by [her] father" when she was a young girl (CW 896), Anna begins to break from her family's church quite early in her life. At fourteen, she "demand[s]" to be transferred from Catholic to public school (AP 25). Her explanation to the nuns—"I know you thought I had a calling. . . . I don't. I want to live in the world, one bigger than Charlotte. I want to go out and see everything that's going on" (AP 26)—implies that she perceives Catholicism to be oppressive and limiting.[12] One can find in Anna's elaboration upon her reason for wanting to leave the school a foreshadowing of her eventual rejection of the South because of the threat of its appeal: "I like it here, where things are very old and feel like part of the earth, but out there, at the public school, are other things I need to know. So I won't get caught up in one thing. Like my mother. She does the same things every day" (AP 26). Clearly, Anna does not want to sleepwalk through a life of routine as her mother does—and as Edna Pontellier has done through that part of her life prior to her "awakening."[13]

Significantly, both protagonists sleep a lot in their novels. In The Awakening, Edna's sleeping reminds the reader of the fact that prior to this point in her life she has been symbolically asleep.[14] In the course of the novel, she becomes increasingly "awake" to the world around her until, significantly, she does not sleep at all the night before her death. Her suicide, then, is, paradoxically, a refusal to close her eyes again, to go back to sleepwalking through life. Indeed, the night before her death, referring to the years of her life prior to her recent awakening, she tells Dr. Mandelet that "the years that are gone seem like dreams" (CW 996). She considers, briefly, that all would have been all right "if one might go on sleeping and dreaming" but then reconsiders and asserts that "it is better to wake up after all, even to suffer, rather than to remain a dupe to illusions all one's life" (CW 996).

Similarly, Anna's fatigue is a symptom of her debilitating disease, and her sleeping reflects the effect that this disease will have on her lifestyle. Anna commits suicide to escape such debilitation as well as inevitable pain. She would rather die while she is still in some control of her life than after she has been admitted into a hospital to be cared for by medical personnel and her family. Her aversion to such a death is expressed in the first chapter of the novel when Anna is present at the death of her friend and agent who had cancer, "had spent the last two years of her life being tortured in hospitals and [had] died anyway" (AP 14). Leaving the death-bed of this friend, Anna says, "I wouldn't die like this. . . . No one will ever make me die in a hospital" (*AP* 14–15). Before fulfilling this vow two years later by committing suicide, Anna writes a note to her niece Olivia in which she explains that she "can't be in the power of other people, even in a hospital" (*AP* 160), thereby reaffirming her refusal to be out of control of her own life.

Edna's experience at the bedside of a suffering friend is also a factor in her choice to die. After watching Adèle Ratignolle suffer labor pains, she recognizes that the consequence of an active sex life is pregnancy and childbirth, which would result in her returning again and again to the situation in which she has just seen her friend. It is not the pain of childbirth that Edna fears, having been through the same ordeal twice herself and recalling only "faintly an ecstasy of pain, the heavy odor of chloroform, a stupor which had deadened sensation, and an awakening to find a little new life to which she had given being" (*CW* 994); rather, it is the oppressiveness of motherhood reflected in Adèle's pain that troubles her, as evidenced by her vision of her children when she later contemplates the events of the evening: "The children appeared before her like antagonists . . . who had overpowered and sought to drag her into the soul's slavery for the rest of her days. But she knew a way to elude them" (*CW* 999).[15] At Adèle's bedside Edna realizes, much as Anna does when she learns that she has cancer, that she is unable to control her own body. If she continues to have affairs, she will inevitably get pregnant again. And she knows that she will continue to have affairs: her recent behavior has revealed to her the power of her newly awakened desires over her prudence.

Here again a connection can be made between Anna's cancer and Edna's social oppression. Concluding her discussion of the pregnancy imagery used to describe cancer, Susan Sontag remarks that the victim of cancer is indeed "'invaded' by alien cells, which multiply, causing an atrophy or blockage of bodily functions" (14). Just as Anna's cancer will debilitate her physically, so do Edna's sons (and so would any other children she might have) curtail their mother's activity. Otis B. Wheeler points out how Edna "is a prisoner of the social order, through obligations to her children and through the cast-iron respectability of people like Robert, and of the biological order, through the sensuality of her nature" (127), that is, her newly developed sexual passions. One can view Anna's death as an escape from a similar double prison: she is a prisoner of the biological order, in that she is powerless to stop the cancer from growing within her; and she is a prisoner of the social order, which would have her hospitalized and at the mercy of doctors and drugs. This social order can be seen both depicted in the book—represented by friends who urge her to have her cancer treated and, later, by family members who do not understand why she committed suicide when there are such treatments available—and reflected in those reviews of the novel that criticize Anna's avoidance of hospitals and treatment.

Though Edna, too, commits suicide because she will not be allowed to control her own life, until the last few months of her life, she has never been in such control. Anna, on the other hand, has maintained control of herself, as well as of many of the people with whom she comes into contact, through most of her life. Even when Anna was a child, "her brothers and sisters went to find her during recess, told her what had happened, asked her what to do, checked in" (*AP* 25)—that is, while she attended the Catholic school with her siblings. Some three decades later, she spends her last year of life trying to put these same siblings' lives and the lives of their children back in order.[16] Her own life has been full. She is a successful writer, has seen much of the world, and has had several intense love affairs. To compensate for the one endeavor at which she had not been successful—having children—she writes books, bringing characters to life instead, and is devoted to her nieces and nephews. Heading out to the last adventure of her life, she thinks, "I have lived my life. I have not forgotten to be alive. I was glad to be here" (*AP* 144).

Anna refuses, finally, to live less fully merely so as to continue breathing for a while longer. Her choice of immediate rather than prolonged death, then, is a life-affirming choice, a recognition that the quality of life is more important than its length. Just after adopting a philosophy of life similar to Anna's—to live life fully regardless of social strictures—Edna realizes that she cannot do so because of the harm her actions would bring to her children. Rather than return to an unfulfilling existence, she, too, chooses to die.[17] In contrast to Edna's view of her children as oppressors, Anna views the nieces and nephews she leaves behind as a medium through which her life will continue after her death; and her only regret about her life is that she was unable to bear children.[18] Ironically, this failing, an intertextual reading of the two novels reveals, has served her life well: unlike Edna, she has not had to worry about the effects of her lifestyle on her children. Furthermore, in killing herself she does not take a mother away from a child, as some readers criticize Edna for doing.

When considering Edna's suicide as a triumph over social oppression, one cannot overlook the fact that in taking her own life, Edna leaves her children motherless, to be raised, one can assume, by the woman who raised their father. Consequently, the conservative views of women's roles held by Léonce Pontellier will continue to be held by the next generation of Pontellier men. In defense of Edna, one might apply the arguments made in the previous chapter in defense of Caddy Compson's desertion of her daughter. Furthermore, one might note that prior to Edna's death the raising of her children had often been turned over to nurses and her mother-in-law. Thus, her suicide does not mean that these children will grow up with any different ideology than that which they would have learned otherwise. That is where Edna fails for me: in killing herself before passing on her new values to her sons.

In spite of having no children of her own, Anna also leaves children behind, in particular, two of her nieces, her brother Daniel's daughters Olivia and Jessie, in whose lives she has played a significant role. In contrast to Edna, who gladly hands the responsibility for her children over to her mother-in-law at one point in Chopin's novel, Anna often usurps responsibility for these nieces. One of her last major acts before her death is to bring her brother's older daughter Olivia, who has been raised in Oklahoma by her deceased mother's family, to North Carolina to meet the family. Another, narrated in the novella "Winter" in I Cannot Get You Close Enough, is to track the mother of Daniel's younger daughter Jessie through Europe, finding evidence to support a case against her so that she will be unable to take her daughter away from Daniel and the Hand family. In both cases, Anna's actions reflect her desire to be a mother and remind the reader of the one gap Anna feels in her life.[19]

Although Anna's death does remove her physical presence as a role model from these nieces, both of whom adore her, her memory is still with them. Again, the difference of the placement of the suicide in each novel becomes significant. Chopin ends her novel with Edna's. The story of a woman who awakened to a recognition of her oppression is over. Edna lives on in the reader's memory as a heroine, but Chopin provides no indication of how she will be remembered by her family and friends or how they will view her death. The reader does know, however, that neither Léonce nor Adèle understood what was happening within Edna, and one can infer from this incomprehension that they will not understand why she has committed suicide—if, indeed, they view her death by drowning as suicide. They could decide it was an accident.

Half of Gilchrist's novel, on the other hand, is a "wake" for the deceased heroine, during which her family and friends talk about her incredible life and come to terms with her choice to kill herself. Indeed, *The Wake* would have been an appropriate title for this novel (and its echo of Chopin's title would have provided handy evidence that Gilchrist consciously started her novel where Chopin left off). Given the focus on Anna's life at the wake and no body to emphasize the end of this life, Anna's nieces and nephews, Olivia and Jessie in particular, can continue to view Anna as a positive role model.

Furthermore, unlike Edna, Anna has left "papers"—including her journals, works-in-progress, and notes explaining her actions—for those she leaves behind (hence the title Gilchrist gives her novel). Surprisingly, these papers most influence her conservative sister Helen, a character comparable to Edna's friend Adèle. As Adèle fails to understand Edna's recent actions, Helen has never understood Anna's lifestyle. However, as a result of reading her sister's papers, Helen, as Maggie Paley explains, "discovers the Anna in her own nature" (16).[20] Then, in her section of *The Anna Papers*, Helen begins to write and has an affair with the other executor of Anna's papers. Eventually, as reported in "A Summer in Maine," the third novella of *I Cannot Get You Close Enough*, she leaves her husband and (grown) children to find herself. Hence, Helen's behavior becomes comparable to Edna's as it moves toward being comparable to Anna's. Indeed, as Paley remarks about "the magic [Helen] inherits from Anna" being "principally sexual," adding that in this novel "good sex is a form of thinking for oneself" (16), so, too, is this the case in Chopin's novel: Edna's sexually satisfying affair with Alcée Arobin and her desire to consummate her relationship with Robert Lebrun are part of her rejection of social mores in favor of following her own desires. Also, in the later novella, Helen's thoughts regarding her niece Jessie's unplanned pregnancy are reminiscent of Edna's realization at Adèle's bedside that, as Shirley Foster puts it, "childbearing . . . [is] a biological snare, a harsh edict of nature which renders women helpless in an unchosen role" (165): Helen recalls a time in the past when "a woman's body was completely at the mercy of nature. If she married or was fucked then she was impregnated until she died" (*AP* 386).

In *The Anna Papers*, while Helen is at Anna's house supposedly sorting through Anna's papers with the other executor, who is by this time her lover, her husband Spencer calls to tell her that their daughter DeDe needs her because she is "in trouble" (*AP* 261). In answer to Helen's inquiries, Spencer says merely that DeDe has broken up with her boyfriend. The subsequent exchange between husband and wife may at first remind the reader of Edna and Léonce's exchange about her perfor-mance as a mother when, feeling neglected himself, Léonce insists that one of their sons is ill and that Edna has thus neglected him. Like Edna, Helen begins to dismiss her husband's belief that her child needs her, but unlike Edna, she does not ultimately find that DeDe is indeed well. Rather, when she calls her daughter, she learns that DeDe is not only heart-broken but also pregnant.[21] Significantly, Helen has been prompted to call DeDe by the last of a series of thoughts that occur to her as she looks across the room at her lover while she is talking on the phone to her husband: "I am so fortunate. . . . I'm beginning to be as lucky as Anna was. I could go home and make love to Spencer too. My God, I'm becom-ing a sex maniac. Unless the children die. Then my luck would stop" (*AP* 261). Here, the significant difference between Helen and Anna—and Edna and Anna—is underlined. Unlike Helen and Edna, Anna could for-get about a husband and take off for a weekend of illicit passion without worrying about sick or troubled children needing and not being able to reach her.

More differences can be seen between Edna's and Anna's lives and deaths, reflecting a development in character from the earlier to the later rebel. As Anna approaches her death, the narrator remarks that she is "leaving behind a man she could finally really love" (*AP* 9). This man, Philip, is introduced in the last story of the *Drunk with Love* collection, which was published two years before *The Anna Papers*. In that story, "Anna, Part I," Anna notes two things about Philip on the night they first meet: "His hands were beautiful and clean and freckled, *like her own*" and "His hair [was] the exact color *of her own*" (*DL* 225, emphasis added). These details hint at why she can "finally really love" this man and not the many men who preceded him in her life: it is a narcissistic love, and Anna has never had any difficulty loving herself. Reading the two novels together illuminates the similar narcissism of Edna's attraction to Robert. In describing Robert, the narrator notes that "in coloring he was not un-like his companion [Edna]. A clean-shaved face made the resemblance more pronounced than it would otherwise have been" (*CW* 883). Edna and Robert are also shown to be similar in character when the narrator remarks upon how "Robert talked a good deal about himself. He was very young, and did not know better. Mrs. Pontellier talked a little about herself for the same reason" (*CW* 884). Edna's attraction to Robert, then, may also reflect her developing appreciation of herself—which would not have been acceptable in a society that viewed women as mere reflections of their husbands and children and believed that a woman's desires should be sacrificed for her husband's and children's needs. Indeed, the novel's reviewers and the other characters in the novel criticize such "selfishness" exhibited by Edna. Surprisingly, almost a century later, Anna receives similar criticism from the other characters in her novel and from the novel's reviewers.

A similarity can also be noted between Robert and Philip in that each man considers, but ultimately rejects, the possibility of running away with his beloved. Indeed, the scene in which Philip tells Anna of his mental deliberations on the subject echoes remarkably the scene in which Robert tells Edna of his. First of all, both exchanges take place just after a passionate scene between the lovers: in *The Awakening*, just after Robert and Edna kiss for the first time; in *The Anna Papers*, at the end of a weekend Philip and Anna spend together. Although there seems to be quite a difference between these two encounters (a mere kiss versus a whole weekend of lovemaking), given the difference between the times in which these two novels are set, these scenes are actually quite comparable in the degree that each pair has broken social decorum. Second, similar to Robert's telling Edna that he had "dream[ed] of [her] some way becoming [his] wife . . . . dream[ed] of wild, impossible things, [like] men who had set their wives free" (*CW* 992), Philip tells Anna that in thinking over their situation, he had decided briefly that "we should . . . just leave it all and go away and live somewhere" (*AP* 115). Ultimately, however, both men are too "honorable" for such actions. Explaining the futility of his leaving his wife, Philip remarks, "We would take the baggage of our lives with us" (*AP* 115). He believes that neither he nor Anna could truly divorce themselves from their families in their quests for a lasting love. Similarly, Robert says that he "realized what a cur [he] was to dream of such a thing, even if [she] had been willing" (*CW* 992). Such "honor" reveals to Edna that life with him would ultimately be no different from life with Léonce: he, too, merely wants to trap her in a conventional marriage.

Surprisingly, at this point she seems to be less conservative than Anna, for it is Anna who has been pushing Philip to divorce his wife and marry her, while Edna wants only to love Robert, not to marry him.[22] She does not want to be his possession. On the other hand, Edna leaves Robert at this point to keep her promise to Adèle, an action which might indicate that, like Robert, she ultimately does the "honorable" thing: if she keeps this promise to Adèle when her beloved begs her to stay with him, might she not also ultimately keep her "promise" to Léonce—that is, her wedding vows?[23] In contrast, in the exchange between Anna and Philip, Anna moves from desiring marriage to accepting Philip's argument against running away together and agreeing to continue in the role of mistress. Marriage is no longer important to her. Like Edna, she has not had much success with marriage in the past. Unlike Edna, though, she believes that "this is [her] last, [her] very last" love (*AP* 115)—that is, the love that will last.[24] Therefore, she is not willing to lose it just because she cannot have it under "proper" social strictures.

In spite of finding out that she is dying so soon after finally finding the love she has longed for all of her life, as Anna plans her death she can still tell herself, "Let go . . . leave the world. It's okay. They won't even miss you in a year or two" (*AP* 145). Apparently, she is not troubled by the fickleness of the human heart. Rather, she takes comfort in the thought that her family will eventually get over their loss of her. For one thing, it relieves her guilt over the sadness they will suffer upon learning of her death; for another, such fickleness is merely a fact of human nature that Anna accepts. In contrast, during the last night of Edna's life, as she thinks about her affair with Alcée Arobin and her love for Robert, she is dismayed to realize that "to-day it is Arobin; tomorrow it will be some one else" and that, as with the infatuations of her youth, "the day would come when [Robert], too, and the thought of him would melt out of her existence" (*CW* 999). Unlike Anna, Edna is unable to see an advantage in the inconstancy of desire or love.

In Donald A. Ringe's evaluation of Edna's relationships with men, her children, and Adèle, he explains that "as the story develops, one begins to suspect that Edna's self is by its very nature a solitary thing, that she is utterly incapable of forming a true and lasting relationship with another" (586). He continues, "Since Edna cannot give herself to anyone, but instead remains aloof from any true relationship with another, she is doomed to stand completely alone in the universe, a position that is clearly symbolized by the final episode in the book: her solitary swim far out into the emptiness of the Gulf" (587). Anna, too, is a loner to a certain extent. As a writer, she needs her privacy and so shuts herself away from the rest of the world for varying periods of time. Also, until the last few years of her life, she has had one brief relationship after another with men, some of which have gone as far as marriage but none of which has lasted. The members of her family repeatedly call Anna selfish, thereby offering an explanation for these failures. Her selfishness, however, is not necessarily to be condemned. Her story shows that self-centeredness has helped her to become the successful writer she is. More important, it has aided her resolve to live fully. Nothing and no one has kept her from doing whatever she wanted to do—and ultimately that has included loving "the red-haired baby doctor," as she refers to Philip (this "man she could finally really love"), even though he was married to someone else. Interestingly, this description of Anna's life echoes in content, though not in tone, one reviewer's summation of *The Awakening* as "the sad story of a Southern lady *who wanted to do what she wanted to*" (rev. of *Awakening* 96)—though the only thing "sad" about Anna's story is its brevity, due to her disease and death. Anna herself sums up her life in the closing words to her description of another affair she once had with a Norwegian sea captain: "I have not missed much. Thank God for that. I was here. I was definitely here and all the time I was here I played" (*AP* 225).

Edna's comparable behavior toward the end of her life does not result in such self-satisfaction. She is disconcerted by her discovery that desire can exist outside of love and that love does not last.[25] She realizes, too, that the desires awakening within her may give her pleasure but may also ultimately hurt her children. And she perceives that her awakening has exacted a price: the illusions of her former life have all been permanently dispelled. Therefore, she cannot return to the dull comfort of her former respectable life, and society will never accept her new sense of self. The only choice she sees is death.[26]

The contrast between Edna's and Anna's different reactions to their sex lives brings up another difference between the two women: whereas through much of Edna's story one sees that she is not comfortable with her awakening sexuality, Anna's last thoughts before taking cyanide and stepping into the ocean are unashamedly of an illicit, passionate affair she once had with a shallow "social climber," as she labels this lover. She remembers "how wild and selfish he had been . . . match[ing] her own selfishness," and she thinks to herself regarding the affair, "nobody needed to be ashamed of themselves" (*AP* 9). With this thought she is rejecting shame for either her life or her death. When Gilchrist later narrates the events leading up to this moment, it is revealed that on her way to the ocean, Anna stops to call a young lover from her recent past, after which she is ashamed of herself for doing so. She thinks, "Shame will be a nice final emotion," but then again rejects shame in favor of selfishness, recalling that one of her former husbands told her that "when we died the world would still owe us plenty so not to worry about any happiness we could steal" (*AP* 149).

In spite of the difference between their reactions to their sexuality, Anna's thoughts about her "selfish" nature do recall Edna's words to Adèle early in the novel: "I would give up the unessential; I would give my money, I would give my life for my children; but I wouldn't give myself" (*CW* 929). Such a connection between the characters of these women further supports the contention that Anna has evolved from the literary predecessor whose death hers emulates. As already suggested, she picks up where Edna leaves off—in character and action. In the course of her novel Edna is only just awakening to her sexuality. Anna's casual attitude toward sex—evidenced by her use of vulgar terminology when referring to various sex acts, her thorough enjoyment of her sexual relationships, and her habit of questioning others about their sex lives—contrasts remarkably with Edna's prudish embarrassment regarding the apparently racy novel being passed around her social circle, her discomfort with the discussion of Adèle's "condition" in "mixed company," and her dismay upon realizing that she could desire a man whom she does not love. Again, one might argue that this difference reflects the different times in which each novel is set: nineteenth-century Victorian America and twentieth-century post–sexual revolution America. However, such an argument is undermined, first, by the lack of embarrassment shown by Adèle regarding the same book that troubles Edna or in talking about her pregnancies and, second, by the prudery Anna's sister Helen displays in their conversations with each other and when Helen reads her sister's "scandalous" writing. Thus, this difference between Edna and Anna can, indeed, be seen as reflective of the evolution of the character type.

The evolution of character from Edna to Anna is also reflected in Anna's achievements as a writer. At the start of her story, she is an established author, whereas Edna only just begins to exercise her artistic talents at the end of her life. Like Anna, who isolates herself from the world when she writes, Edna secures a place for herself, which Carol P. Christ likens to Woolf's "room of one's own" (34), the pigeon house where she is free, not only "from emotional and financial dependence on men" but also "from the constant interruptions of household duties and children" (Christ 33).[27] In addition, and closer in character to Anna, Edna is developing as a storyteller, as well as an artist, according to Joseph R. Urgo, who traces her progress in narration from the novel's beginning, when she cannot express to Léonce the humor of her adventure with Robert in the water, to her "first attempts to narrate," which include her account to Adèle of walking through a meadow in Kentucky, a bedtime story she tells her children (another failure, since it only serves to excite them rather than to put them to sleep), and the story she tells at the dinner table which completely enthralls her husband and Dr. Mandelet (Urgo 25–28). The latter story's success, Urgo argues, reveals that Edna is just awakening to "the art of telling, of making her desires and her emotions into narrative form" at the time of her death (23).

Edna dies before developing her talents as a painter as well. According to Wayne Batten, Edna's artistic drive reflects her desire to have some control over the world around her, "to become herself a creator and manipulator of illusion in the self-conscious and socially recognized role of artist" (85). Batten rightly points out regarding Edna's failures, however, that "she has difficulty making the transition from amateur to professional. The discipline she needs has not been part of her upbringing" (85). A second reason for her failure, according to Batten, is society's reaction to her early attempts at creating art. For example, Chopin's narrator reports that Adèle is "greatly disappointed to find that it [Edna's portrait of her] did not look like her" (CW 891). Adèle's implicit judgment of Edna's painting is undermined both by the narrator's comment that while Edna painted "she handled her brushes with a certain ease and freedom which came, not from long and close acquaintance with them, but from a *natural aptitude*," and by the narrator's evaluation of the painting: "it was a fair enough piece of work, and in many respects satisfying" (CW 891, emphasis added).[28] As many critics have pointed out, the portrait of Adèle reflects Edna's unique view of the world. However, such a view brings frustration to the artist when others do not understand it or recognize its value. The artist is tempted to give up to avoid criticism. Indeed, Edna's actions at the end of this scene reflect just such resignation: "After surveying the sketch critically she drew a broad smudge of paint across its surface and crumpled the paper between her hands" (CW 891–92). Then, at the end of the novel she gives up her life, in part to escape such social judgment, though more for her children's sakes than her own.

Like Léonce and Adèle, the Hands are dismayed by Anna's choice to seclude herself in her rented house after she has returned to her hometown of Charlotte, North Carolina, and they have no qualms about dropping in on her or giving her phone number out to friends. In response, Anna disconnects the doorbell, unplugs the telephone (gestures comparable to Edna's refusal to keep her reception day), and continues her work. Anna's family appreciates her writing little more than Léonce appreciates Edna's painting. Like Edna, Anna has a unique view of the world, most evident in her description to Philip of her childhood home: "If I looked out my window in the spring I saw twenty pear trees in full bloom and in the fall oaks and maples and in the winter the architecture of a dozen different species of trees" (*AP* 30). The narrator reports that several years after Anna's death, Philip "drove alone down the street where she had grown up and lived and was amazed at how ugly and ordinary it all seemed" (*AP* 30).

Philip is not alone in failing to appreciate Anna's world view. Her brother Daniel's exasperated response to Anna for interfering in his daughter's life holds a not-so-subtle criticism of her writing: "If you want to do something for Jessie, get her to read something. . . . But not your books. She isn't ready for that yet" (*AP* 80). At another point in the novel, after visiting a nephew in a drug rehabilitation hospital, Anna is admonished by her sister-in-law, "Don't go writing about this . . . don't go putting this in some stories" (*AP* 84). Finally, after Anna's death her sister Helen does not wait for the other literary executor before starting through Anna's papers: "I thought I'd better go on and see if there is anything that will embarrass Momma to death. If so, I would just put that away for later" (*AP* 208). In addition, throughout her section of the novel, Helen repeatedly blanches at what she finds among Anna's work, most of which was probably to be part of "the Tom Jones thing" Anna had spoken of with her editor early in the novel (42), apparently a collection in progress of anecdotes of Anna's various love affairs. Such a project in the works shows that Anna—unlike Edna, who tears up Adèle's portrait—has not allowed her family's opinion of her writing to influence her. The comparison reminds the reader, too, however, that later in Chopin's novel Edna does continue to paint after her husband expresses his desire that she not allow it to distract her from her other duties.

It appears from her final work-in-progress that Anna views her life as comparable to that of Fielding's picaresque hero Tom Jones. In her mind, then, her life has been a comedy, rather than a tragedy, in spite of the death of an early love, her inability to have children, finding the love of her life in a married man, and contracting cancer. In contrast, the story of

Edna's last year has been compared to the stories of Emma Bovary and Anna Karenina in that adultery has been a factor in her decision to die.[29] Although, as Lawrence Thornton points out, Edna's despair is not, like Emma's, a result of not "find[ing] the man of her dreams" but rather results from her not being allowed the "freedom to do as she likes" (58), and even though, as Judith Fryer notes, Edna is not "guilt-ridden like Anna [Karenina]" over her extramarital affair (243), still, her awakening to her sexuality is not a positive experience for her.[30] Rather, it adds another dimension to her life that she believes will not be fulfilled. In contrast, Anna's sex life is quite fulfilling. This difference is, of course, another reflection of the different time periods in which the two novels are set. Edna has matured under the sexual repression of Victorian America, while Anna became sexually active during the American sexual revolution of the 1960s. At the same time, again the difference between Edna's and Anna's attitudes toward their sexuality also supports the view of Anna as an evolution of Edna: Edna awakens to sexual pleasure in the course of her novel; Anna, then, her literary daughter, takes pleasure in sex from the very start of her sexually active life.

The perception of Anna as an evolution of Edna is further illustrated by the fact that Anna has been swimming since she was a young child, whereas Edna has only just learned to swim in her twenty-ninth year. Indeed, as pointed out by Eleanor Wymard, though "she has spent many summers on the Gulf coast, Edna is fearful of the water" (379)—that is, until the last year of her life. Carol Christ notes how the sea in *The Awakening* is "empowering" (30). She cites as evidence the "feeling of exultation [that] overtook [Edna], as if some power of significant import had been given her to control the working of her body and her soul" (*CW* 908). Anna, too, equates swimming with power, a means of control, when she recalls her cousin Phelan's instructions on how to swim in cold weather: "You can will yourself not to freeze" (*AP* 130).

After her first successful swim, Edna leaves the water before everyone else in order to contemplate alone this new medium in which she feels empowered (she has defied the "quick vision of death" [*CW* 908] that seized her during her first successful swim) and in control (recall her "impression of [the] space and solitude" [*CW* 908] of this medium—in water, she feels herself isolated from society and thus in control of herself).[31] Edna's next swim is taken as a means of escaping the unwanted company of Mademoiselle Reisz, whose criticism of the Spanish girl

Mariequita is disconcerting to her. Functioning as the judgmental voice of society at this point, Mademoiselle Reisz labels Mariequita "a bad one" (CW 930), implicitly blaming her for the fight between Robert and Victor. Although Edna does not perceive the reason she feels "depressed, almost unhappy" in Mademoiselle Reisz's company at this time (CW 930), the reader can understand how the woman's opinion of Mariequita would be discomforting to Edna, who, just as Mariequita was when Robert and Victor fought over her, is caught between two men, Robert and her husband. She decides suddenly to go swimming, leaves Mademoiselle Reisz on the beach, and this time "she remained a long time in the water" (CW 931). Still, when she finally does return to land, society's representative has not disappeared—Mademoiselle Reisz is waiting for her. Realizing that society will always be waiting for her, Edna, after her last swim in the novel, does not get out of the water at all. Chopin ends the novel as Edna tires, far from the shore.

An evolved Edna, "Anna had *always* been the one who stayed in the water the longest" (AP 130, emphasis added). Not long before her death, but before she discovers the lumps in her breast, on a day when she is feeling particularly run-down, Anna impulsively wades into a pond: "She floated for a minute, then began to swim. She swam out to the dam, gingerly at first, then with more abandon" (AP 138). In the water, she "feel[s] better than she had felt in days" (AP 138). This episode is comparable to Edna's swimming to soothe her sense of loss after Robert has left Grand Isle for Mexico.[32] Finally, also like Edna, Anna later walks into a body of water never to walk out again. It is significant that she takes a cyanide pill before stepping into the water. She is such a strong swimmer that she will not tire as easily as Edna did. Also, she may fear that, unlike Edna, she will try to save herself rather than so easily give up to the ocean the life she values so highly.

The mourners gather for the second half of Gilchrist's novel after the notes Anna left, rather than her body, are found. The last image of Anna, then, like that of Edna, is a vibrant one. Sandra Gilbert explains the significance of the ending of *The Awakening*:

> In depicting Edna's last swim Chopin seems quite consciously to have swerved from precursors like Flaubert . . . [who] not only show the beautiful and desirous Aphroditean woman dead but actually linger over the details of her mortification. . . . By contrast, Kate Chopin never allows Edna Pontellier to become fixed, immo-

bilized. Neither perfected nor corrupted, she is still swimming when we last see her, nor does she ever in Dickinson's phrase, "Stop for Death." (57–58)

Neither does Gilchrist ever portray the dead Anna. The absence of a body troubles some of Anna's survivors, and yet, due in large part to this absence, the second half of Gilchrist's novel deals with an Anna as alive as the Anna of the first half. Those who gather for her wake focus much more on her life in their talk with each other than on her death.

In contrast, however, the imagery of the ending to *The Awakening*, as pointed out by Jane P. Tompkins, is "contradictory" (24). For example, in the final scene, the narrator describes a "bird with a broken wing . . . beating the air above, reeling, fluttering, circling disabled down, down to the water" (*CW* 999), an image "impl[ying] defeat," according to Tompkins (24), thereby undermining one's sense of Edna's swim as a triumph over oppression. On the other hand, Anna's thoughts at the time of her death are not "reeling, fluttering, circling disabled down," like the bird Edna sees but, rather, borrowing the imagery from Anna's earlier description of her plans for her last weekend with Philip, are "burst[ing] apart and sail[ing] out across the stars" (*AP* 145). Furthermore, when she steps off the pier into the ocean, Anna is fully and elaborately dressed, whereas Edna undresses completely on the beach, and, "for the first time in her life . . . stood naked in the open air, at the mercy of the sun, the breeze that beat upon her, and the waves that invited her" (*CW* 1000). Edna's removal of the vestiges of civilization is a sign that she is rejecting the world which has oppressed her. Throughout *The Anna Papers*, in contrast, Anna repeatedly accepts the world as it is, flaws and all, and her death is not so much a rejection of society (she wears its most outrageous vestments proudly) as it is a rejection of having to live the rest of her life at its mercy.

One can perceive the end of *The Awakening* positively, too, however, by realizing that, according to the narrator, Edna does stop thinking of the things that troubled her thoughts during the previous night—Adèle's suffering, Robert's desertion, her children's oppressiveness—before walking down to the beach. In fact, at that point she might not be consciously planning to commit suicide, for she does ask Victor what time they will have dinner and remarks that she hopes it will be soon since she is hungry.[33] Once she reaches the beach, Edna concentrates on "how strange and awful it seemed to stand naked under the sky! how delicious! She felt like a new-born creature, opening its eyes in a familiar world that it had never known" (CW 1000). She feels the chill of the water, "but she walked on. . . . She remembered the night she swam far out, and recalled the terror that seized her at the fear of being unable to regain the shore. She did not look back now, but went on and on" (CW 1000).

Gilchrist narrates Anna's last moments with comparable details. Parallel to Edna's conversation with Victor about food, Anna tells Philip that she is going out for marmalade when she leaves him to drive to the ocean. Neither is it the season for swimming in Gilchrist's novel, so that here, too, the water is cold: "the ocean lay before [Anna], gray and stormy and real. Cold and real. It was possible to turn back but [like Edna] she didn't want to" (AP 149). Anna thinks of that which has driven her to this decision, "the alternative . . . a bed in a hospital and knives and terror"; of her sister Helen, who will "never figure this one out"; of the other members of her family, whom "time will heal"; and of a former lover, a younger man who she worries may never get over her (AP 149). Finally, she remembers that meaningless affair she had years before with the young tennis-playing social climber, and with that thought she steps into the ocean. Edna's thoughts, as she swims out to sea, are, like Anna's, of her family—first her husband and children, then her father and sister—and a past love interest, the cavalry officer. At the last, she hears "the hum of bees" and smells "the musky odor of pinks" (CW 1000). Her senses are awake, then, as she becomes one with the universe, and when she is reincarnated as Anna Hand in Ellen Gilchrist's 1988 novel, she is a sensual being, actively defiant of any oppressive forces in the world that would attempt to curb this sensuality.

6

No Conclusion Possible

An Organic Story Cycle

We need to know the writing of the past, and know it differently than we have ever known it; not to pass on a tradition but to break its hold over us.

Adrienne Rich, "When We Dead Awaken: Writing as Re-Vision"

Not that anything I wrote about them is untrue, far from it. Yet when I wrote, the full facts were not at my disposal. The picture I drew was a provisional one, like the picture of a lost civilization deduced from a few fragmented vases, an inscribed tablet, an amulet, some human bones, a gold smiling death mask.

Lawrence Durrell, *Clea*[1]

Reading Ellen Gilchrist's fiction intertextually with the fiction of four other American writers illuminates particular achievements in her work and allows one to trace, as well, the author's development as a writer. For example, as was done in chapter 2, one might examine Gilchrist's writing against the writing of Ernest Hemingway, an author directly alluded to and echoed in her fiction. His works, particularly his short story collections, provide an example of how a collection of short stories can form a short story cycle. However, reading Gilchrist's stories against works by Hemingway, whose novels and stories advocate stoicism in the face of tribulation, reveals, too, how her characters differ from his: Gilchrist's protagonists rarely respond with "grace under pressure." Rather—and this the reader for the most part finds admirable, not troublesome—they scream out and fight back against their oppression. With her characters' actions, then, Gilchrist undermines the notion that expressing one's emotions is shameful. If Gilchrist did, indeed, model her story collections after Hemingway's or learn from his development of a composite personality, she also ultimately (consciously or unconsciously) rejects qualities within the model which her protagonists would find debilitating. Since the majority of her protagonists are women, silent suffering is not ennobling. Indeed, such is the practice of these characters' not-so-admirable mothers, whose behavior allows the patriarchy and the protagonists' oppression within it to continue.

Finding a male writer so emblematic of the patriarchal tradition of American literature ultimately incompatible with Gilchrist's focus on women-centered issues, her reader might turn to another writer of short stories, Katherine Anne Porter, as a more likely exemplar of the tradition out of which Gilchrist has emerged, as was done in chapter 3. Besides helping to answer the criticism of the handling of racial issues in some of Gilchrist's stories, Porter's work serves well to illuminate Gilchrist's depiction of the immutable South versus the rebellious southern woman as this conflict is developed in her fiction. Although both writers create female characters who defy their oppression by rejecting the roles assigned to women and by pursuing their own desires, neither author provides a sense of an ultimately positive future for these women. The many parallels between the fiction of these two women writers, then, reveal that there has been no substantial change in the status of women—either in or outside the South, since neither woman confines her stories to a southern setting—from the early to the late twentieth century.

Whereas Gilchrist may have used Hemingway's and Porter's stories and story cycles as models for her own stories, her first two novels seem to be responses to novels by William Faulkner and Kate Chopin, respectively, as illustrated in chapters 4 and 5. *The Annunciation*, quite simply, gives Caddy Compson's side of the story told in *The Sound and the Fury*. Beginning her novel during World War II, Gilchrist picks up where Faulkner leaves Caddy in his appendix to the novel, in which he depicts her as the apparent mistress of a Nazi general. Taking her novel as far as the 1980s, Gilchrist shows that until "Caddy" tells her own story and thereby and otherwise takes control of her own life, a change in the status of women, which one notes to be lacking when reading Gilchrist's stories with Porter's, will not occur. Similarly, Gilchrist presents her second novel, *The Anna Papers*, in such a way that the death of Kate Chopin's Edna Pontellier is re-viewed and her life reexamined by members of a similar character's family and community as well as by the reader of both novels. Rather than tell only what leads her own character to suicide and then end her novel with that death, Gilchrist focuses much of *The Anna Papers* on the family and community who do not at first approve of her heroine's character. Until Anna's life is appreciated, Gilchrist's novel shows, women will continue to feel compelled to suppress their desires—either through suicide, as Edna does, or by conforming their minds as well as their actions to comply with society's view of proper behavior, as Anna's sister Helen does until she begins to model her behavior after Anna's.

After *The Anna Papers*, one hears fewer echoes of earlier writers in Gilchrist's works, and the intratextual nature of her canon becomes more complicated. In other words, Gilchrist responds to, revises, and transforms her own earlier works rather than works by her mentors. Therefore, the short fiction collected in *Light Can Be Both Wave and Particle*, the novellas collected in *I Cannot Get You Close Enough*, the novels *Net of Jewels*, *Starcarbon*, and *Sarah Conley*, and her most recent collections of short stories *The Age of Miracles* and *The Courts of Love* in various ways modify her own vision rather than the vision of another writer.[2]

For a brief time after *The Anna Papers*, Gilchrist's work reinforced the reader's sense of the prototype's potential for achievement, which the characterization of Anna Hand provides. In her first book after *The Anna Papers*, the collection of short fiction *Light Can Be Both Wave and Particle*, Gilchrist returns to the medium of the short story, and in the first three stories in this volume, she returns as well to Rhoda Manning (which is exactly what she did in *Victory over Japan* after her first novel *The Annunciation*). The reappearance of Rhoda reminds the reader that Anna is an evolution of this prototype and thus demonstrative of Rhoda's potential. It is significant, therefore, that Rhoda is a child in these three stories. Her strong character is still intact. However, Gilchrist concludes *Light Can Be Both Wave and Particle* with a novella ("Mexico") in which an adult Rhoda is at the center, and the consequences to her character of her constant battles with her parents, brother, and lovers are most evident in her characterization in this work. This novella reveals, too, that Gilchrist's optimism about her prototype's ability to overcome the forces against her does not permeate her works very far beyond *The Anna Papers*, though it returns in her most recent books.

The first of the Rhoda stories in *Light Can Be Both Wave and Particle*, "The Tree Fort," is quite similar to the story "Revenge" from Gilchrist's first collection. In both works the central conflict is between Rhoda and her brother Dudley Manning, Jr. In "The Tree Fort," Rhoda reports that "once again Dudley had found a way to ruin [her] life": he and some neighborhood boys are building a fort, and if Rhoda "want[s] to help" she can "go in the house and get [them] some water" (*LWP* 4)—that is, serve them rather than work side by side with them. When she asks if she will be allowed to play in the fort with them, Dudley predictably tells her, "I doubt it. You're a girl. Girls aren't supposed to be in everything" (*LWP* 7). Again, Rhoda's duties and privileges (or lack thereof) are determined by her gender. Still, the story ends on a more positive note than the ending to "Revenge," in which an older Rhoda states her belief that her successful pole vault was the highlight of her life. "The Tree Fort" ends with Rhoda's sense of empowerment:

> I was eight years old. In five years darker blood would pour out from in between my legs and all things would be changed. For now, I was pure energy, clear light, morally neutral, soft and violent and almost perfect. I had two good eyes and two good ears and two arms and two legs. If bugs got inside of me, my blood boiled and ate them up. If I cut myself, my blood rushed in and sewed me back together. If a tooth fell out, another one came in. . . . It was Saturday. I had nothing to do and nowhere to go and I didn't have to do a thing I didn't want to do and it would be a long time before things darkened and turned to night. (*LWP* 13)

There is, however, still a sense of foreboding hovering around these thoughts, which is not surprising since they are inspired by her brother's loss of an eye. The younger Rhoda is both relieved that such an accident did not befall her and frightened by the close call: if such a thing can happen to her brother, it can happen to her. Also contributing to the tone of apprehension is the way that this story works intra*textually with other Rhoda stories. The reader of Gilchrist's earlier work is given a reason in this passage for why Rhoda Manning might resist maturity: a character who quite early in her life rejects the notion of God (though not by the time of this story, in which her fears of the dark have to do with the threat of damnation), Rhoda fears death. She might be as strong as Anna Hand in character, but with age her body will weaken and become susceptible, as Anna's did, to diseases that could end her life.

Rhoda continues to ponder the mystery of death in the second story of this collection, "The Time Capsule," and it is here that she rejects the comforting promise of heaven offered by Christianity to soothe one's fear of death. "The Time Capsule" takes place shortly after "The Tree Fort," and soon after its beginning the narrator repeats Rhoda's sense of her invulnerability: "No, she would never die. She was not the type. It was probably a lie like everything else they told you. She smelled her arms. They smelled alive. She lifted her head. She tossed her hair. To hell with death. . . . Let them come with death. She would smash them in the face" (*LWP* 15). One recalls that in the preceding story, although Rhoda and Dudley fight, she admires his bravery, which she sees in "his ability to stand up to and get along with [their] father" and in the fact that he "took punishment like a man" (*LWP* 7). In "The Time Capsule," on the other hand, she watches Dudley cry because he "was afraid to go to a different school so soon after he lost his eye" (*LWP* 22). Now she is the brave one. This inversion rocks the foundation of her world, and consequently, she questions other foundations, namely religion and God. The story then ends on a less upbeat note than does "The Tree Fort": first, Rhoda's bravado about her family's impending move to Indiana does not last, and second, she comes to the conclusion that the duality of existence is not life and afterlife but life and death. Still, she determines at the close of the story to "keep moving" (*LWP* 25). Like Anna, she plans to live her life while she can.

The third Rhoda story in this collection, "Some Blue Hills at Sundown," recalls Anna's story in its portrayal of a victim of cancer. Rhoda's own life is not threatened by cancer, but her boyfriend's life is. In this story, Rhoda demands that her parents allow her to visit Bob after his latest operation. As in the previous story, she is still haunted by death and wishes to confirm her own vitality in the face of it, this time by consummating her relationship with Bob. Although her plans are thwarted, it is the only time in all the Rhoda stories that she offers herself to a man and he does not use her for his own pleasure, unmindful of her feelings.[3] Furthermore, just as she and Dudley exchanged roles in the previous story, she and Bob are now each playing the role society expects of the other: she tries to seduce him, and he tells her they must wait for the right time. The story ends positively in that Rhoda has not been used, and Bob, according to the narrator, is not going to die in the next two years but, rather, will live "a lifetime after all" (*LWP* 30).[4]

Nora Jane Whittington, the first embodiment of Gilchrist's second generation of protagonists, also reappears in this volume. Within her story one begins to see Gilchrist's ambivalence about whether or not her second generation of women is going to measure up to Anna's potential any better than the other women in Anna's generation do. In "The Starlight Express," Nora Jane claims to be prepared to raise her twins without a father after she has once again been deserted by Sandy (whose original desertion of her in "The Famous Poll at Jody's Bar" in *In the Land of Dreamy Dreams*, as noted, led Nora Jane to rob a bar for money to follow him to California). In spite of her resolute move toward independence, she turns to another former lover (who is as likely as Sandy to be the twins' father) for support just before the babies are born. Also, the birth of these babies is not without a sense of foreboding. Not only is it another case of a woman having a difficult time giving birth (one recalls here Rhoda's cesarean sections), this time almost dying from the ordeal, but also Gilchrist ends the story with the thoughts of one of the new babies as she screams out her first demand for attention: "This is me, Tammili Louise Whittington, *laying my first guilt trip on my people*" (*LWP* 59, emphasis added). Gilchrist seems to be suggesting here that, from birth, one must begin perfecting the art of manipulation, which will be necessary to receive the attention one needs. It must be remembered, however, that, though younger than Rhoda, Nora Jane was created at about the same time (both appear in Gilchrist's first volume of fiction). Thus, when Nora Jane was initially developed, Gilchrist was still modeling her characters upon Rhoda.

In contrast, in the title story of *Light Can Be Both Wave and Particle*, which branches off from Nora Jane's story, a new female protagonist is developed whose characterization is more comparable to Anna's than to that of the original prototype. Indeed, Margaret McElvoy could be viewed as Anna's spiritual daughter. Her story begins as she—quite significantly, given Anna's death in the preceding book—stands on the bridge from which, the reader is told, her cousin has recently jumped to his death. Gilchrist also links Margaret to Amanda McCamey, whose characterization is a step from Rhoda to Anna in Gilchrist's development of the prototype. Amanda, one recalls, moves to Fayetteville, Arkansas, in the second half of *The Annunciation*, where she is able to put her creative writing abilities and her skill with languages together to become a successful translator of poetry.[5] Similarly, Margaret reports that she is from Fayetteville, that she knows several languages, and that her father is a poet. It is interesting to note that in this story, although Gilchrist characterizes Margaret's mother as another of the former southern belles who worry about their daughters' sexuality and strength, the author does not give her protagonist the more debilitating handicap of a money-

and power-hungry father who pays attention to his daughter only through telling her how she fails to measure up to his expectations. Rather, Margaret's father recognizes that his daughter has her life under control and supports, for example, her choice for a husband—a young Chinese medical student. After meeting Lin Tan Sing, he thinks to himself, "I did good . . . I raised a girl with a brain in her head, hitting on all cylinders the morning she plucked this one from the sea. So, we'll let go. Let her go. Lose her. Maybe never see her again" (*LWP* 83). When he considers the chance that Lin Tan Sing will take Margaret to his own country, this father does not offer to set them up in a house and with jobs near him, as Rhoda's father repeatedly does for Rhoda and her first husband Malcolm. In turn, unlike Rhoda, Margaret recognizes the possible connection between her deep love for her father and her attraction to Lin Tan Sing. She tells the young man, "We have to be careful. I could just be getting you mixed up with my dad. He talks like that all the time. . . . I don't want to fall in love with someone just because he talks like my father" (*LWP* 68). One recalls that in *The Anna Papers*, Anna, too, has such an insight. Thinking of her father, she exclaims to herself, "That glorious old man. . . . My God, I love him. Every man I ever loved is just a replay of those emotions. I remember every word he's ever said to me" (*AP* 136).[6]

Margaret McElvoy's relationship with and imminent marriage to Lin Tan Sing further reflect the optimistic view of human potential of *The Anna Papers*, especially in light of many of Gilchrist's earlier depictions of relationships between people of different races. In "The Lower Garden District Free Gravity Mule Blight or Rhoda, a Fable" in *Victory over Japan* and "Memphis" in *Drunk with Love*, the white female protagonists have relationships with black men for specious reasons. In the Rhoda story, which focuses on her cheating an insurance company by claiming to have lost a ring she has pawned, Rhoda is working on getting a divorce from a husband named Jody. She needs money, which means either that her father does not support this divorce or that she is trying to keep him out of it this time so that she will not simply go from the entrapment of marriage back to the entrapment of her father's home, as she did after her first divorce (from Malcolm in *Net of Jewels*). Her situation affects the reader's view of her decision to have an affair with the black insurance agent who handles her case. The reader senses that her attraction to Earl has little to do with Earl himself. Rather, her planned affair with him

seems to be a part of her rebellion against her husband and, if one knows
her history, against her prejudiced father.[7] As Betty A. Matthews argues,
the affairs some of Gilchrist's women have with black men are merely a
"struggle for independence, a breaking away from traditional mores"
(73). Another example is Baby Kate's relationship with a black man in
"Memphis," which begins as a way to get her father's attention or to
show the world that her father is not the wonderful, open-minded liberal
he is reputed to be. Indeed, he has his prejudices, as well as his other
flaws—such as being so wrapped up in his own glory that he ignores his
wife and daughter. Baby Kate's father might fight for desegregation of
schools, but he throws his daughter out of his house when she brings
home a black man. Finally, reading the love story of Margaret McElvoy
and Lin Tan Sing calls back to mind, too, Gilchrist's "The Emancipator,"
in which a young white woman marries a Lebanese student and is eventually killed by him. But Gilchrist has become more optimistic about
human nature and, relatedly, about interracial relationships, since the
publication of the volume of stories in which "The Emancipator" and
"Memphis" appeared, as is indicated by the uplifting rather than tragic
love story between people of two different races in "Light Can Be Both
Wave and Particle."

Also within the collection *Light Can Be Both Wave and Particle,* Gilchrist
adds a "happy ending" to her earlier novel *The Annunciation.* More accurately, she adds two more chapters to the novel. In the first, "The Song of
Songs," she picks up with Amanda's daughter Barrett Clare just after
Amanda's lover Will has left Barrett with information about the identity
of her mother. In "The Song of Songs," Barrett decides she will go to her
mother, and the story ends at the point of Barrett and Amanda's reunion
on Christmas day. Then "Life on Earth" revives Will from his seemingly
fatal car accident at the end of the novel and tells how he lived through it
after all. Neither chapter adds much to the novel. The latter, in fact, seems
incredible in light of the description of Will's accident in the novel and
can only be explained as a desire Gilchrist must have had to have her
novel end "happily ever after"—that is, with the implication that the
"hero" and "heroine" would be reunited.[8] A case can be made, however,
that the novel already had a happy ending, in spite of Will's apparent
death, for, as discussed in chapter 4, in the original ending Amanda finally claims her life and her children as her own. Mary A. McCay argues
similarly that "the first ending [makes] clear that Gilchrist sees her

protagonist's independence in terms of freedom from men who would define her. . . . Amanda frees herself from her cousin and her husband, and fate frees her from Will" (*Ellen* 81).

As these additional chapters continue *The Annunciation*, Gilchrist's next book, *I Cannot Get You Close Enough*, continues *The Anna Papers*. It is a collection of three novellas, the first of which, "Winter," is a manuscript found after Anna's death. The manuscript details Anna's adventures while tracking her niece Jessie's mother in order to provide evidence that would declare this woman unfit to have custody of her child. The second novella, "De Havilland Hand," fills in much of the story begun in *The Anna Papers* of Anna's niece Olivia de Havilland Hand's discovery of her father's identity and then continues Olivia's story beyond Anna's death. The third novella, "Summer in Maine," brings Olivia and Jessie Hand, their father Daniel (Anna's brother), and, briefly, their aunt Helen (Anna's sister) together with Crystal Weiss's family and friends.

In these three novellas, the sense of hope for the character type pervading *The Anna Papers* and evident in the characterization of Rhoda, Nora Jane, and Margaret in *Light Can Be Both Wave and Particle* is almost entirely missing. Anna's characterization in "Winter" is not nearly as positive as it was in "Anna, Part I" and *The Anna Papers*. Although the reader might determine from Jessie's mother's actions that she is, indeed, an unfit mother, still one wonders at Anna's motivation for working so hard to declare her as such. Anna's thoughts keep returning to her concern that Sheila will take Jessie away from the Hands—or, more particularly, away from Anna, who seems to view Jessie at this time as a surrogate daughter (she has yet to discover Olivia). By the time of this novella, then, Anna has apparently not yet come to view her books as a fulfilling substitute for the children she cannot have.

In the continuation of Olivia's story in this volume, Olivia reminds the reader of the lying, scheming Rhoda Manning rather than of her aunt Anna. She forges report cards, for example, to prove herself worthy of her father's attention, and, sexually active at only fifteen, she talks more to her boyfriend about his paying for an abortion should she become pregnant than she does about their taking precautions to prevent a pregnancy from occurring. Rhoda and Malcolm, one recalls, are very careless about birth control in both the short story "Adoration" in *Drunk with Love* and the novel *Net of Jewels*. Olivia's characterization regresses further in the last novella as she continues to lie about her scholarly potential and concocts a crazy story, which she half believes herself, that Anna is not really dead. Furthermore, instead of modeling her life after Anna's *life*, she considers following her aunt to her death and, in lieu of such drastic action, becomes something of a devotee to her aunt's memory. Jessie, too, regresses in this novella. Her marriage to King Mallison (Crystal's son) at the end of the novella is quite similar to Rhoda's first marriage, the details of which are narrated in the novel *Net of Jewels*: both marriages come about after the young women discover sex rather than love and wind up pregnant, and both marriages show signs of imminent end within the first few months.

It seems that when Gilchrist resurrected Anna for "Winter," she based Anna's characterization upon, rather than developed it from, the Rhoda prototype. This seeming inconsistency is easily explained: at the point in her life when the events of "Winter" take place, Anna has not yet developed into the character she becomes by the time in her life of *The Anna Papers*, for it must be remembered that the events in the novella do (of course, since Anna dies in the novel) occur before the events of the earlier-published novel. At the same time, this different—though not necessarily inconsistent—portrait of Anna supports the argument that the story cycle made up of all of the works in Gilchrist's canon is continually evolving. When one examines the tone and imagery of these three novellas, one notices a darkening voice and vision from which it can be inferred that the author writing these works after the death of the character who inspired them is no longer rejoicing in the triumph of that death but, rather, is now in mourning for the loss. One might think here of criticism of *The Awakening* from the last couple of decades, which, while proclaiming Chopin's achievements with Edna Pontellier, at the same time notes the sad state of affairs when a woman must choose death in order to be free. Gilchrist, too, seems to have been troubled by having created a woman whose control of her life cannot last: she is struck down finally by something entirely out of her hands—cancer. Whereas the works preceding *The Anna Papers* seem to build up to its sense of triumph, those following do not all continue to carry this tone or the sense that Anna's character is indicative of the prototype's potential rather than being an anomaly.

All that is left of Anna after her death, according to Gilchrist's more recent work with Anna at its center, are papers like the manuscript that makes up "Winter," the tone of which is all too "Rhoda." For example,

Anna passes judgment upon her former sister-in-law, Jessie's mother Sheila, while blind to the implications of her own behavior. The loss of Anna's vitality is further reflected in the transformation of the water imagery in "Summer in Maine." Typically in Gilchrist, water is representative of the source of life—even when it is the medium through which one passes to death, as in *Drunk with Love*'s "The Blue-Eyed Buddhist" and in *The Anna Papers* (and nearly so in *The Annunciation* when Amanda almost drowns). In "Summer in Maine," however, the ocean—the same ocean in which Anna has died—is viewed as sinister and threatening by the characters. Again in the role of chronicler, Traceleen is the first to describe it as such: "To tell the truth the ocean looked mean up here in Maine, gray and uninviting" (*IC* 219). Although the anticipation of their first walk on the beach cheers the group after their disappointment upon seeing the house in which they are to spend their summer, Traceleen again describes the water in negative terms when they reach it: "So dark and cold and far out in all directions. . . . This water seemed to come from a darker place" (*IC* 223). Later, Olivia visits the ocean one night to be closer to Anna, and though her thoughts begin positively—"I walked in up to my knees and thought about how close I was to her. She isn't dead because her spirit is everywhere. Her spirit is free because she left her body behind"—the reader is disturbed by the direction in which they immediately turn: "I could walk out into the ocean and join her spirit. Drowning might hurt for a moment, but so what? It hurts to be alive and have to fight, fight, fight every minute to have people like you" (*IC* 297).

It seems, then, that Gilchrist has reconsidered Anna's position as a positive role model for her nieces even after death. In this novella, one no longer sees these young women benefiting from the role Anna played in their lives. Olivia contemplates suicide because "it hurts to be alive." Explaining her choice to consummate her relationship with King, Jessie remarks that Anna "would understand. . . . She gave up anything for love. She told me that. And she didn't mind if she had to be sad in the end" (*IC* 290–91). However, following her aunt's credo on love does not end well for Jessie. By the close of the novella, she is about to have a baby and already she is planning to leave her husband, as well, perhaps, as the baby.[9] Even the brief glimpse of Anna's sister Helen, who seems to be on the way to transforming her life for the better at the end of *The Anna Papers*, is disappointing. She is depicted in "Summer in Maine" as foolishly chasing after the co-executor of Anna's papers.[10]

Finally, in "Summer in Maine," even Crystal and Traceleen are characterized less positively than they have been presented in earlier works. One is not so surprised by Crystal's regression since her most recent appearance prior to this novella (in "Traceleen Turns East" in *Light Can Be Both Wave and Particle*), for like Rhoda's, Crystal's triumphant moments are not usually lasting. For example, at the end of "Traceleen, She's Still Talking" (in *Victory over Japan*), Crystal seems to win her latest battle with her brother: she wreaks havoc on his mock safari, wrecking his new Mercedes Benz in the process. During the plane ride home, however, she tells Traceleen a story about one of her brother's victories when they were children and ends the narration with a pathetic cry: "Traceleen, are you listening? Can you hear me? This is everything I know about love. I'm telling you. Everything I know about everything" (*VJ* 277). Her distress reveals that, like Rhoda's triumphant moments, her exhilaration is false; the reality is that in some way she has lost another battle for love.

Given this pattern in her and other Gilchrist protagonists' stories, one is not surprised that the sense of triumph in "Traceleen Turns East," consistent with the positive tone of the other stories in *Light Can Be Both Wave and Particle*, does not continue into the later novella. In "Traceleen Turns East," Crystal abandons her continuous dieting in order to stop grinding her teeth in her frustration at not being able to keep her waistline down to the size it was when she was younger. Such a choice is a positive step for the vain Crystal, but even more positive in this story is Crystal and Traceleen's relationship—again, perhaps the most positive relationship between any two people in all of Gilchrist's fiction. Beginning her report of how she and Crystal tricked a man who held them at gunpoint, Traceleen tells the reader that "the reason we were saved is that Miss Crystal and I are so used to working together and have honed the skills of cooperation so well that we knew how to read each other's minds when we had to" (*LWP* 125), and the reader thereby knows that they found during this adventure the strength in each other that is typical of their stories.

In "Summer in Maine," however, Crystal is depicted as once again caught between her sexual desires and longing for romantic love, on the one hand, and her husband's money, her unfulfilling love for her husband, and giving her daughter and son a stable home, on the other. Whereas in earlier stories Crystal tries to stop taking pills in order to be a better role model for her son, who has a drug problem (in "Miss Crystal's

Maid Name Traceleen, She's Talking, She's Telling Everything She Knows" of *Victory over Japan*), and gives up alcohol after her drinking almost results in the death of her daughter in a fire (in "Traceleen at Dawn" of *Drunk with Love*), in "Summer in Maine" she does not act in such a way as to provide her children with a more stable home environment. To begin with, since her husband does not accompany them to Maine, she invites her lover to join her family there. This angers her son King, who does not like the young man, and distracts Crystal from noticing her daughter Crystal Anne's distress over Olivia's stories about Anna still being alive. Later in the novella, Crystal usurps the children of others to fulfill some of her needs—much as Anna does in her involvement in the lives of Olivia and Jessie. First, in spite of Daniel's disapproval, Crystal encourages Jessie to marry her son, hoping Jessie will be a stabilizing influence upon King. Reflecting his sense that Crystal is stealing his child from him, Daniel tells her, "You can't have her. You can't take her away from me" (*IC* 356). Second, as her friend Lydia indicates in her criticism of Crystal's support of the impending marriage and birth, Crystal regards Jessie's unborn baby as a chance to make up for her mistakes with her son: "Are you going to sacrifice them for the sake of some baby you think will do it for you? . . . King wouldn't do it for you so you think this baby's going to?" (*IC* 345).

Even Traceleen no longer measures up to her earlier characterization. Although other characters continue to comment upon how wonderful Traceleen is, the reader is disturbed by some of Traceleen's attitudes expressed in this novella. She is no longer as open-minded and tolerant as she is in the earlier stories. For example, she repeatedly expresses her displeasure over her niece Andria's attraction to King, not because of his past drug problem but because he is white, and Traceleen does not believe in relationships between men and women of different races. Also, to the reader's surprise, Traceleen is less accepting, even critical of Crystal at times in this work. She seems to condemn Crystal for not trying to work out her relationship with her husband, while she repeatedly expresses her admiration for Manny Weiss's character. Both attitudes disturb the reader who recalls the events of the very first Crystal/Traceleen story, "Miss Crystal's Maid Name Traceleen, She's Talking, She's Telling Everything She Knows." In that story Traceleen believes that this same Manny whom she so admires in "Summer in Maine" pushed his wife down a staircase in his anger at her for flirting with a young man.[11] Finally, one begins to compare Traceleen's attitude toward Crystal Anne to the other instances of someone usurping another's child that occur in this volume, and her attention to the child is no longer seen in such positive terms. Like Anna, Traceleen does not have children; perhaps also like Anna, this lack leaves her unfulfilled.

Toward the end of "Summer in Maine," and thereby of the volume *I Cannot Get You Close Enough*, Anna speaks from the grave:

> I cannot get you close enough, I said to him, pitiful as a child, and never can and never will. We cannot get from anyone else the things we need to fill the endless terrible need, not to be dissolved, not to sink back into sand, heat, broom, air, thinnest air. And so we revolve around each other and our dreams collide. It is embarrassing that it should be so hard. Look out the window in any weather. We are part of all that glamour, dreams, change, and should not be ashamed. (*IC* 387)[12]

Here again, Anna's tone is less than triumphant, although it is a step closer to the Anna who went to her death rejecting any feelings of shame for her life. Still, the other voices closing the volume are, for the most part, filled with regret: Jessie is sorry she chose to marry King and go through with the pregnancy; Olivia is sorry for Jessie; King is sorry for himself; and Crystal "do[es]n't know what went wrong" (*IC* 391). Only Traceleen's last words, the last line of the book, offer, if not hope, then at least the sense that "this too shall pass away" (*IC* 391). At the same time, however, her word choice connotes death ("pass away"), a marked contrast with *The Anna Papers*, which may also end with a woman's death but is still a celebration of life.

From earlier references to Gilchrist's *Net of Jewels* in the preceding chapters, one can already see how Gilchrist again presents a darker view than that which is found in *The Anna Papers* of her characters' potential to develop in spite of the forces against them. Like the other works providing glimpses of Rhoda as an adult, *Net of Jewels* reveals that Rhoda has yet to achieve the sense of her own self-worth that Anna has achieved by the time of *The Anna Papers*. In the preface to her novel, Rhoda states that this story "is about [her] setting forth to break the bonds [her father] tied [her] with" (*NJ* 3). Although she continues, "In the end I got free, so it sort of has a happy ending" (*NJ* 3), upon completing the novel, the reader wonders about this claim. At the end of the last chapter, Rhoda asks her father to help her out of yet another mess and then rests peacefully under his protection. The adventures covered in this novel, in which Rhoda is in her late teens and early twenties, show Rhoda going around in circles: she ventures out from her father's dominion, gets into some kind of trouble, calls him for help, and then allows him to run her life for a while before she rebels again. Finally, the coda that ends *Net of Jewels*, which reports that Rhoda is now fifty-five years old, reveals that she is still lying to herself about her father's power over her. She discusses with her friend Charles William Waters a time—when she was over twenty years old!—he witnessed her father literally chasing her in the front yard. She tells Charles William, "I only gave in because you were there. If I'd been alone I could have gotten away" (*NJ* 357). She believes that, at the time of the incident, she was concerned that her father would "say something about [Charles William] being gay" (*NJ* 358). Like the reader, Charles William is incredulous regarding Rhoda's contention that she was "trying to protect [him]," and Rhoda responds to his skepticism, "I remember it that way" (*NJ* 358). One recalls here the narrator's comment in the early story "1957, a Romance" that "she always believed her own stories as soon as she told them" (*LDD* 82) and then realizes that Rhoda is still avoiding the truths about her life. One of those truths is that she is too self-centered to have been concerned with Charles William's feelings in the midst of one of her own "tragedies." Another is that she still has not escaped her father's domination.

From an interview with Gilchrist, Wendy Smith reports that *Net of Jewels* "was a difficult book to write . . . partly because there was little room for the humor that has always enlivened her work" (46). The absence of humor may be what distinguishes Gilchrist's later books from the earlier ones. Certainly there are humorous scenes in each of these books, but the pervading tone is not that of comedy but of drama. As her main characters get older, the fact that they must continue to fight the same battles against society's view of their roles as women becomes less comical. As these women's "children" get older and are confronted still with the same conflicts, the author and reader are even less amused, even more troubled. One can see this difference in tone by contrasting the narration of Rhoda's abortion in "1957, a Romance" of Gilchrist's first book of fiction with the narration of the same abortion in *Net of Jewels*. Rhoda's turning to her father for help in paying for the abortion in the beginning and her delusions of independence in the end of this episode in the novel are no longer even wryly humorous, as in the short story; and no longer is this a story about a particular spoiled and willful young woman who does not want to have a baby and will do anything to keep from doing so. The focus is now on the community's role in Rhoda's situation. Gilchrist explained to Smith that she does not find amusing "a world where if you got pregnant you *had* to have the baby; the only way you could get out [of it] was by putting your life in danger" by having a back-street abortion (W. Smith 46)—or by prostituting yourself, as Rhoda does, in order to get the name of a legitimate doctor who would perform the operation.

In her recent work, Gilchrist seems also to be pointing out how little progress women have made since the 1950s when a woman had to have sexual relations with one doctor to get the name of another who would give her a safe abortion. In a novella set thirty years later, which Gilchrist had published just prior to *Net of Jewels*, young Jessie Hand becomes so caught up in a romantic fantasy of marriage and motherhood that, though she has a legal choice about whether or not to have a baby she has not planned and is not ready for, she chooses to go through with the pregnancy as well as to marry a man too much like her alcoholic father— the latter action also reminiscent of Rhoda's marriages. Consequently, as revealed in *Starcarbon*, published just after *Net of Jewels*, Jessie, again like Rhoda, is in constant conflict with the men in her life.

Also in *Starcarbon*, as pointed out by reviewer Trev Broughton, Olivia Hand, the central character of the novel, "seems to be fighting exactly the same battles as her southern foremothers: how to keep two men [her father and her lover] happy and still have time for an education" (21). She ultimately resists her father's wish that she finish school in North Carolina, where she will be near him and thus in range of his control; however, she seems to be moving toward giving in to her lover's pressure. She accepts an engagement ring, in spite of her determination not to marry and "have babies" too young and before completing her education and launching a career. This latest supplement to the Hand portion of the story cycle made up of Gilchrist's entire canon therefore reveals that it is in content, as well as in form, indeed a story *cycle:* the young women of the latest generation are little different from the prototypical member of the previous generation of Gilchrist's characters, the reason being, as already mentioned, that the social pressures are not letting up. These women are no less oppressed than their literary mother Rhoda Manning, grandmothers Caddy Compson and Miranda Gay, and great-grandmother Edna Pontellier. Indeed, as Gilchrist shows in the historical novel *Anabasis*, the pressure upon women to get married, as well as their lack of control over their own bodies, can be traced back to ancient times.

On a more positive note, the development of the protagonist of *Anabasis* is reminiscent of the Anna Hand of her novel. Perhaps in some way related to this similarity, the Rhoda one meets in some of the stories in Gilchrist's next collection of short stories, *The Age of Miracles*, is also more comparable to Anna. Her development in such stories as "A Wedding in Jackson," "Paris," and "The Uninsured" seems to have been influenced by the evolution of herself for the creation of Anna. In these stories, Rhoda is approaching sixty, pleased with her appearance but not focused on attracting men, at peace with her family and serving as peacemaker within it, and successful as a writer, which seems to be a major source of her self-satisfaction and inner strength. Although Gilchrist does not explain how this transformation of character came about, the first story of the collection, "A Statue of Aphrodite," does provide something of a transition to the other middle-aged Rhoda stories. In this first story, Rhoda tells about the ridiculous lengths and expense she went to at one point during her fifties in order to have an affair with a doctor she was not really attracted to but who, due to his profession, she believed would probably not infect her with AIDS. A significant difference in tone can be detected between this story and other stories of affairs Rhoda has had: in this one she is laughing at rather than feeling sorry for herself. Again, though, the reader does not know how she achieved the ability to see the humor in her adventures, except for the reason already suggested: Rhoda's characterization has finally become part of the evolution of the composite personality of Gilchrist's canon, of which she is, after all, the prototype.

Following "A Statue of Aphrodite," "A Wedding in Jackson" begins with Rhoda remarking on a younger man with whom she recently "spent all [her] time and money" in order to "show the world [she] was still physically attractive" (*AM* 35). After admitting, "What a bore I must have been" (*AM* 35), she explains that she has since ended the affair and focused her attention on her family. By the time of this story, then, she is no longer bitter toward her father and is on much better terms with her mother than she has been in previous works. She sums up her reconciliation with her family with: "At fifty-eight I have finally left my adolescence behind me" (*AM* 44). In this story, Rhoda not only plays peacemaker within her family but also recognizes her role in the discord. The story centers on her attempts to reconcile her grandson to his mother's new boyfriend. Rhoda realizes that it is to some extent because she left her first husband, the father of her children, that her son left his wife: to punish Rhoda, who he knows loves her daughter-in-law very much. Such insight once again distinguishes this characterization of Rhoda from her earlier incarnations.

The focus of "A Wedding in Jackson"—on the relationship of a younger couple—is repeated in "Paris"; and in "The Uninsured" the focus is on Rhoda's superb health as she anticipates her sixtieth birthday. Although she mentions a relationship with a younger man toward the end of this collection of letters (to insurance companies regarding whether she will renew, transfer, or drop her policy), it is not at all central in the story but rather merely a means of corroborating her vitality. Indeed, this story contrasts provocatively with "The Lower Garden District Free Gravity Mule Blight or Rhoda, a Fable" in *Victory over Japan*, in which Rhoda also deals with an insurance company. The difference between "The Uninsured" and the earlier story reflects Rhoda's development. In "The Lower Garden District," as mentioned previously, Rhoda falsely reports to an insurance company having had a ring stolen, in order to get money that will facilitate leaving her husband. She then seduces the adjuster who comes to investigate the claim, only to realize in the end that it is she who has been used. In "The Uninsured," Rhoda is not trying to get any money out of the insurance company to which she writes. Rather, she gloats in her letters about her good health and cancels her policy. This decision to quit paying for what she does not need seems to be part of a determination to live by her own rules with no backup support to cover her if consequences ensue.

In contrast to these middle-aged and matured Rhoda stories, *The Age of Miracles* does have Rhoda stories that the reader finds reminiscent of a more familiar Rhoda: "The Stucco House," "Joyce," "Love of My Life," and "Going to Join the Poets." Similar to "A Wedding in Jackson" and "Paris," the first of these does not focus on Rhoda as much as it does on the next generation: in this case her youngest son Teddy (not the son who later divorces the favored daughter-in-law). In a change of perspective, Teddy is the protagonist and a thirty-something Rhoda his antagonist: her drunken adventures threaten his security with his beloved new stepfather Eric. At the same time, the story does prepare for Rhoda's departure for graduate school in Fayetteville, Arkansas, which becomes the subject of the other two stories from this period of Rhoda's life—"Joyce" and "Going to Join the Poets." In these stories, Rhoda engages in an adulterous affair with a fellow graduate student while her husband Eric takes care of her sons in her absence from their home in New Orleans. Again, this behavior is more familiar to the reader of Gilchrist's canon. The Rhoda who narrates "Love of My Life," which takes place some years before these other three stories, during the period following her divorce from her first husband Malcolm, is even more reminiscent of the Rhoda encountered in *Net of Jewels:* Rhoda and her sons are being supported by her father, and the story centers on her affair with a married man who reminds her of her father. Her satisfaction with her appearance in this story differs significantly from the satisfaction she expresses in the stories in which she is older: it is all focused on her outward appearance; it has come about with the help of diet pills; and she will use it to attract friends and lovers. In other words, Rhoda has not yet reached the point of self-satisfaction for her own sake.

The Age of Miracles also includes several stories with new central characters, though they are either connected to the Rhoda stories via place (set in Fayetteville) or age and role of the narrator (for example, Virginia of "Love at the Center," like Rhoda in "A Wedding in Jackson" and "Paris," tells the story of a budding romance between two young people at her health club), or they are comparable to other characters or plot lines in Gilchrist's canon, thus reminding the reader once again that this book is another volume in a larger story cycle. In still further support of this perception of her canon, in other stories in the collection, Crystal and Nora Jane reappear. Crystal is not much changed but getting along better with her husband. Just as the older Rhoda is not obsessed with finding a lover, the younger Nora Jane in "The Blue House" is not yet focused on having a boyfriend. This Nora Jane story, a prequel to the earlier ones, focuses on her relationship with the origin of her strength of character, her grandmother, and the death of this same grandmother, which left Nora Jane in the sole care of her alcoholic mother.

Soon after the appearance of *The Age of Miracles* on bookstore shelves, it was joined by *Rhoda, A Life in Stories,* which collects most of the Rhoda stories from the previous volumes along with a couple of new ones. Even collected in this way, the volume does not provide the whole story of Rhoda's life, as earlier noted. The reader is left with some of the same questions spurred by the previous collection's stories: what exactly inspired the fifty-year-old adolescent to grow up, and how did she do it? Also, the reader wonders what kinds of adventures Rhoda had during her forties; perhaps they hold the key to her ability to regroup her earlier strengths in order finally to reach in her late fifties the potential suggested by her earlier character. The answer seems to be connected to

Rhoda's writing. As these stories in *The Age of Miracles* indicate, Rhoda begins her writing career during her forties.

That Gilchrist also began her writing career in her forties may be why she has not yet provided more than glimpses of this decade of her character's life. Because Rhoda's adventures are so closely based on her own life and given the amount of time she spent writing during her forties, she may be finding it difficult to find much material for a story from that period. However, she has included another story of Rhoda's graduate study in her most recent short story collection, *The Courts of Love*, which along with the stories in *The Age of Miracles* suggests that she is preparing to fill in this period of Rhoda's life.

There is also still much to hear about Gilchrist's other recurrent characters. Seeming to recognize this, in both *The Age of Miracles* and *The Courts of Love*, Gilchrist provides prequel chapters to her Nora Jane adventures and in the latter several chapters that pick up and continue Nora Jane's ongoing adventures with Sandy, Freddy, and their twins. She has also given her readers much to anticipate—the histories and further adventures of some of her other characters, including some of the one-time-only manifestations of the composite personality who can be found throughout Gilchrist's canon. Reminding the reader that the story cycle is continually evolving in various directions, Gilchrist has included in *The Courts of Love* another story with a protagonist named Aurora, who, having first appeared in *The Age of Miracles*, promises to be a new recurring character in the canon. The last story in *The Courts of Love*, entitled "Excitement, Part I," also promises a sequel. The reader is reminded that just before the novel *The Anna Papers*, Gilchrist had closed *Drunk with Love* with a story entitled "Anna, Part I." "Excitement, Part I" brings the reader back to New Orleans, and the first-person narrator mentions a cousin named Ingersol, which is the name of one of Rhoda's brothers. The reader waits for an explanation of the connection between this character and Rhoda in stories or novels to follow. In the meantime, Gilchrist gives her reader a whole new cast of characters but still another manifestation of her composite personality in her latest novel, *Sarah Conley*.

In other words, the reader of Gilchrist's fiction gets caught up in a world that continues to spin what I have termed an organic story cycle.

NOTES

1. Tradition and an Individual Talent

1. Reviewing Gilchrist's *Victory over Japan*, fiction writer Beverly Lowry comments that this second collection of stories, in which characters from Gilchrist's first collection reappear, is "not [a] sequel but [a] complement" to the earlier work (18). Similarly, in his review of Gilchrist's *Light Can Be Both Wave and Particle*, novelist Roy Hoffman remarks that "followers of Ms. Gilchrist's writing will appreciate many links to earlier works, but it is not essential to be already acquainted with her fictional family to enjoy this collection" (13)—although he sees the two stories in this collection that provide a new ending to *The Annunciation* as exceptions to this sense of autonomy. A contrasting opinion on the interrelatedness of Gilchrist's fiction can be found in the review of this same collection in *Kirkus Reviews:* "Gilchrist's stories call out to each other: this collection, middling on its own, should be read in tandem with *Victory over Japan* and *Drunk with Love* to fully appreciate her delicate and nervy talent" (rev. of *Light* 1096).

2. See Jonathan Yardley's review in *Book World* and Gene Lyons's backward glance at *The Annunciation* in his review of *Victory over Japan*.

3. Surprisingly, and I believe inaccurately, several reviewers compliment Gilchrist's depiction in this novel of the conflicts that arise within various familial and sexual relationships, viewing her development of these conflicts as realistically "gritty" (McCay, "Star-Struck" E-9), "wise" (Bosworth 19), and unsentimental (Seaman 876).

4. See in particular the review in *Publishers Weekly* (rev. of *Age*), Donna Seaman's review in *Booklist*, Susan Duncan's review in *Southern Living*, and Bharat Tandon's review in the *Times Literary Supplement*.

5. The *Publishers Weekly* reviewer of this volume mistakenly remarks that the years missing are 27 to 39. I am not sure how this number was reached, for there are several stories in which Rhoda is in her thirties ("Drunk Every Day," "Joyce," and "Going to Join the Poets"—as well as "The Lower Garden District Free Gravity Mule Blight or Rhoda, a Fable," from *Victory over Japan*, which is inexplicably not

included in the Rhoda collection). I also wonder at this reviewer's notion that the abrupt transition in Rhoda's character is "between the spoiled, impetuous rich girl who gulps diet pills, drinks a lot, and, while reading Hemingway, comments about his 'terrible looking' wife and the middle-aged Rhoda who . . . places her work with the *Paris Review* as easily as she might buy a new outfit" (rev. of *Rhoda* 242), for at the same time that Rhoda is having her first stories accepted for publication, she is engaged in another adulterous affair while living apart from her husband Eric (see "Joyce" and "Going to Join the Poets"), not unlike the affairs she had in her twenties while married to her first husband (see *Net of Jewels*).

6. Amanda McCamey's story is also continued chronologically; however, her case is different from Nora Jane's since she has only reappeared in Gilchrist's fiction in one book since *The Annunciation:* in *Light Can Be Both Wave and Particle* Gilchrist includes two stories—or, more accurately, two additional chapters—which, as mentioned previously, provide a new and more obviously happy ending to the novel by having Amanda's lover actually survive the wreck that seems to take his life at the end of the novel and by narrating the reunion between Amanda and the daughter she gave up for adoption thirty years before.

7. It must be pointed out, however, that Traceleen is Crystal's servant; so, although theirs is the most positive relationship between characters in Gilchrist's fiction, it is still problematic. Reviewing *Victory over Japan* for the *Times Literary Supplement,* David Sexton remarks upon the fact that in spite of Gilchrist's new step in narrating her story—"the story-telling is delegated to the heroine's black maid['s] uncritically loyal report[ing] of the war against fathers, husbands and brothers"—Gilchrist's "real interest still lies with Crystal, rather than Traceleen, the maid, who is reduced to a narrative servant" (573).

8. Crystal, in contrast, does not have such a tool for self-awareness, a medium through which she can undermine the power exerted over her by the men in her life; but she does have Traceleen, who tells Crystal's story in much the same way (and to the same ends) that Anna and Rhoda write theirs.

9. See Noel Polk's afterword to his edition of Faulkner's *Sanctuary: The Original Text* for a discussion of the similarities between Quentin and Horace (298–301).

10. The best study of the evolution of this Faulkner character type is John Irwin's article, "Horace Benbow and the Myth of Narcissa," in which he shows why Gavin is able to survive while Quentin and Horace are destroyed (562–65).

11. Jeanie Thompson and Anita Garner make a similar argument as they contrast Amanda with Gilchrist's earlier protagonists:

> With the creation of Amanda McCamey . . . Gilchrist may be reversing the trend set by Rhoda, LeLe, Matille, even LaGrande McGruder and Lelia McLaurin [some of the protagonists of the stories of *In the Land of Dreamy Dreams*]. Amanda is possibly Gilchrist's first female protagonist who may be elevated to the class of *hero*. Although Amanda has in common with her "sisters" a penchant for the downhill slide, a heavy cargo of guilt, and a similar Mississippi Delta/New Orleans background, she redeems herself

with an honest attempt to flee "the world of guilt and sorrow," to borrow a phrase from Flannery O'Connor, by literally asserting her will against the forces that would slow her down in her bid for a self-directed, meaningful life. (105)

Similarly, Mary A. McCay notes that "the progress of Amanda McCamey in this one text [*The Annunciation*] mirrors the progress that women like Rhoda make over several volumes of short stories" (*Ellen* 81).

12. Because Traceleen is not in any way self-centered, she cannot be said to have developed from the Rhoda prototype (this is why she has been left out of the discussion of Gilchrist's major recurring characters), although in many ways her character is also a movement toward Anna Hand's.

13. Riffaterre's focus on the reader reminds one of what separates intertextual studies from influence studies: as Jay Clayton and Eric Rothstein explain, studies of a work's intertexts are reader-centered, while influence studies are author-centered (Clayton and Rothstein 22).

2. Gilchrist's Composite Personality and Story Cycle: Transforming Ernest Hemingway

1. In a more recent study, Maggie Dunn and Ann Morris have used the term *composite novel* and defined it similarly: "*The composite novel is a literary work composed of shorter texts that—though individually complete and autonomous—are interrelated in a coherent whole according to one or more organizing principles*" (2, their italics). Although they insist that what they are referring to is distinguishable from the short story cycle, their definition and most of their examples belie this claim. The difference seems only that their term allows also for collections of works other than short stories (like the mixture of poetry, prose sketches, and drama in Jean Toomer's *Cane* or the mixture of poetry and autobiographical essays in Judith Ortiz Cofer's *Silent Dancing*). Their definition might therefore seem more appropriate for my purposes since, for example, one of Gilchrist's collections is a collection of novellas rather than short stories and, indeed, Dunn and Morris devote an entire chapter to books like it. However, at the start of their study, they do insist that "the composite novel resides under one cover" (16). I am arguing, in contrast, that Gilchrist's whole body of fiction is a story cycle; thus, their terminology is ultimately not appropriate for my study.

2. It is interesting to note that Gilchrist also makes a war part of the characterization of another recurring character of her fiction even though she is a generation younger than Rhoda: Nora Jane Whittington's father died in the Vietnam War, leaving his daughter in the care of his wife, who drinks heavily to escape the grief of her loss, and his mother, who dies when Nora Jane is only fourteen.

3. Although they do refer to it as blasphemy, Jeanie Thompson and Anita Garner's response to Amanda's version of the Lord's Prayer is similar to mine: they argue that it reflects her reaching for "self-respect, forgiveness and love" (113). In response to another incident of Amanda revising Christ's words to apply

to herself, they add, "There is nothing irreverent in Amanda's creation of her own liturgy as she accepts motherhood and acknowledges a degree of selflessness shortly before she goes into labor" (113).

4. This novel's epigraph is also taken from Hemingway (from a 1925 letter to F. Scott Fitzgerald): "Love is also a good subject, as you might be said to have discovered."

5. Joseph Flora points out that "in its structure and its use of symbolism, 'Hills Like White Elephants' may remind readers of 'The End of Something'" (*Ernest* 33). Therefore, he concludes, "one might ask if the unnamed protagonist is Nick Adams. If so, this story would give us the most unflattering picture of Nick to be found in any of the Nick stories, which characteristically show a perplexed but essentially idealistic character" (*Ernest* 33).

6. In "Adoration," too, however, Rhoda's second pregnancy is described as "ecstatic," and her reaction to that cesarean is mild: "They cut her open and took him out and sewed her back up" (*DL* 62). Furthermore, the narrator reports that afterward Rhoda wrote to her father and he "sent her some money" and that "her mother came and stayed and took care of her and got her a new maid" (*DL* 62), all of which undermines somewhat Rhoda's fears in "1957, a Romance" about being "cut open" again. In addition, twice in "Adoration" Rhoda risks pregnancy by failing to use birth control during intercourse with her husband. The first time results in the second baby mentioned above, and during the second time she thinks to herself, "she was making a baby right that very minute and she knew it and she didn't give a damn because it was her birthday and she thought it was funny" (*DL* 64). I have argued elsewhere that this playful, careless lovemaking produces the child Rhoda aborts in "1957, a Romance" ("Water" 84).

7. Mrs. Manning's criticism of Rhoda is somewhat specious, however, given the narrator's comment that Rhoda's mother is "a gentle, religious woman who lived her life in service to her family and friends. But she had spells of fighting back against the terrible inroads they made into her small personal life. This was one of those spells" (*LDD* 84). Mrs. Manning is feeling resentful toward Rhoda, not only because Rhoda has dropped the responsibility for her children unexpectedly upon her mother, but also, one might infer from these narrative comments regarding Rhoda's mother, because Mrs. Manning is somewhat envious of her daughter's strength of character, which she apparently lacks. This view is confirmed in one of the most recent Rhoda stories, "A Wedding in Jackson" in *The Age of Miracles*, even while it is softened: "I have acted out for her the life she never got to lead," Rhoda remarks, along with admitting to causing her mother "heartbreak and disappointment" and to being "selfish, spoiled, [and] hot-tempered" (*AM* 37). Clearly, by the time of the story in this later collection, which a fifty-eight-year-old Rhoda narrates, she is no longer a source of envy and frustration for her mother, but rather a source of fulfillment and satisfaction.

8. In Gilchrist's canon, too, pregnancy and childbirth are depicted almost solely in negative terms: besides Rhoda, for example, both Crystal Manning and Nora

Jane Whittington almost die during childbirth, and Anna Hand has several bloody miscarriages.

9. In the Rhoda novel *Net of Jewels*, which also covers the events of this story and the story "Adoration," Gilchrist changes some of the details surrounding Rhoda's pregnancies and abortion (and, as discussed in chapter 6, the tone of the story). After her abortion in the novel, Rhoda does not go back to Malcolm. Once again, I learn from Malcolm Cowley's experience with Faulkner's inconsistencies and apply to Gilchrist his realization about Faulkner: "His [or in this case her] creative power was so unflagging that he [she] could not tell a story twice without transforming one detail after another" (46).

10. Also comparable to the ending of "Indian Camp," at which point Nick "felt quite sure that he would never die" (*IOT* 19), is Rhoda's similar sense of invulnerability at the beginning of the story "The Time Capsule" in *Light Can Be Both Wave and Particle:* Rhoda, who is about eight years old in this story, is "thinking about fate. Anything could happen to anyone at any time," including the fact that "you could die" (*LWP* 15). Like Nick, however, Rhoda rejects this thought, "No, she would never die. She was not the type" (*LWP* 15).

11. Rhoda speaks out directly to her mother against double standards in "A Wedding in Jackson" in *The Age of Miracles*. When Mrs. Manning complains that the man whom the ex-wife of one of Rhoda's sons is dating is "too young" for her, Rhoda responds, "You don't care how young Dudley's wives are [or] Ingersol's girlfriends" (*AM* 45). Within her apology to her former daughter-in-law for coercing her to attend the wedding, Rhoda alludes even more directly to the double standard under which her family lives when she describes Jackson, Mississippi, as "the shrine of the double standard" (*AM* 48).

12. In his chronological grouping of *The Nick Adams Stories*, Philip Young places the third and fourth Nick Adams stories, "The End of Something" and "The Three-Day Blow," after Nick returns from war. However, this placement is unique with him. I agree with the majority of Hemingway critics who view these stories as occurring during Nick's adolescence.

13. Another example can be found at the end of *The Annunciation* when Amanda remarks that she will write "a novel about love . . . everything I know about love and everything I can find out" (*A* 349); Gilchrist's much later novel *Starcarbon* is subtitled "A Meditation on Love."

14. Actually, Gilchrist's fiction has had "metafictional" references since *Victory over Japan:* as mentioned in chapter 1, Anna Hand is first introduced in the short story "Looking over Jordan" as the author of a novel called *The Ascension*, which the protagonist reviews. This story is discussed in chapter 3. Patricia Lattin remarks upon Chopin's practice of "placing the same person in more than one work" ("Kate" 20)—another point of comparison between Gilchrist and Chopin besides those discussed in chapter 5. In both women's canons, a minor character in one story sometimes becomes a major character in another and vice versa. Lattin's summary of the effect of this technique upon Chopin's work illuminates Gil-

christ's accomplishments with her own interrelated characters: "This technique contributes to the creation of a believable fictional world with a dense social reality and also serves to make characters fuller, more complex human beings than they would be within the confines of one piece of fiction" ("Kate" 20). In addition, Lattin's comments regarding the "remarkable complexity" that results from "the presence of the same characters in several works" is discussed in my concluding chapter in connection with Gilchrist's work: "one story fills in facts omitted by another, and details from one world color our understanding of another" ("Kate" 29).

15. Rhoda's married life, as it is developed in later works, particularly the novel *Net of Jewels*, also recalls that of the woman in "Cat in the Rain," as Debra Moddelmog describes her: "Like the cat in the rain, she feels shut out, unwanted, unnoticed, unloved; she and her husband do not make each other happy anymore" ("Unifying" 27). This description can also be applied to several other married protagonists in Gilchrist's canon.

16. Flora examines in detail the significance of eating in "Big Two-Hearted River" (*Hemingway's* 161–63) and in other Nick Adams stories (*Ernest* 53).

3. The New Order: Picking Up Where Katherine Anne Porter Left Off

1. Stout explains: "Beset by a devastating combination of dire forces—the flu epidemic, the war, the forced patriotism all around her, the shortage of money, her sense that her love is doomed—[Miranda] has no refuge but style, her manner or way of suffering them. . . . The way she chooses, the only way she can choose, is the way of the stiff upper lip" (138). Sarah Youngblood also refers to Hemingway in her discussion of "Pale Horse, Pale Rider": "War . . . creates the necessity for a 'code' or 'system' among the younger generation, much like the code of Hemingway's characters, which makes possible for them a 'proper view' of chaos, a proper existentialist formula of casualness and flippancy for maintaining cynical control: because the situation is absurd, behave as if it were amusing" (131–32). In addition, William L. Nance makes two comparisons between Hemingway and Porter. First, he compares the "attitude of sensitive knowledgeability" of the "American fool" Kennerly of "Hacienda" to "the Hemingway stance" (52). In a more favorable comparison, he compares Porter's writing style to "the stylized understatement of Hemingway, to whose work hers bears some close resemblances" (213). Interesting, too, is Willene and George Hendrick's comment that, like Hemingway, Porter "became an aficionado [of bullfighting], drawn in fascination to the spectacle of death in the ring" (124).

2. William Nance also groups together protagonists of Porter's fiction who are comparable to Miranda in that they are "semiautobiographical or subjective" (5), and in his readings of Porter's stories he repeatedly points out the characteristics Miranda shares with these other protagonists. Gilchrist herself has said that Rhoda is autobiographically based (*FS* 152), and one can find autobiographical details in the characterizations of many of her other protagonists.

3. Jeanie Thompson and Anita Miller Garner have already made a brief com-

parison between works by Gilchrist and Porter. Referring to Gilchrist's LeLe Arnold of "Traveler," they write:

> Her gutsy actions are . . . reminiscent of Katherine Anne Porter's Miranda stories, stories in which the female characters gain more than petty desires and whims by their actions. What LeLe gains by swimming the lake has much in common with what Miranda's idol, Aunt Amy, gains by riding off to Mexico astride a horse in "Old Mortality." Just as Miranda's dull life is reshaped by this socially rebellious event, LeLe cannot forget when she returns to hum-drum Indiana how "the water turned into diamonds in [her] hands" that day. (103)

4. In the introduction to her collection, Magee alludes to both the positive and the negative sides I see in the relationship between the fiction of Gilchrist and Porter:

> To discuss the ways that women writers have flourished in the South is to pay tribute to their talent and determination and the relationships between them. . . . This heritage is one not lost to the writers of today as they write in a world more accepting of what they may have to offer and providing more opportunities for interaction but not always receptive to who they are. Southern women writers of the past and present in offering "friendship and sympathy" to one another transcend the boundaries of time and space, of rigid definitions of literature and life, and they bear witness to a vibrant literary unfolding. (xxvi)

5. In comparison, however, both authors began these novels as short stories. Porter's biographer Joan Givner traces the development of *Ship of Fools* from its beginning as a short story entitled "Promised Land" (256, 300, 310, 323, 328, 350). In the preface to *Net of Jewels*, Rhoda reports that she "meant this as a book of short stories and . . . started writing it that way. Then the stories started to bleed into each other" (*NJ* 3). Given Gilchrist's habit of having her characters talk about her own writing, as noted in chapter 2, it is probable that what Rhoda says about the novel's development from short stories is exactly what happened.

6. See Eils Lotozo's review in the *New York Times Book Review* (18), Ann G. Sjoerdsma's review in the *Washington Post* (C9), and Rhoda Koenig's review in *New York* (101). On the other hand, Barbette Timperlake, writing for the *School Library Journal* (151); Carol Anshaw, writing for the *Chicago Tribune* (6); and the reviewer for *Publishers Weekly* (rev. of *Net* 86) recognize Rhoda's lack of development to be consistent with the novel's statement about the society within which she is struggling to mature.

7. Mary A. McCay's volume on Gilchrist for the Twayne United States Authors Series is the only substantial source available on Gilchrist's biography (*Ellen* 4–19).

8. Porter had previously written and published some children's stories, but according to Joan Givner, "she designated ['María Concepción'] as her first" story (163).

9. Joan Givner discusses the genesis of "María Concepción" in her biography of

Porter (161–62). In an interview for the American Audio Prose Library, Gilchrist explained that "Rich" was motivated "by a rash of suicides in New Orleans. . . . All the darkness of these suicides rose up out of my unconscious mind and became one suicide, one terrible and desperate suicide" (Interview). This explanation of the source of "Rich" reveals again how Gilchrist's method of organizing memory into story is similar to Porter's. Robert H. Brinkmeyer explains of "Noon Wine," for example, that it "was not merely a reporting of events from her upbringing but instead was a recreation of a number of events and characters from her past that at that earlier time were unrelated" (141).

10. See Darlene Unrue's discussion of María Concepción's return to "primitive ways" in dealing with this crisis in her marriage despite her earlier pride in her Catholicism (*Truth* 17).

11. See my article on Gilchrist's New Orleans stories for a discussion of the other closing paragraphs ("Ellen" 95).

12. Janis Stout notes two of the same similarities between Thompson and Helton: "Helton kills his brother abruptly and apparently without warning on a hot day; Mr. Thompson suddenly and without thought kills Hatch on a day of 'almost unbearable' heat . . . Helton is a stranger in the land; Mr. Thompson, for all his family roots and his familiarity, becomes a stranger after his act of murder" (122). Stout also remarks upon how both Thompson (by Hatch) and Helton (by Thompson) are mistaken for Irishmen, a detail which is comparable to the mistaken belief voiced at the end of Gilchrist's story by the neighbors that Helen is Tom's illegitimate child.

13. Helen's dyslexia is as suspect as Tom's vision troubles, which are probably either psychosomatic or have something to do with his heavy drinking. Dyslexia seems in this context to be a vogue and acceptable explanation given to Helen's parents and community for the child's psychological problems. Indeed, the narrator defines dyslexia as "a complicated learning disability that is a fashionable problem with children in New Orleans" (*LDD* 10).

14. An echo can be heard in the names of these characters—Thompson/Tom and Helton/Helen—which supports the connection I perceive between these two stories.

15. Since I discuss parallels between Gilchrist's work and Kate Chopin's, particularly *The Awakening*, in chapter 5, it is interesting to note here that in Chopin's novel, Edna, too, is dismayed to realize the effect that being a nonconformist seems to have on one's demeanor, as evidenced by her repulsion for Mademoiselle Reisz.

16. Or grandmother (singular)—they might actually have the same grandmother, though this is not directly indicated. Both girls' grandmothers own a plantation in Mississippi named Esperanza. Amanda grew up there after her father's death in World War II. Rhoda visits there during the summer while her father is overseas during this same war. The two characters do not, however, appear in any works together, and when Amanda is mentioned in a later Rhoda story called "Joyce" (*AM* 161), no familial relationship is suggested. Perhaps more compelling than the notion that they are related is the possibility that they are different mani-

festations of the same character, as is suggested not only by their both spending summers on Esperanza but also by their both marrying men named Malcolm and both participating in the writing program at the University of Arkansas. I would still argue, however, that Amanda's character reflects evolution of the prototype, though not so much as does the characterization of Anna Hand, discussed in chapter 5.

17. Darlene Unrue also views the hole in the dove's breast as representative of heartlessness, though in a different way. She associates it with Miranda at the time of her visit to the grave site when, "without the awareness of her own mortality and the attendant suffering and appreciation for life that the awareness will bring, she exists in only an animal, or physical state. The silver dove . . . reflects at that early point in the story Miranda's own physical but 'heart-less' or 'spirit-less' existence" (*Truth* 50).

18. Again, one might note a comparison to Chopin's *The Awakening:* Edna sheds her clothes, the vestiges of civilization (as discussed in another context in chapter 5), just before taking her final swim. This parallel serves to undermine further the sense of Rhoda's triumph since Edna's last swim ends in her death.

19. In terms similar to this mixture of victory and defeat, Barbara Harrell Carson compares "the painful victory of the old mare" in "Old Mortality" to "the victories of the human females in Porter's Miranda stories. For them, too, triumph and defeat are virtually indistinguishable" (239).

20. In several of the stories in *The Age of Miracles,* Rhoda comments on the confines of motherhood. She reports in "Love of My Life" that some unknown "*They* had tried to kill me with the babies. They had tried to ruin and kill me and make me ugly" (*AM* 221, emphasis added). At that point in her life, separated from her first husband and living near her parents, with whom she can leave her children when she wants to do something, she feels she has "outwitted [this unknown] them" (*AM* 221). Later, though, remarried and in her thirties, she no longer seems to think so: in "The Stucco House," her new husband Eric reveals her frustration to the reader when he reads from her daybook, "I'll never be a painter. . . . All I am is a mother and a wife" (*AM* 118); and in "Going to Join the Poets," she tells him directly, "I have to have my turn. I never had a turn. . . . All I had were babies" (*AM* 260).

21. Although Amanda McCamey's Jewish husband Malcolm is reported to have been a generous and devoted husband—"He had never done an unkind thing to her. He had never told her a lie or denied her anything he had the power to give her or threatened or broken a promise to her. For years he had devoted himself to Amanda morning night and noon whether she wanted him to or not" (*A* 62)—this point of characterization is undermined not only by its implication that he is crowding his wife but also by a comment that soon follows this description of his treatment of her, a comment that destroys the reader's trust in him: "He was very wealthy. He could buy anything he wanted, even a wild Christian girl from Mississippi" (*A* 63). Ultimately, then, Malcolm is viewed as an antagonist to the more sympathetic Amanda. Thus, he joins Gilchrist's other rather "unlikable

Jews." One might be further disturbed by the narrator's emphasis upon the fact that Malcolm is Jewish during the description of the couple's brief courtship. The narrator's tone, along with this emphasis, leaves the reader feeling certain that the marriage will not last—though not certain why, except that Malcolm's being Jewish is part of the reason: as though his ethnicity is metaphorically indicative of the irreconcilable differences between him and Amanda.

22. One exception is David Sexton, who, in his review of *Victory over Japan*, does express his disappointment that Traceleen "is reduced to narrative servant" in the stories she tells about her employer (573). More recently, Jerry W. Ward, Jr., discussing the difference between Gilchrist's perspective on the South (as a white woman writing) and his own (as a black man reading), points out that he finds in her fiction "stereotypes of the Chinese, the Jews, and Southern blacks (perpetuating myths of kindness, innocence, and sexuality)" (49).

23. One could also turn to "The Old Order" for further evidence against racism in Porter's fiction. In the sketch entitled "The Journey," Sophia Jane rebukes Nannie for her fears that God, too, might be prejudiced: "Nonsense! I tell you, God does not know whether a skin is black or white. He sees only souls. Don't be getting notions, Nannie—of course you're going to Heaven" (*CS* 336). Perhaps the best analysis of the subject of racism in Porter's fiction is a paper read by Cheryl Cunningham at the Northeast Modern Language Association's 1993 convention (see bibliography for complete citation).

24. On the other hand, as Betty A. Matthews points out, Gilchrist's "interracial pairings do not appear to be an effort on the part of the author to validate the Civil Rights Movement" either (74). Matthews believes that Gilchrist "simply perceived herself to be telling another part of the truth about the South, a truth ignored, despised, and frequently denied" (74).

25. Guttenplan responds to this passage after admitting that he does not ultimately think Gilchrist is a racist—"at least no more than the rest of us" (54). He remarks that "the whole topic made [him] uncomfortable" and that this "may well have been [Gilchrist's] intention," with which point I would agree. Hence, in spite of his criticism of her placement of the two stories depicting violence in mixed marriages, he concludes that the problem was more his own than a flaw in the collection.

26. In the novella "Summer in Maine" in *I Cannot Get You Close Enough*, Crystal's friend Lydia reports that "Crystal was so sick after Crystal Anne's birth [that] Traceleen nursed [Crystal Anne] for the first few months of her life" (*IC* 287). It is interesting to note the reversal of this situation in Porter's story: Sophia Jane, impervious to scandal, insists upon being *wet*nurse to Nannie's fourth child herself while Nannie recovers from puerperal fever.

27. See, in particular, "Miss Crystal's Maid Name Traceleen, She's Talking, She's Telling Everything She Knows" in *Victory over Japan* and "Traceleen at Dawn" in *Drunk with Love*. In light of events in the first of these—Crystal's husband pushes her down a staircase for flirting with a younger man—it is interesting

to note that according to the petition filed by Porter asking for a divorce from her first husband John Koontz (which he countersigned), Koontz threw his wife down some stairs. Joan Givner remarks that before accepting as actual fact this and the other statements of violence against Porter made in the petition, "allowance must be made for the fact that some exaggeration may have been necessary to expedite the legal proceedings, since divorce at that time would not have been granted on slender grounds" (91). However, Mrs. Treadwell of *Ship of Fools,* whom critics, including Givner, have noted to be somewhat autobiographical, has been abused by her husband. Mrs. Treadwell's disappointment with how her experience of love has not measured up to her romantic expectations is similar to Crystal's disappointment with each of her husbands and lovers. Furthermore, Mrs. Treadwell's flirtation with the young ship's officer is comparable to Crystal's flirtation in this story with a younger man—which enrages her husband and thus results in her "accident." Porter also has another character who is disappointed in marriage and attracted to younger men—Rosaleen of "The Cracked Looking-Glass." Similarly, several other Gilchrist characters have affairs with younger men.

4. *The Annunciation* as a Dialogue with William Faulkner: Giving Caddy Compson a Fighting Chance

1. Also seeing a comparison between Gilchrist's work and Faulkner's, and also implying that Gilchrist rewrites Faulkner, Frances Taliaferro points out that Amanda's departure from the Delta is a "goodbye to Faulknerian romance" (76). According to Taliaferro, Gilchrist's heroine "will no longer be exploited by those who would turn her into a Southern fiction and deprive her of her child, her brains, and her spunk." Rosellen Brown points out similarly that "Amanda will survive by grit and shamelessness. . . . Three men are sacrificed along the way, but the belle of Issaquena County . . . prevails" (53), a fact of the novel that brings up another point of comparison as well as contrast with *The Sound and the Fury:* in Faulkner's novel three men—Caddy's brothers—sacrifice (rather than are sacrificed by) the belle of Yoknapatawpha County.

2. Her criticism thereby anticipates the criticism of the heroine of Gilchrist's second novel, *The Anna Papers,* discussed in the next chapter.

3. In her review of Gilchrist's novel, Frances Taliaferro is perhaps alluding to this parallel when she writes, "Readers of the School of Faulkner will recognize the McCamey plantation in the Mississippi Delta; the old family retainers; the bayou, the bridge, the river, the levee, the flat delta farmlands, and the cotton gin; and the star-crossed cousins, Amanda and Guy, whose childish love turns carnal when Amanda is fourteen and Guy makes her pregnant" (76).

4. Gilchrist remarks on this common phenomenon of "the fate of the strong . . . be[ing] the prey of the weak or unhealthy" in her later novel, *Sarah Conley:* "Of course they gravitate to you and want to latch on to you," the protagonist/title character of that novel is warned, to which she responds, "How do I protect myself? . . . One can't just leave the world and not love people" (*SC* 151). Her

analyst then advises, "You keep the proper distance. . . . That is more difficult than it seems because they are always thinking about you. Devising ways to move into your sphere, to get closer, to make you guilty" (*SC* 151).

5. Since I read a portion of this chapter at the Mississippi Philological Association Annual Meeting in Jackson, Mississippi, in 1989, Betty A. Matthews has briefly noted in her article on Gilchrist's women the similarity between these two pairs and their incestuous relationships (70–71).

6. The list of marriages declared incestuous by Mississippi Code 93–1–1, which law was in effect at the time this part of the novel is set (post–World War II), includes first cousins: "nor shall the children of brother or sister, or brothers and sisters intermarry being first cousins by blood" (*Mississippi Code* 1972, vol. 20, p. 268). Mississippi Code 97–29–5, then, remarks upon the criminality of sexual relations between "persons being within the degrees within which marriages are prohibited by law to be incestuous" (vol. 21, 256–57). Therefore, according to Mississippi law, it is accurate to refer to the sexual relationship between Amanda and Guy as incestuous.

7. André Bleikasten is in apparent agreement with Thompson's notion, for he writes that because of the name Caddy chooses for her child, "symbolically, Quentin II is . . . the fruit of the imaginary incest" (224).

8. John Irwin points out that Quentin's narcissistic view of Caddy is particularly evident in a scene in which Quentin looks down upon Caddy lying in the water: "The narcissistic implication is that his sister lying on her back in the stream is like a mirror image of himself" (*Doubling* 41).

9. Charles Stubblefield describes Amanda and Guy's lovemaking as "natural and free and open" and remarks that "the harm comes not in the love, but in the aftermath of it and what is done to Amanda as a result of it" (109).

10. Later, she may find further corroboration of this view that she must pay for her past actions when she is unable to conceive during her marriage to Malcolm. Then, when Guy tells her he wants to find their child, her response implies that she believes in some kind of retribution, "*Don't talk about it.* There's something terrible about it. She's blind or crippled or dead. Or she'll come for me and kill me for deserting her" (*A* 57). She repeats this belief in the child paying for the sins of the, in this case, mother when Guy reports to her later that he has seen their daughter: "She's blind, isn't she? I know she's blind. I've always known she would be blind" (*A* 286).

11. Apparently, Guy's deal with God has expired. The reader is no more surprised than Amanda appears to be, it being weak in the first place. Although he would not have intercourse with her when he visited in college, he saw no problem with either fondling or oral sex. One finds it difficult to take such hypocrisy seriously. Guy's reasoning about this matter is as ridiculous as Quentin's apparent determination that he, Caddy's brother but an aristocrat, would be a better sexual partner than Dalton Ames, whom Quentin would consider poor white trash, or that Caddy would be better off running off with her brother, a gentleman, than marrying "that blackguard" Herbert Head.

12. Melvin Backman also writes about Mrs. Compson's responsibility for her children's incestuous relationship. He believes that the "complex brother-sister relationship [between Quentin and Caddy] had its roots in their childhood and in the negativity of their mother. . . . Incapable of love, sacrifice, or charity, [Mrs. Compson] failed her family as a mother. For the love she did not provide, Quentin turned to his sister. But the love that grew between brother and sister was subject to invasion by sex" (18).

13. Although I believe that Mrs. Compson's neglect of her children leads to their unhealthy relationships with each other, I do not disagree with recent feminist critics who defend Mrs. Compson and point out that she, like Caddy, is presented from the perspective of others. Furthermore, one should not overlook Mr. Compson's responsibility for his dysfunctional family. I merely do not discuss his alcoholism and nihilism because it is not paralleled in *The Annunciation*—Amanda's father is deceased.

14. I develop this argument further in my article "'I have sinned in that I have betrayed the innocent blood': Quentin's Recognition of His Guilt."

15. Elizabeth M. Kerr might also agree with the view of Miss Quentin as the Christ figure, given her notion that Caddy's love for her daughter "might be the only means of saving Caddy" (11). One can also infer agreement with this argument from the connection Douglas B. Hill makes between Caddy and the Virgin Mary (35).

16. Karen Kaivola sees Miss Quentin's departure as a further reflection of the absence of the female voice in the novel. She notes that in the last section, which does not focus on Caddy and thus "suggest[s] that femininity is . . . lost" (38), Miss Quentin somewhat "fills the gap Caddy leaves, but she, too, is banished from the textual world—and the appendix holds out less hope for her than for Caddy" (39).

17. Another parallel can be seen here between Amanda's and Caddy's daughters. As Brian Morton points out in his review of Gilchrist's novel, "Mother and daughter, both poets, lead parallel lives, masking their emotional and artistic infertility in obsessive tasks, games and self-examinings" (368). Similarly, Miss Quentin's behavior echoes her mother's.

18. I refer here to the Rhett Butler in the novel as opposed to the movie. For a discussion of the evidence of Rhett's destruction by novel's end, a result of having lost his daughter and being repeatedly disappointed by his wife, see my article on *Gone with the Wind*, in which I also point out that, in contrast, Scarlett remains standing after losing many more loved ones, including the same daughter, and, after realizing it is Rhett she loves, him, as well ("'Put'" 175–77).

5. The Reincarnation of Kate Chopin's Edna Pontellier in *The Anna Papers*

1. I make this comparison between Gilchrist's Helen and Chopin's Désirée on the basis of my reading of "Désirée's Baby" (see bibliography for citation of my article in which this reading can be found), in which I argue that the lack of surprise or remorse shown by Armand as he burns every trace left of Désirée's existence, along with the letter from his mother to his father revealing his racial heri-

tage, are evidence that he knew of the letter all along and thus knew the truth of his parentage and chose a wife with that in mind: should his own racial heritage reveal itself in his progeny's features, he could blame his wife, whose parental heritage was a mystery to all. See my article on "Désirée's Baby," too, for a more complete explanation of society as the story's villain.

2. See Anne M. Blythe's reading of "Charlie," which refutes earlier readings of this story, particularly Per Seyersted's, that view the relationship between Charlie and her father as unhealthy, even incestuous (Blythe 206–7, 212–13).

3. See Gilchrist's Net of Jewels (77–78).

4. Rhoda leaves her first husband Malcolm in the short story "1957, a Romance," to get an abortion without his knowledge, and in the novel Net of Jewels several times (including the time she goes home to enlist her father's help in paying for that same abortion). She leaves a husband named Jody in the short story "The Lower Garden District Free Gravity Mule Blight or Rhoda, a Fable," in Victory over Japan. She leaves still another husband, Eric, to move to Fayetteville, Arkansas, in order to enroll in the creative writing graduate program at the university there (see "Joyce" and "Going to Join the Poets" in The Age of Miracles).

5. Similarly, Emily Toth argues that Chopin's "At Chênière Caminada" "was a preliminary sketch for The Awakening, with many of the same local characters, and much of the sensuous atmosphere: the sea and the sky, the power of love and the power of music, birds and water, love and death, and the magical atmosphere of [Grand Isle]" (60). Gilchrist, too, wrote short stories that seem to be the germs from which she developed her novels. For example, "There's a Garden of Eden" and "Summer, an Elegy" include elements that eventually found their way into The Annunciation.

6. Reviewer Clare O'Brien, in contrast to those quoted, praises Anna for "choos[ing] cyanide in preference to the lingering indignities of incurable disease" (32).

7. Although Anna's physical absence from but central role in the rest of her novel may remind the reader of Faulkner's Caddy Compson, a significant difference reminds the reader again of the discussion in chapter 4 of how, in The Annunciation, Gilchrist transforms Faulkner's novel into the story of a female central character (rather than of her effect on the men in her life). After Anna's death, The Anna Papers also continues to focus on its female characters, in particular, Anna's sister Helen and her niece Olivia.

8. Similarly, but more condemning in tone and not entirely accurate, Pat Ellis Taylor interprets Anna's cancer as a reflection of the fact that she is "so spoiled that when love is withheld from her for the first time she lets her obsession take over her body" (8). Actually, love is not withheld from Anna when she falls in love with a married man, as Taylor implies. In fact, her lover's marriage does not affect their relationship very much at all, as I discuss later.

9. Shirley Foster also argues that "in choosing to commit suicide [Edna] is making the ultimate bid for freedom. . . [Thus,] she dies . . . in control of her own actions" (168, emphasis added).

10. Eleanor Wymard argues similarly that "suicide is . . . the only way that the real Edna sees to attack the conforming Edna who has drained all of her creative potential" (384).

11. Gilbert even associates Edna with Aphrodite, a figure from Greek mythology, thereby, too, confirming the appropriateness of judging Edna's actions by ancient Greek standards.

12. As has been pointed out of Rhoda, Anna also has a problem with the cruelty of Christianity, as evidenced in her telling the nuns, "You should not have the girls kneel in the gravel at the Feast of Saint Mary. . . . It is not a good thing to do and hurt my knees so much and Helen cut hers" (*AP* 26). At this point, unlike Rhoda, who by about the same age has already rejected the Christian God, Anna still believes in Jesus. It is only Christianity with which she has a problem, as evidenced in her additional remarks to the nuns: "I do not believe that Jesus wanted children to cut their knees and there wasn't any gravel long ago when He lived. He put the names of flowers into the Bible. . . . You should concentrate on things like the flowers, not when He was nailed to the cross or kneeling in the gravel. The Stations of the Cross are terrible things to look at" (*AP* 26). Similarly, in "Perils of the Nile," the reader is told that Rhoda "didn't want anything to do with . . . people nailed up on crosses or eaten by lions or tortured by Romans" (*LDD* 134). And in *Net of Jewels*, as a young adult Rhoda remarks, "One of the things I hate about the church is that goddamn cross. Imagine worshipping an instrument of torture. Every time I see one of those things . . . I don't think about [Jesus] rising from the dead or any of that. I just think about him being nailed up there" (*NJ* 245).

13. James H. Justus argues, on the other hand, that Edna's awakening actually "begins . . . in childhood" (108), quoting the following passage from the novel to support his contention: "Even as a child she had lived her own small life all within herself. At a very early period she had apprehended instinctively the dual life—that outward existence which conforms, the inward life which questions" (*CW* 893). Such a reading would also support the view that Edna is the original prototype upon which Anna was created.

14. Although I must credit an article by George Arms for calling to my attention the amount of sleeping Edna does in the novel, my reading of the significance of her sleeping is quite different from his. Arms views Edna's sleeping as ironic, rather than symbolic: "It is almost as if the author were saying: here is my heroine who at the critical points of her progress toward an awakening constantly falls asleep" (219). Also addressing the amount of time Edna sleeps in the novel, James Justus argues that, indeed, it is symbolic, but symbolic of "The Unawakening of Edna Pontellier"—the title of his article. Sleeping, he explains, "is a state which neutralizes any determined struggle to construct a new self, or even to uncover deeper levels of the old one. In a fine touch of characterization [referring to Edna's sleeping], Kate Chopin never allows her protagonist to understand fully what it is she is awakening *to*" (119).

15. Similarly, Priscilla Allen reads Edna's "strong expression of the children's power over [Edna as] based on her knowledge that consideration for their future

could force her return to her husband's house, to his bed and board, to the oppression she has just escaped" (235). One might recall here previous references to stories in *The Age of Miracles* in which Rhoda feels oppressed by her children.

16. In an article comparing *The Awakening* and Atwood's *Surfacing*, Jeanee P. Sacken makes a similar point about Edna and Atwood's unnamed protagonist (as well as George Sand's Indiana of the novel named for the protagonist): "The effort to transform first their own lives and then perhaps the lives of those around them precipitates these heroines' flights from domesticity" (20).

17. As argued by Priscilla Allen, "her infidelities . . . make no difference to her as far as [Léonce] is concerned . . . but they would make a difference to her children" (237). Allen remarks upon how Edna takes her life soon after visiting them at her mother-in-law's home and finding that her sons "have no need of her; they are perfectly happy with their grandmother" (237). According to Allen, Edna realizes that "they have need only of her honor and good reputation, which she cannot give them without sacrificing daily her independence and full life" (237).

18. It is ironic that, after several miscarriages, Anna finally has something growing successfully inside of her—cancer. In her discussion of the pregnancy imagery used to describe the disease, Susan Sontag calls cancer "a fetus with its own will" (13).

19. See Jane Taylor McDonnell's similar reading of Anna's "appropriation of the lives of others" (189): "Anna . . . recover[s] a lost 'spiritual' daughter . . . and in the process . . . write[s] Olivia . . . back into the story of the Hand family"; later, she tries also to "write another competing mother [Jessie's] *out* of the Hand family history" (188).

20. See also Jane McDonnell's article on *The Anna Papers* for her discussion of Helen "becoming like Anna" (191) and Mary A. McCay's discussion of the effect of Anna's papers on Helen (*Ellen* 93–94).

21. Possibly. DeDe claims to be pregnant, but the reader is not sure whether to believe her or not. Although she "began to recite her problems" as soon as she answered her mother's call, she does not say she is pregnant until her mother asks her directly, "Are you pregnant?" (*AP* 262). Recalling Léonce's motivation for telling Edna that Raoul has a fever—that he is annoyed with Edna for failing to show any interest in his evening's adventures—one wonders if DeDe, too, sensing her mother's distraction, is just trying to get Helen's attention. On the other hand, DeDe is indeed pregnant in the later novel *Starcarbon*.

22. In this case, *The Annunciation*'s Amanda more directly echoes Edna when she tells Guy, "I don't want to be anyone's woman, yours or Malcolm's or anyone's. I want to find out what I really want in the world" (*A* 59). Like Edna, too, then, Amanda leaves her husband to pursue her art.

23. I must credit Dorothy H. Jacobs's article with pointing out to me Edna's regression in this scene when her "confidence about being no one's possession" and her desire for "a romantic future for her and Robert disappear in the urgency of her response to the exaggerated but nevertheless compelling entreaty of her female friend" (92). Jacobs concludes from this scene that "for *both* characters

[Edna as well as Robert], the assumption of a noble task results in devastating *personal* revelations" (92, emphasis added). Edna not only realizes that Robert is not so unlike Léonce as she had thought but also that she is not so unlike Adèle when it comes to fulfilling her "duties."

24. In further illustration of the composite personality in Gilchrist's fiction, this statement echoes Alisha in "There's a Garden of Eden," who muses to herself similarly about her new young lover: "This is the very last time I will ever love anyone. . . . I will love this boy until he leaves me. And then I will never love another human being" (*LDD* 47). Noting the difference between the two characters' similar comments provides support for my theory of the composite personality having evolved in the creation of Anna Hand. Anna's statement is made in assertion of her intention of continuing her affair, whereas Alisha's statement is reflective of a defeatist attitude: she is resigned to the probability that the affair will not last.

25. Martha Black's assessment of this realization is remarkably applicable to Gilchrist's earlier characters, particularly Rhoda, Crystal, and Nora Jane. Black argues that "because romantic ideals deluded her into desiring 'the acme of bliss' that equates love with sexual desires, and because reality taught her that erotic satisfaction can be divorced from love, Edna is trapped by her delusion that without a man, she is incomplete" (111). Such is the delusion of Gilchrist's prototype, though as this prototype evolves—into such characters as Amanda McCamey and ultimately Anna Hand—Gilchrist has them recognize their value as autonomous individuals.

26. Carole Stone argues similarly: "Edna drowns herself because she cannot live as a conventional wife or mother any longer, and society will not accept her newfound self. The solitude she enjoys makes for artistic growth, but she is bound to children, home, social duty. She will not sacrifice her new autonomy" (30).

27. On the other hand, as John Carlos Rowe argues, "Edna's room of her own [also] represents . . . the confinement of a yearning spirit" (137), in that it is acquired from income "derive[d] from the patriarchy she flees" (136). He recalls, for example, that Edna's father is in control of the money her mother left her and that he only hands it out to her "by driblets" (*CW* 963). Thus, her elation with this house, as well as her party celebrating her departure from Léonce's—the bills for which, she admits, Léonce will pay—are both as mistakenly felt as is the elation Gilchrist's Rhoda Manning feels upon getting her abortion, which was paid for by her father and which may free her somewhat from her husband but binds her more closely to her father.

28. Deborah E. Barker argues that Adèle may not have been satisfied with the portrait because it was not "a realistic depiction" of her and, "given the emphasis on realistic art in the mid-nineteenth century, Adèle [would] assum[e] that the painting should resemble her" (66). Barker proceeds with a provocative discussion of what artistic talent Edna's portrait of Adèle might actually have exhibited (66–68).

29. As Mary Jane Lupton argues, "it must be recognized that . . . [Edna's] self-

destruction is partly a response to being rejected by Robert, whom she loves" (97).

30. Martha Black develops further the significant differences between Emma and Edna and their deaths: "Chopin's heroine, a sensuous, intelligent American refinement on Emma, was perhaps even more disturbing because she more clearly chose her fate, thus raising the issue of a person's right to control her own life and even choose her own death" (99). Similarly, almost a century later, the American public still has a problem with the individual assuming such control, as indicated by the negative responses to Gilchrist's fictional Anna Hand for committing suicide rather than seeking treatment for her cancer, as well as by the legal action against Dr. Jack Kevorkian, commonly referred to as "the suicide doctor," who helps real people with terminal illnesses to commit suicide.

31. The "quick vision of death" Edna perceives as she gauges "the stretch of water" between herself and the shore, which suddenly "assume[s] the aspect of a barrier which her unaided strength would never be able to overcome" (CW 908), is comparable to the near-drowning experience of Gilchrist's Amanda McCamey in *The Annunciation*. Though she has been swimming since she was a child, tossed from a canoe into a rushing river, Amanda "had never known such helplessness" (A 245). Similar to Edna's "quick vision of death," Amanda thinks, "This is what it is to die" (A 246). Also like Edna, Amanda emerges from the water an awakened woman, ready to start life over again, to make up for the past by doing what she wants to do in the present. Therefore, as previously suggested about Anna's sister Helen, Amanda can also be viewed as a step in the evolution from Edna to Anna.

32. In addition, just as Edna also begins to apply herself more seriously to her painting at this point, Anna spends the next few months working on a new book.

33. In agreement with this reading, Marco A. Portales remarks that "Edna goes for a swim with the intention of returning for supper.... Like all her previous acts, one act [swimming] simply leads to another [suicide]" (435). As suggested to me in a discussion with Mary E. Papke, however, it is also possible that Edna asks Victor about dinner in order to make her suicide appear to be an accident so as to protect her children from shame.

6. No Conclusion Possible: An Organic Story Cycle

1. Gilchrist uses this passage as the epigraph to *Light Can Be Both Wave and Particle*.

2. I do not include the novel *Anabasis* in this list and only mention it in concluding this chapter, since it is a historical novel set in ancient Greece, thus a departure into a new realm, and therefore a subject for a study of her entire canon, including her poetry. I have also left *Rhoda, A Life in Stories* out of this list, since all but two of the stories within it are reprints from the earlier collections. This collection is, however, discussed at the end of this chapter.

3. In "Music," she loses her virginity to a boy who "had set out to fuck the boss's daughter" (VJ 47). In "The Lower Garden District Free Gravity Mule Blight or Rhoda, a Fable" (also in *Victory over Japan*), the black man with whom she is planning to have an affair lies to her about not being married. In *Net of Jewels*, she has

an affair, first, with the shallow husband of a friend and, second, with a doctor who will, in turn, give her the name of an abortionist. In later-published Rhoda stories of *The Age of Miracles*, the pattern continues: her young lover during her first year in graduate school turns on her after she has published a story (in "Joyce"), and the man she considers the "Love of My Life" (title of story) lies to her repeatedly in order to continue their affair. Of course, in each of these cases, Rhoda freely puts herself in the position of being used; still, the reader sympathizes with a woman with such low self-esteem that she needs this kind of validation of her desirability.

4. Like Bob, another character in this volume will survive cancer: the protagonist of "The Man Who Kicked Cancer's Ass." Although this story is not connected to any of the others in *Light Can Be Both Wave and Particle*, it is part of the story cycle of the volume and part of Gilchrist's evolving story cycle due to its employment of the cancer motif. Like Anna, this character does not allow cancer to stop him from living. He does not, however, commit suicide; rather, when he leaves the hospital after treatment, he picks up his life at the point where he left it, refusing to live as an invalid.

5. Rhoda, too, winds up in Fayetteville, Arkansas, in the stories in *The Age of Miracles*. She goes there when she is in her thirties to study writing; later in her life, as indicated by some of the other stories in that collection, she settles there, at which time she shows evidence of having matured. Thus, in these later Rhoda stories, she seems finally to be developing toward the character of Anna Hand.

6. In "Love of My Life," Rhoda, too, realizes that one of her lovers reminds her of her father: "My father was that strong. His shoulders were that powerful, that wide, that still. Maybe this man was my father to the tenth power" (*AM* 226). The difference between this recognition and Margaret's questioning her attraction to Lin Tan Sing is that Rhoda merely notes this comparison and continues her affair with this man who repeatedly deceives and hurts her. Also, the reader gets no sense of the insight that Anna has when she admits to the connection between her lovers and her father.

7. Rhoda reports in *Net of Jewels* that one of the topics of discussion on her father's porch each evening is "how soon it would be before the niggers took us over" (*NJ* 30). His view of civil rights is that "now the niggers will be all over us. . . . They'll take us over. They'll mongrelize the races. . . . You turn the niggers loose and the women will be right behind them" (*NJ* 233).

8. In an essay for *Southern Magazine*, Gilchrist writes of a trip she took with a man she refers to as the Trout Fisherman to find the source of the White River. Before making the trip, Gilchrist realized that they would have to drive on the same mountain road "where [she] once killed a character named Will Lyons in a novel called *The Annunciation*" ("White" 65–66). She continues, "The character was based on the Trout Fisherman, and I meant the death to be a reckless driving warning to a lot of wild boys I knew, but all it did was confuse and sadden my readers and make the Trout Fisherman stop speaking to me for several months" ("White" 66). This reference to her novel may explain her motivation for later rewriting this part of the ending.

9. She does not go through with this plan, however, at least not by the end of the novel *Starcarbon*, which picks up about where these novellas leave off.

10. On the other hand, this depiction of Helen is somewhat undermined by the fact that she is portrayed from the point of view of other characters, who do not approve of her leaving her husband and children to pursue this man.

11. One cannot dismiss the events of the earlier story as an example of Gilchrist rewriting a character, for in "Summer in Maine" Crystal's friend Lydia recalls a letter Crystal wrote her several years before, in which she told Lydia, "Manny threw me down the stairs. Give this to me if he tries to tell me how much he loves me" (*IC* 333).

12. Though much briefer, Anna's section is reminiscent of Addie Bundren's section in Faulkner's *As I Lay Dying:* she is dead and she speaks only this once, and like Addie's, Anna's section sums up the central conflicts of the book. This similarity to *As I Lay Dying* is not surprising given the structure of this novella, which is reminiscent of *As I Lay Dying:* the chapters are divided into sections, each beginning with the name of the person whose point of view will follow.

APPENDIX

The following is a list of the criticism published thus far on Ellen Gilchrist, including entries in reference books but not including reviews and interviews, which, if cited within this study, are listed in the bibliography. Those articles cited within the preceding chapters are listed in both this appendix and the bibliography.

Bain, Robert. "Ellen Gilchrist." In *Contemporary Fiction Writers of the South: A Bio-Bibliographical Sourcebook*. Ed. Joseph M. Flora and Robert Bain. Westport, Conn.: Greenwood Press, 1993. 169–84.

Bauer, Margaret D. "Ellen Gilchrist's False Eden: The New Orleans Stories of *In the Land of Dreamy Dreams*." *Xavier Review* (1996): 88–107.

———. "The Evolution of Caddy: An Intertextual Reading of *The Sound and the Fury* and Ellen Gilchrist's *The Annunciation*." *Southern Literary Journal* 25.1 (1992): 40–51.

———. "Traveler" by Ellen Gilchrist. In *Masterplots II: Short Story, Supplement*. Pasadena: Salem Press, 1996. 4212–14.

———. *Victory over Japan* by Ellen Gilchrist. In *Masterplots II: Women's Literature*. Ed. Frank N. Magill. Pasadena: Salem Press, 1995. 2409–12.

———. "Water and Women: Ellen Gilchrist Explores Two Life Sources." *Louisiana Literature* 7.2 (1990): 82–90.

Bolsterli, Margaret Jones. "Ellen Gilchrist's Characters and the Southern Woman's Experience: Rhoda Manning's Double Bind and Anna Hand's Creativity." *New Orleans Review* 15.1 (1988): 7–9.

Cobb, James C. *The Most Southern Place on Earth: The Mississippi Delta and Roots of Regional Identity*. New York: Oxford University Press, 1992.

Darden, Donna Kelleher. "Southern Women Writing about Southern Women: Jill McCorkle, Lisa Alther, Gail Godwin, Ellen Gilchrist, and Lee Smith." In *Southern Women*. Ed. Caroline Matheny Dillman. New York: Hemisphere Publishing Corporation, 1988. 215–21.

"Ellen Gilchrist's and Clifton Taulbert's Portrayals of Glen Allan." *Notes on Mississippi Writers* 24.2 (1992): 59–65.

Johnson, Tonya Stremlau. "Ellen Gilchrist's Rhoda: Managing the Fiction." *Southern Quarterly* 35.4 (1997): 87–96.

LaRue, Dorie. "Progress and Prescription: Ellen Gilchrist's Southern Belles." *Southern Quarterly* 31.3 (1993): 69–78.

Matthews, Betty A. "The Southern Belle Revisited: Women in the Fiction of Ellen Gilchrist." *Publications of the Arkansas Philological Association* 16 (1990): 63–81.

McCay, Mary A. *Ellen Gilchrist.* Twayne United States Authors Series 690. Boston: Twayne Publishers, 1990.

McDonnell, Jane Taylor. "Controlling the Past and the Future: Two-Headed Anna in Ellen Gilchrist's *The Anna Papers.*" In *The Anna Book: Searching for Anna in Literary History.* Ed. Mickey Pearlman. New York: Greenwood Press, 1992. 187–93.

Riddel, Maria del Carmen. "El suicidio incidente estructurante en la narrativa feminina contemporanea: Presente profundo de Elena Quiroga y *The Anna Papers* de Ellen Gilchrist." In *Literatura feminina contemporanea de Espana.* Ed. Juana Arancibia, Adrienne Mandel, and Yolanda Rosas. Westminster, Calif.: Inst. Literario y Cultural Hispanico, 1991. 139–48.

Thompson, Jeanie, and Anita Miller Garner. "The Miracle of Realism: The Bid for Self-Knowledge in the Fiction of Ellen Gilchrist." *Southern Quarterly* 22.1 (1983): 100–114. Rept. in *Women Writers of the Contemporary South.* Ed. Peggy Whitman Prenshaw. Jackson: University Press of Mississippi, 1984. 233–48.

Wagner-Martin, Linda. "*The Anna (Aspern) Papers.*" *Notes on Contemporary Literature* 21.1 (1991): 2.

Ward, Jerry W., Jr. "Voices: Racial Reading." *Southern Exposure* 22.2 (1994): 47–49.

Woodland, J. Randal. "'New People in the Old Museum of New Orleans': Ellen Gilchrist, Sheila Bosworth, and Nancy Lemann." In *Louisiana Women Writers: New Essays and a Comprehensive Bibliography.* Ed. Dorothy H. Brown and Barbara C. Ewell. Southern Literary Studies Series. Baton Rouge: Louisiana State University Press, 1992. 193–210.

BIBLIOGRAPHY

Rev. of *The Age of Miracles. Publishers Weekly* 13 Mar. 1995: 58–59.

Allen, Priscilla. "Old Critics and New: The Treatment of Chopin's *The Awakening*." In *The Authority of Experience: Essays in Feminist Criticism*. Ed. Arlyn Diamond and Lee R. Edwards. Amherst: University of Massachusetts Press, 1977. 224–38.

Alvarez, A. *The Savage God: A Study of Suicide*. London: Weidenfeld, 1971.

Rev. of *Anabasis: A Journey to the Interior. Kirkus Reviews* 1 July 1994: 867–68.

———. *Publishers Weekly* 8 Aug. 1994: 382.

Rev. of *The Anna Papers. Kirkus Reviews* 15 Aug. 1988: 1175–76.

———. *Publishers Weekly* 12 Aug. 1988: 439–40.

Anshaw, Carol. "An Ellen Gilchrist Heroine, Lost in the Mid-1950s' South." Rev. of *Net of Jewels. Chicago Tribune* 29 Mar. 1992, sec. 14: 6.

Arms, George. "Kate Chopin's *The Awakening* in the Perspective of Her Literary Career." In *Essays on American Literature in Honor of Jay B. Hubbell*. Ed. Clarence Gohdes. Durham: Duke University Press, 1967. 215–28.

Arthos, John. "Ritual and Humor in the Writing of William Faulkner." *Accent* 9 (1948): 17–30.

Atwood, Margaret. *Surfacing*. New York: Popular Library, 1972.

Auden, W. H. *Collected Poems of W. H. Auden*. Ed. Edward Mendelson. New York: Random House, 1940.

Rev. of *The Awakening. Nation* 31 Aug. 1899: 96.

Backman, Melvin. *Faulkner, the Major Years: A Critical Study*. Bloomington: Indiana University Press, 1966.

Bakhtin, M. M. *The Dialogic Imagination: Four Essays*. Ed. Michael Holquist. Austin: University of Texas Press, 1981.

Barker, Deborah E. "The Awakening of Female Artistry." In Boren and Davis. 61–79.

Barthes, Roland. *The Rustle of Language*. Trans. Richard Howard. New York: Hill and Wang, 1986.

Bassett, John Earl. "Family Conflict in *The Sound and the Fury*." *Studies in American Fiction* 9 (1981): 1–20.

Batten, Wayne. "Illusion and Archetype: The Curious Story of Edna Pontellier." *Southern Literary Journal* 18.1 (1985): 73–88.

Bauer, Margaret D. "Armand Aubigny, Still Passing After All These Years: The Narrative Voice and Historical Context of 'Désirée's Baby'." In *Critical Essays on Kate Chopin.* Ed. Alice Hall Petry. New York: G. K. Hall and Company, 1996. 161–83.

———. "Ellen Gilchrist's False Eden: The New Orleans Stories of *In the Land of Dreamy Dreams." Xavier Review* (1996): 88–107.

———. "'I have sinned in that I have betrayed the innocent blood': Quentin's Recognition of His Guilt." *Southern Literary Journal* 32.1 (1999): forthcoming.

———. "'Put Your Heart in the Land': An Intertextual Reading of *Barren Ground* and *Gone with the Wind." In Ellen Glasgow: New Perspectives.* Ed. Dorothy M. Scura. Tennessee Studies in Literature series 36. Knoxville: University of Tennessee, 1995. 162–82.

———. "Water and Women: Ellen Gilchrist Explores Two Life Sources." *Louisiana Literature* 7.2 (1990): 82–90.

Baum, Catherine B. "The Beautiful One: Caddy Compson as Heroine of *The Sound and the Fury." Modern Fiction Studies* 13 (1967): 33–44.

Bedford, Sybille. "Voyage to Everywhere." Rev. of *Ship of Fools. Spectator* 16 Nov. 1962. 763–64.

Benson, Jackson J. "Patterns of Connection and Their Development in Hemingway's *In Our Time." In Critical Essays on Ernest Hemingway's In Our Time.* Ed. Michael S. Reynolds. Boston: G. K. Hall and Company, 1983. 103–19.

Black, Martha Fodaski. "The Quintessence of Chopinism." In Boren and Davis. 95–113.

Bleikasten, André. *The Most Splendid Failure: Faulkner's The Sound and the Fury.* Bloomington: Indiana University Press, 1976.

Blythe, Anne M. "Kate Chopin's 'Charlie'." In Boren and Davis. 207–15.

Boren, Lynda S., and Sara deSaussure Davis, eds. *Kate Chopin Reconsidered: Beyond the Bayou.* Southern Literary Studies Series. Baton Rouge: Louisiana State University Press, 1992.

Bosworth, Sheila. Rev. of *Starcarbon. Gambit* [New Orleans] 24 May 1994: 19.

Bowling, Lawrence E. "Faulkner and the Theme of Innocence." *Kenyon Review* 20 (1958): 466–87.

Brinkmeyer, Robert H., Jr. *Katherine Anne Porter's Artistic Development: Primitivism, Traditionalism, and Totalitarianism.* Baton Rouge: Louisiana State University Press, 1993.

Broughton, Trev. "Too Many Hands." Rev. of *Starcarbon, a Meditation on Love. Times Literary Supplement* 1 July 1994: 21.

Brown, Georgia. "Look at Me! The Writer as Flasher." Rev. of *The Anna Papers. Mother Jones* Dec. 1988: 46–47.

Brown, Rosellen. "Coming up Short." Rev. of *The Annunciation. Saturday Review* July–Aug. 1982: 53–54.

Burhans, Clinton S. "The Complex Unity of *In Our Time." In Critical Essays on*

Ernest Hemingway's In Our Time. Ed. Michael S. Reynolds. Boston: G. K. Hall and Company, 1983. 88–102.

Carper, Leslie. "Deep South, Deep Roots." Rev. of *Victory over Japan. Women's Review of Books* June 1985: 4–5.

Carson, Barbara Harrell. "Winning: Katherine Anne Porter's Women." In *The Authority of Experience: Essays in Feminist Criticism.* Ed. Arlyn Diamond and Lee R. Edwards. Amherst: University of Massachusetts Press, 1977.

Childress, Mark. "Books about the South." Rev. of *In the Land of Dreamy Dreams. Southern Living* Aug. 1982: 60.

Chopin, Kate. *The Complete Works of Kate Chopin.* Ed. Per Seyersted. Baton Rouge: Louisiana State University Press, 1969.

Christ, Carol P. *Diving Deep and Surfacing: Women Writers on Spiritual Quest.* Boston: Beacon Press, 1980.

Clayton, Jay, and Eric Rothstein. "Figures in the Corpus: Theories of Influence and Intertextuality." In *Influence and Intertextuality in Literary History.* Ed. Jay Clayton and Eric Rothstein. Madison: University of Wisconsin Press, 1991. 3–36.

Comley, Nancy R., and Robert Scholes. *Hemingway's Genders: Rereading the Hemingway Text.* New Haven: Yale University Press, 1994.

Cowley, Malcolm. *The Faulkner-Cowley File: Letters and Memories, 1944–1962.* New York: Viking Press, 1966.

Culler, Jonathan. *The Pursuit of Signs: Semiotics, Literature, Deconstruction.* Ithaca: Cornell University Press, 1981.

Cunningham, Cheryl. "'I want the little monkey': Race and Katherine Anne Porter's *The Old Order*." Northeast Modern Language Association Conference. Philadelphia, 26 Mar. 1993.

Davis, Thulani. "Rednecks, Belles, and K Mart Gals: Southern Women Stake Their Claim." Rev. of *The Annunciation, Victory over Japan, In the Land of Dreamy Dreams* (as well as works by other writers). *Village Voice Literary Supplement* Feb. 1986: 10–13.

DeFalco, Joseph. *The Hero in Hemingway's Short Stories.* Pittsburgh: University of Pittsburgh Press, 1963.

DeMouy, Jane Krause. *Katherine Anne Porter's Women: The Eye of Her Fiction.* Austin: University of Texas Press, 1983.

Drabble, Margaret. *The Waterfall.* London: Weidenfield, 1969.

Duncan, Susan. Rev. of *The Age of Miracles. Southern Living* June 1995: 121.

Dunn, Maggie, and Ann Morris. *The Composite Novel: The Short Story Cycle in Transition.* Studies in Literary Themes and Genres Series. New York: Twayne Publishers, 1995.

Eliot, T. S. *Selected Prose of T. S. Eliot.* Ed. Frank Kermode. New York: Farrar, Straus and Giroux, 1975.

Faulkner, William. *The Portable Faulkner.* 1946. Ed. Malcolm Cowley. Rev. and exp. ed. New York: Viking Press, 1967.

———. *Requiem for a Nun.* New York: Random House, 1951.

———. *The Sound and the Fury.* 1929. New, corrected ed. New York: Random House, 1984.

Felber, Lynette. *Gender and Genre in Novels without End: The British Roman-Fleuve.* Gainesville: University of Florida Press, 1995.

Ferguson, Sarah. Rev. of *Starcarbon, a Meditation on Love. New York Times Book Review* 19 June 1994. 33.

Flora, Joseph M. *Ernest Hemingway: A Study of the Short Fiction.* Twayne Studies in Short Fiction Ser. 11. Boston: Twayne Publishers, 1989.

———. *Hemingway's Nick Adams.* Baton Rouge: Louisiana State University Press, 1982.

Foster, Shirley. "The Open Cage: Freedom, Marriage and the Heroine in Early Twentieth-Century American Women's Novels." In *Women's Writing: A Challenge to Theory.* Ed. Moira Monteith. Sussex: Harvester Press, 1986. 154–74.

Fowler, Doreen. "The Ravished Daughter: Eleusinian Mysteries in *The Sound and the Fury.*" In *Faulkner and Religion.* Ed. Doreen Fowler and Ann J. Abadie. Proc. of Faulkner and Yoknapatawpha Conference, 1989. Jackson: University Press of Mississippi, 1991. 140–56.

Friedman, Susan Stanford. "Weavings: Intertextuality and the (Re)Birth of the Author." In Clayton and Rothstein. 146–80.

Frow, John. "Intertextuality and Ontology." In *Intertextuality: Theories and Practices.* Ed. Michael Worton and Judith Still. Manchester: Manchester University Press, 1990. 45–55.

Fryer, Judith. *The Faces of Eve: Women in the Nineteenth-Century American Novel.* New York: Oxford University Press, 1976.

Furman, Nelly. "Textual Feminism." In *Women and Language in Literature and Society.* Ed. Sally McConnell-Ginet, Ruth Borker, and Nelly Furman. New York: Praeger, 1980.

Gallagher, Susan. "To Love and to Honor: Brothers and Sisters in Faulkner's Yoknapatawpha County." *Essays in Literature* 7 (1980): 213–24.

Gilbert, Sandra M. "The Second Coming of Aphrodite: Kate Chopin's Fantasy of Desire." *Kenyon Review* 5.3 (1983): 42–56.

Gilchrist, Ellen. *The Age of Miracles.* Boston: Little, Brown and Company, 1995.

———. *Anabasis, a Journey to the Interior.* Jackson: University Press of Mississippi, 1994.

———. *The Anna Papers.* Boston: Little, Brown and Company, 1988.

———. *The Annunciation.* Boston: Little, Brown and Company, 1983.

———. *Drunk with Love.* Boston: Little, Brown and Company, 1986.

———. *Falling Through Space: The Journals of Ellen Gilchrist.* Boston: Little, Brown and Company, 1987.

———. *I Cannot Get You Close Enough: Three Novellas.* Boston: Little, Brown and Company, 1990.

———. *In the Land of Dreamy Dreams.* Fayetteville: University of Arkansas Press, 1981. Boston: Little, Brown and Company, 1985.

———. *The Land Surveyor's Daughter.* Fayetteville, Ark.: Lost Roads, 1979.

———. *Light Can Be Both Wave and Particle*. Boston: Little, Brown and Company, 1989.

———. *Net of Jewels*. Boston: Little, Brown and Company, 1992.

———. *Rhoda, a Life in Stories*. Boston: Little, Brown and Company, 1995.

———. *Riding Out the Tropical Depression: Selected Poems, 1975–1985*. New Orleans: Faust Publishing, 1986.

———. *Sarah Conley*. Boston: Little, Brown and Company, 1997.

———. *Starcarbon, a Meditation on Love*. Boston: Little, Brown and Company, 1994.

———. *Victory over Japan*. Boston: Little, Brown and Company, 1984.

———. "A White River Journal." *Southern Magazine* Mar. 1987: 64–67+.

Givner, Joan. *Katherine Anne Porter: A Life*. New York: Simon and Schuster, 1982.

Guttenplan, D. D. "Lie Down with Darkness." Rev. of *Drunk with Love*. *Village Voice* 27 Jan. 1987: 54.

Gwynn, Frederick L., and Joseph L. Blotner, eds. *Faulkner in the University: Class Conferences at the University of Virginia, 1957–1958*. Charlottesville: University of Virginia Press, 1959.

Hall, Constance Hill. *Incest in Faulkner: A Metaphor for the Fall*. Ann Arbor: UMI Research Press, 1983.

Hardy, John Edward. *Katherine Anne Porter*. Modern Literature Monographs. New York: Frederick Ungar Publishing Company, 1973.

———. "William Faulkner: The Legend behind the Legend." In *Man in the Modern Novel*. Ed. John Edward Hardy. Seattle: University of Washington Press, 1964. 137–58.

Heilbrun, Carolyn G. *Reinventing Womanhood*. New York: W. W. Norton and Company, 1979.

Helgesen, Sally. "Adventures in Dreamland: Ellen Gilchrist Lives It Up." Rev. of *In the Land of Dreamy Dreams*, *The Annunciation*, and *Victory over Japan*. *Village Voice* 1 Apr. 1986: 55.

Hemingway, Ernest. *Death in the Afternoon*. New York: Charles Scribner's Sons, 1932.

———. *In Our Time*. New York: Charles Scribner's Sons, 1925.

———. *Men without Women*. New York: Charles Scribner's Sons, 1927.

———. *A Moveable Feast*. New York: Charles Scribner's Sons, 1964.

———. *The Nick Adams Stories*. Ed. Philip Young. New York: Charles Scribner's Sons, 1972.

———. *Winner Take Nothing*. New York: Charles Scribner's Sons, 1932.

Hendrick, Willene, and George Hendrick. *Katherine Anne Porter*. Rev. ed. Twayne United States Authors Series 90. Boston: Twayne Publishers, 1988.

Hennessy, Rosemary. "Katherine Anne Porter's Model for Heroines." *Colorado Quarterly* 25 (1977): 301–15.

Hill, Douglas B. "Faulkner's Caddy." *Canadian Review of American Studies* 7 (1976): 26–38.

Hoffman, Frederick J. *The Art of Southern Fiction: A Study of Some Modern Novelists*. Carbondale: Southern Illinois University Press, 1967.

Hoffman, Roy. "Smart Enough for Their Own Good." Rev. of *Light Can Be Both Wave and Particle. New York Times Book Review* 22 Oct. 1989: 13.

Hovey, Richard B. *Hemingway: The Inward Terrain.* Seattle: University of Washington Press, 1968.

Interview with Ellen Gilchrist. Audiotape. American Audio Prose Library Series 6062, Feb. 1986.

Irwin, John T. *Doubling and Incest/Repetition and Revenge: A Speculative Reading of Faulkner.* Baltimore: Johns Hopkins University Press, 1975.

———. "Horace Benbow and the Myth of Narcissa." *American Literature* 64 (1992): 543–66.

Jacobs, Dorothy H. "*The Awakening:* A Recognition of Confinement." In Boren and Davis. 80–94.

Jenkins, Lee Clinton. *Faulkner and Black-White Relations: A Psycho-Analytical Approach.* New York: Columbia University Press, 1981.

Jenkins, Victoria. "Charmed Loves: Ellen Gilchrist's Tale of Privileged People and Safe Romance." Rev. of *Starcarbon. Chicago Tribune* 22 May, 1994, sec. 14: 5.

Johnston, Kenneth G. *The Tip of the Iceberg: Hemingway and the Short Story.* Greenwood, Fla.: Penkevill Publishing Company, 1987.

Jorgensen, Bruce W. "'The Other Side of Silence': Katherine Anne Porter's 'He' as Tragedy." In *Katherine Anne Porter.* Ed. Harold Bloom. Modern Critical Views. New York: Chelsea House, 1986. 107–15.

Joyce, Alice. Rev. of *Anabasis. Booklist* 1 Sept. 1994: 23.

Justus, James H. "The Unawakening of Edna Pontellier." *Southern Literary Journal* 10.2 (1978): 107–22.

Kaivola, Karen. "Becoming Woman: Identification and Desire in *The Sound and the Fury.*" *Reader* 17 (1987): 29–43.

Kerr, Elizabeth M. "William Faulkner and the Southern Concept of Woman." *Mississippi Quarterly* 15 (1962): 1–16.

Koenig, Rhoda. "Rosemary's Babies." Rev. of *Net of Jewels. New York* 6 Apr. 1992: 92+.

Kristeva, Julia. *Desire in Language: A Semiotic Approach to Literature and Art.* Ed. Leon S. Roudiez. New York: Columbia University Press, 1980.

Lattin, Patricia Hopkins. "Childbirth and Motherhood in *The Awakening* and in 'Athénaïse'." In *Approaches to Teaching Chopin's* The Awakening. Approaches to Teaching World Literature Series 16. New York: Modern Language Association of America, 1988. 40–46.

———. "Kate Chopin's Repeating Characters." *Mississippi Quarterly* 33 (1979–80): 19–37.

Leitch, Vincent B. *Deconstructive Criticism: An Advanced Introduction.* New York: Columbia University Press, 1983.

Liberman, M. M. *Katherine Anne Porter's Fiction.* Detroit: Wayne State University Press, 1971.

Rev. of *Light Can Be Both Wave and Particle. Kirkus Reviews* 1 Aug. 1989: 1095–96.

Lodge, David. *The Art of Fiction.* New York: Penguin, 1992.

Lotozo, Eils. Rev. of *Net of Jewels. New York Times Book Review* 12 Apr. 1992: 18.

Lowry, Beverly. "Redheaded Hellions in the Crape Myrtle." Rev. of *Victory over Japan. New York Times Book Review* 23 Sept. 1984: 18.

Lupton, Mary Jane. "Women Writers and Death by Drowning." In *Amid Visions and Revisions: Poetry and Criticism on Literature and the Arts.* Ed. Burney J. Hollis. Baltimore: Morgan State University Press, 1985. 95–101.

Lyons, Gene. "First Person Singular." Rev. of *Victory over Japan. Newsweek* 18 Feb. 1985: B81+.

Magee, Rosemary M. *Friendship and Sympathy: Communities of Southern Women Writers.* Jackson: University Press of Mississippi, 1992.

Mann, Susan Garland. *The Short Story Cycle: A Genre Companion and Reference Guide.* New York: Greenwood Press, 1989.

Matthews, Betty A. "The Southern Belle Revisited: Women in the Fiction of Ellen Gilchrist." *Publications of the Arkansas Philological Association* 16 (1990): 63–81.

McCay, Mary A. "Star-Struck: Ellen Gilchrist Writes a Passionate 'Meditation on Love'." Rev. of *Starcarbon. Times Picayune* [New Orleans] 1 May 1994: E8–9.

———. *Ellen Gilchrist.* Twayne United States Authors Series 690. Boston: Twayne Publishers, 1990.

McDonnell, Jane Taylor. "Controlling the Past and the Future: Two-Headed Anna in Ellen Gilchrist's *The Anna Papers.*" In *The Anna Book: Searching for Anna in Literary History.* Ed. Mickey Pearlman. New York: Greenwood Press, 1992. 187–93.

Moddelmog, Debra A. "Narrative Irony and Hidden Motivations in Katherine Anne Porter's 'He'." In *Katherine Anne Porter.* Ed. Harold Bloom. Modern Critical Views. New York: Chelsea House, 1986. 117–25.

———. "The Unifying Consciousness of a Divided Conscience: Nick Adams as Author of *In Our Time.*" In *New Critical Approaches to the Short Stories of Ernest Hemingway.* Ed. Jackson J. Benson. Durham: Duke University Press, 1990. 17–32.

Mooney, Harry J., Jr. *The Fiction and Criticism of Katherine Anne Porter.* Rev. ed. Critical Essays in Modern Literature Series. Pittsburgh: University of Pittsburgh Press, 1962.

Morgan, Thaïs. "The Space of Intertextuality." In *Intertextuality and Contemporary American Fiction.* Ed. Patrick O'Donnell and Robert Con Davis. Baltimore: Johns Hopkins University Press, 1989. 239–79.

Morton, Brian. "Southern Death." Rev. of *The Annunciation. Times Literary Supplement* 6 Apr. 1984: 368.

Nance, William L., S.M. *Katherine Anne Porter and the Art of Rejection.* Chapel Hill: University of North Carolina Press, 1963.

Rev. of *Net of Jewels. Publishers Weekly* 27 Jan. 1992: 86.

O'Brien, Clare. "Sweet as Nothing." Rev. of *The Anna Papers. Books* Oct. 1989: 32.

Page, Sally. *Faulkner's Women: Characterization and Meaning.* DeLand, Fla.: Everett–Edwards, 1972.

Paley, Maggie. "A Wake in Charlotte." Rev. of *The Anna Papers. New York Times Book Review* 15 Jan. 1989: 16.

Plottel, Jeanine Parisier. Introduction. *Intertextuality: New Perspectives in Criticism.* Ed. Jeanine Plottel and Hanna Charney. Spec. issue of *New York Literary Forum* 2 (1978): xi–xx.

Polk, Noel. Afterword. *Sanctuary: The Original Text.* By William Faulkner. Ed. Noel Polk. New York: Random House, 1981. 293–306.

Portales, Marco A. "The Characterization of Edna Pontellier and the Conclusion of Kate Chopin's *The Awakening.*" *Southern Studies* 20 (1981): 427–36.

Porter, Katherine Anne. *The Collected Essays and Occasional Writings of Katherine Anne Porter.* New York: Delacorte Press, 1970.

———. *The Collected Stories of Katherine Anne Porter.* New York: Harcourt Brace Jovanovich, 1965.

Powers, Lyall. *Faulkner's Yoknapatawpha Comedy.* Ann Arbor: University of Michigan Press, 1980.

Rajan, Tilottama. "Intertextuality and the Subject of Reading/Writing." In Clayton and Rothstein. 61–74.

Rankin, Daniel. *Kate Chopin and Her Creole Stories.* Philadelphia: University of Pennsylvania Press, 1932.

Rev. of *Rhoda, a Life in Stories. Publishers Weekly* 18 Sept. 1995: 124.

Rich, Adrienne. *On Lies, Secrets, and Silence: Selected Prose, 1966–1978.* New York: Warner, 1987.

Riffaterre, Michael. "Syllepsis." *Critical Inquiry* 6 (1980): 625–38.

Ringe, Donald A. "Romantic Imagery in Kate Chopin's *The Awakening.*" *American Literature* 43 (1972): 580–88.

Rowe, John Carlos. "The Economics of the Body in Kate Chopin's *The Awakening.*" In Boren and Davis. 117–42.

Sacken, Jeanee P. "George Sand, Kate Chopin, and Margaret Atwood, and the Redefinition of Self." *Postscript* 2 (1985): 19–28.

Seaman, Donna. Rev. of *The Age of Miracles. Booklist* 1 Apr. 1995: 1377.

———. Rev. of *Starcarbon. Booklist* 15 Jan. 1994: 876.

Sexton, David. "The Wacky Woman's *Whyyyyyy Not* World." Rev. of *Victory over Japan. Times Literary Supplement* 25 May 1985: 573.

Seyersted, Per. *Kate Chopin: A Critical Biography.* Baton Rouge: Louisiana State University Press, 1969.

Showalter, Elaine. "Tradition and the Female Talent: *The Awakening* as a Solitary Book." In *New Essays on* The Awakening. Ed. Wendy Martin. Cambridge: Cambridge University Press, 1988. 33–57.

Sjoerdsma, Ann G. "The Bankrupt Inheritance." Rev. of *Net of Jewels. Washington Post* 9 Apr. 1992: C9.

Smith, Starr E. Rev. of *Anabasis. Library Journal* Aug. 1994: 128.

Smith, Wendy. "*PW* Interviews: Ellen Gilchrist." *Publishers Weekly* 2 Mar. 1992: 46–47.

Solotaroff, Theodore. "*Ship of Fools* and the Critics." *Commentary* 34 (1962): 277–86.

Sontag, Susan. *Illness as Metaphor.* New York: Vintage Books, 1979.

Rev. of *Starcarbon, a Meditation on Love. Kirkus Reviews* 15 Feb. 1994: 162.

———. *Publishers Weekly* 31 Jan. 1994: 74.

Stone, Carole. "The Female Artist in Kate Chopin's *The Awakening:* Birth and Creativity." *Women's Studies* 13 (1986): 23–32.

Stout, Janis P. *Strategies of Reticence: Silence and Meaning in the Works of Jane Austen, Willa Cather, Katherine Anne Porter, and Joan Didion.* Charlottesville: University of Virginia Press, 1990.

Stubblefield, Charles. "A Triumph of the Human Will." Rev. of *The Annunciation. Prairie Schooner* 58.2 (1984): 107–109.

Swiggart, Peter. *The Art of Faulkner's Novels.* Austin: University of Texas Press, 1962.

Taliaferro, Frances. "Fiction." Rev. of *The Annunciation. Harper's* June 1983: 76.

Tandon, Bharat. "Dressed for Success in the South." Rev. of *The Age of Miracles. Times Literary Supplement* 20 Oct. 1995: 23.

Taylor, Pat Ellis. "Suicide Is So Aristocratic." Rev. of *The Anna Papers. Los Angeles Times Book Review* 27 Nov. 1988: 8.

Thompson, Jeanie, and Anita Miller Garner. "The Miracle of Realism: The Bid for Self-Knowledge in the Fiction of Ellen Gilchrist." *Southern Quarterly* 22.1 (1983): 100–14. Rept. in *Women Writers of the Contemporary South.* Ed. Peggy Whitman Prenshaw. Jackson: University Press of Mississippi, 1984. 233–48.

Thompson, Lawrance. *William Faulkner: An Introduction and Interpretation.* American Authors and Critics Series. New York: Barnes, 1963.

Thornton, Lawrence. "*The Awakening:* A Political Romance." *American Literature* 52 (1980): 50–66.

Timperlake, Barbette. Rev. of *Net of Jewels. School Library Journal* May 1992: 151–52.

Tompkins, Jane P. "*The Awakening:* An Evaluation." *Feminist Studies* 3 (1976): 22–29.

Toth, Emily. "Kate Chopin's New Orleans Years." *New Orleans Review* 15.1 (1988): 53–60.

Unrue, Darlene Harbour. *Truth and Vision in Katherine Anne Porter's Fiction.* Athens: University of Georgia Press, 1985.

———. *Understanding Katherine Anne Porter.* Understanding Contemporary American Literature Series. Columbia: University of South Carolina Press, 1988.

Urgo, Joseph R. "A Prologue to Rebellion: *The Awakening* and the Habit of Self-Expression." *Southern Literary Journal* 20 (1987): 22–32.

Rev. of *Victory over Japan. Publishers Weekly* 27 July 1984: 136.

Wadlington, Warwick. "*The Sound and the Fury:* A Logical Tragedy." *American Literature* 53 (1981): 409–23.

Walker, Nancy A. *The Disobedient Writer: Women and Narrative Tradition.* Austin: University of Texas Press, 1995.

Walton, David. "The Zany, Tender, Harrowing World of Novelist Ellen Gilchrist." Rev. of *The Anna Papers. Chicago Tribune Books* 2 Oct. 1988: 6–7.

Ward, Jerry W., Jr. "Voices: Racial Reading." *Southern Exposure* 22.2 (1994): 47–49.

Wheeler, Otis B. "The Five Awakenings of Edna Pontellier." *Southern Review* 11 (1975): 118–28.

Wilder, Amos N. *Theology and Modern Literature.* Cambridge, Mass.: Harvard University Press, 1958.

Wood, Carl. "*In Our Time:* Hemingway's Fragmentary Novel." *Neuphilologische Mitteilungen* 74.4 (1973): 716–26.

Wood, Susan. "Louisiana Stories: The Debut of Ellen Gilchrist." Rev. of *In the Land of Dreamy Dreams. Book World* 21 Mar. 1984: 4+.

Woolf, Virginia. *A Room of One's Own.* New York: Harcourt Brace Jovanovich, 1929.

Wymard, Eleanor B. "Kate Chopin: Her Existential Imagination." *Southern Studies* 19 (1980): 373–84.

Yaeger, Patricia. *Honey-Mad Women: Emancipatory Strategies in Women's Writing.* Gender and Culture Series. New York: Columbia University Press, 1988.

Yardley, Jonathan. "A Talented Short Story Writer Takes on the Novel." Rev. of *The Annunciation. Book World* 29 May 1983: 3.

———. "Knockout 'Victory': The Best Stories Yet from Ellen Gilchrist." Rev. of *Victory over Japan. Washington Post* 12 Sept. 1984: B1+.

Young, Philip. "'Big World Out There': *The Nick Adams Stories.*" *Novel* 6 (1972): 5–19.

Young, Tracy. "Off the Cuff: Ellen Gilchrist, at Last a Short Story Writer with Something to Say." Rev. of *Drunk with Love. Vogue* Sept. 1986: 415+.

Youngblood, Sarah. "Structure and Imagery in 'Pale Horse, Pale Rider'." In *Katherine Anne Porter: A Critical Symposium.* Ed. Lodwick Hartley and George Core. Athens: University of Georgia Press, 1969. 129–38.

Index